TUNBRIDGE WARE

AND RELATED EUROPEAN DECORATIVE WOODWARES

NEW EDITION

Rosewood reading stand with a tessellated geometrical panel in the centre and miniature parquetry bandings, attributable to Edmund Nye c1840. Base 43 x 31.5cm, book rest 109 x 81.5cm (Sotheby's).

TUNBRIDGE WARE

AND RELATED EUROPEAN DECORATIVE WOODWARES

Killarney — Spa — Sorrento

NEW EDITION

Brian Austen

First published 1989
Revised 1996
Extended 2001

foulsham

LONDON • NEW YORK • TORONTO • SYDNEY

Travelling chess set, the board with a surround of miniature parquetry c1840. d:11.5cm (Bracketts).

foulsham

The Publishing House, Bennetts Close,
Cippenham, Slough, SL1 5AP, England

ISBN 0-572-02545-9

Cover photograph
*A rosewood tea caddy decorated with a tessellated view of
Eridge Castle and various floral and leaf bandings c1850
(Canterbury Auction Galleries).*

Printed in Great Britain by St Edmundsbury Press, Bury St Edmunds, Suffolk

CONTENTS

	Page
INTRODUCTION	7

TUNBRIDGE WARE — THE PRE-MOSAIC PERIOD

Chapter 1 — Tunbridge — the Well and the Ware	13
Chapter 2 — The London Tunbridge Ware Industry	21
Chapter 3 — The Brighton Tunbridge Ware Industry	29
Chapter 4 — Tunbridge Ware Production and Sale at Other Centres	35
Chapter 5 — The Nature of Tunbridge Wares Prior to c1830	42

MOSAIC TUNBRIDGE WARE c1830–1939

Chapter 6 — The New Mosaic Wares	63
Chapter 7 — The Victorian Tunbridge Ware Industry 1830–75	69
Chapter 8 — Methods of Production	82
Chapter 9 — Victorian Tunbridge Ware Designs and their Sources	99
Chapter 10 — The Industry in Decline 1875–1939	116
Chapter 11 — Modern Craft Workers in Tunbridge Ware	130
Chapter 12 — Tunbridge Ware Makers	135

RELATED DECORATIVE WOODWARES

Chapter 13 — Killarney Inlaid Woodwares	177
Chapter 14 — Spa Woodwares	196
Chapter 15 — Sorrento Woodwares	209

A Note on Mauchline and Scottish Souvenir
Woodwares   217

NOTES   223

APPENDICES

1. List of articles manufactured in print-decorated and
   painted, or inlaid and mosaic Tunbridge ware   239

2. Topographical prints recorded on items of Tunbridge
   ware   241

3. Topographical mosaic blocks   244

4. Tunbridge ware manufacturers and retailers   248

5. Museum collections of Tunbridge ware   265

6. Killarney arbutus ware manufacturers and retailers 266

7. Museums and houses displaying items of
   Killarney arbutus ware   268

8. Price guide to Tunbridge and other
   decorated woodwares   269

SELECT BIBLIOGRAPHY   278

INDEX   288

INTRODUCTION

The resurgence in the seventeenth century of the health resort was accompanied by a new trade in souvenirs. This book deals with a number of souvenir wares, especially Tunbridge wares, the production and sale of which extended well beyond the area of west Kent responsible for their genesis. The highly decorative nature of Victorian Tunbridge wares has made them objects for collection for many decades and this has resulted in a considerable literature, mainly in periodicals, devoted to the decorative arts and antiques. However, no attempt to write a full-length book on the subject was made until 1949 when Ethel Younghusband produced *Mansions, Men and Tunbridge Ware*. The paucity of information then available on the subject was reflected in this book, which devoted more of its space to the buildings depicted in the mosaics than to the development of the industry and its products. No further book appeared until 1970 when Edward and Eva Pinto produced *Tunbridge and Scottish Souvenir Woodware*. This book had a much greater impact because of the reputation of the authors as collectors and students of treen, and their earlier writings in this field. One significant addition to the subject to appear in 1972 was a series of articles written for *Practical Education* by R.G.E. Sandbach, at that time Curator of the Tunbridge Wells Museum. Unfortunately, it was published in a periodical likely to be overlooked by collectors and students of the subject.

Although these three works were all valuable contributions in their way towards the study of the subject, the authors were hampered by the lack of source material that has bedevilled study in this field. No significant business records of any Tunbridge ware makers have survived. In 1931, a Tunbridge Wells antique dealer, Colin Rich, bought a considerable collection of equipment, tools, veneers, designs and documents originally belonging to the business of Edmund Nye. These were offered in their entirety to the Tunbridge Wells Museum for £220, but at that period a small local museum had little chance of raising such a sum and an appeal to the Carnegie Trustees was unsuccessful. The items were auctioned in February 1933. Fortunately, much of the equipment, as well as tools and designs, were purchased by the Museum or by Edward Pinto and are now permanently preserved for study. The documents were acquired privately and their whereabouts is unknown. To compensate for this absence of business records, attempts were made to interview people who had been employed in the industry or who were related to important nineteenth-century makers. Although the information collected was of interest, like most oral evidence it depended too often on the memory of elderly people which was not always reliable.

The present study is not based upon any dramatic new discovery. It does, however, examine a considerable range of material which previous writers have either overlooked or only imperfectly researched. It throws light on the period prior to the introduction of the Victorian mosaic wares, which up to now has been imperfectly understood, and demonstrates the important part played by London and Brighton makers in this phase. Statements made by previous writers have been critically appraised and, in a number of cases, corrected. Collections, both public and private, have been examined carefully for new evidence. The research has proceeded over a period of ten years and the findings represent in many areas a considerable advance over our previous knowledge. The author is, however, only too aware of the lack of information currently available about certain facets of the subject and new evidence may emerge from time to time which will extend our knowledge and even necessitate a review of material published here.

Tunbridge ware had clear associations with certain other European decorative woodwares and these are also dealt with in this study. In the case of Killarney marquetry and inlay wares, little information is in print, and the researches presented here, based on a detailed examination of sources in Great Britain and Ireland, are the most comprehensive account of the industry yet. Again, no business records appear to have survived. The section on the Spa industry is of a different nature. Here, research has been carried out and published in France and Belgium, but has never been translated into English. Although some new source material has been investigated, the account given relies considerably on published writings. For the Sorrento industry, a valuable study has recently been published in Italy. I am greatly indebted to Alessandro Fiorentino of Sorrento for sharing his researches with me, and this information, together with material researched personally by the author, is the basis for the account offered here.

I am indebted to a large number of people who offered their assistance during the research period. R.G.E. Sandbach and Margaret Gill, former Curators of Tunbridge Wells Museum, and Mike Rowlands and Ian Bevis, the present Curator and Assistant Curator, have been frequent sources of information, as has Linda Fletcher, the Keeper responsible for the Pinto Collection at the City of Birmingham Museum. Amongst other museum staff who have provided assistance, Simon Jervis and Clive Wainwright of the Victoria and Albert Museum, Amanda Herries of the Museum of London, Kedrun Laurie of the Geffrye Museum, Caroline Dudley of the Brighton Museum, M.I. Moad of the Guildhall Museum,

Rochester, and the late Christopher Gilbert of Temple Newsam, Leeds, must be mentioned, but this list is far from exhaustive. I am greatly indebted to the staffs of the Public Records Office and the Kent and East Sussex Records Offices and to the Department of Prints of the British Museum. Libraries used ranged from major national institutions such as the British Library, through the Guildhall Library and the Institute of Historical Research of the University of London, to countless county library branches, especially in Kent and East and West Sussex. A special word of thanks must go to the staff of Brighton Reference Library. Individuals who have provided much assistance include John and Jill Ford with Brighton prints and the Ackermann records, the late L.J. Green with information about his father's business and Peter and Daphne Bejamin, Albert Fickling, Robert Vorley and Len Garrett about their productions. Henry Smith, Derek Roberts, Kenneth King, R.J. Goulden and Derek Deadman have shared their expertise with me, much to my benefit, and Robert Bowman and Patricia Brown of Sotheby's as well as many others in various auction houses have fed me with useful illustrative material. For the Killarney wares, special thanks must go to the late Edmond Myers and his staff at Muckross House, the late John Teahan of the National Museum of Ireland, Michael Robinson of the Ulster Museum and Desmond Fitzgerald, the ever-efficient staff of the National Library in Dublin and the staffs of the public libraries in Killarney, Tralee and Cork. The Spa chapter owes much to Dr. A. Henrard of the Musée de la Ville d'Eaux, Spa. Lastly I must thank Geoffrey Beard, formerly Director of the Visual Arts Centre of Lancaster University, for reading the text and offering helpful suggestions and John Upton for the considerable photographic assistance provided. Those whose names are omitted are assured that their contribution is no less esteemed. Where source material is so scattered, no adequate research is possible without the co-operation of many to whom I am eternally grateful.

Much painstaking effort is needed to convert an author's manuscript into an attractive book that will serve the needs of the reader. In this respect I am greatly indebted to many on the staff of the publishers who have seen the various editions of the book through their many stages with commendable efficiency.

TUNBRIDGE WARE –
THE PRE-MOSAIC
PERIOD

Chapter 1

TUNBRIDGE – THE WELL AND THE WARE

The growth of the spa town in Britain in the seventeenth and eighteenth centuries depended upon the widely held belief that water naturally impregnated with certain minerals and salts had curative properties. This belief was popularised at a time of accelerating economic expansion based on improved techniques in agriculture and industry, and the development of deep-water trade to the Americas and the Far East. The income from such sources permitted country gentleman and city merchant to travel over an improving road network to the curative waters, and financed the urban development and also diversions and amusements which rapidly eclipsed the waters as the major attraction.

The curative powers of water had been exploited from classical antiquity, and even in Britain the Romans developed the thermal spring of Aquae Sulis (Bath). Medieval man, too, found water beneficial to promoting health, and pilgrimages were made to such places as St. Ann's Well, Buxton and St. Winifred's Well at Holywell (Clywd). Pilgrimages and holy wells were regarded with disfavour during the Reformation and discouraged. This disfavour was not, however, to last long, for on the Continent a growing interest in medicinal waters was developing by the sixteenth century, as witnessed by a number of English merchants and diplomats. By the early years of Elizabeth I's reign, evidence of some revival was present at Bath, Bristol and Buxton, and the first literature advocating the usage of their waters was being published. At this date, however, only the dedicated and desperate would endure journeys on poorly maintained roads to reach such spas and suffer the indifferent standard of accommodation provided there.[1]

The early resurgence in spa patronage occurred at centres like Bath, which already had a long tradition of usage. It did not, however, escape the notice of landowners, physicians and entrepreneurs that the discovery of the new wells and springs might be financially advantageous, resulting in their proliferation from the late sixteenth century onwards. Tunbridge Wells was one of these. The date of the discovery of this spring on the Kent and Sussex border is usually accepted to be 1606, based on an account in

T. Benge Burr's *History of Tunbridge Wells* published in 1766. Another work places it in 1615 or 1616, but both agree that it was Dudley, third Baron North, who discovered the spring. He was a nobleman at the court of James I who had been advised by his physician to leave London to repair his health, so he went to stay at his friend Lord Bergavenney's hunting seat at Eridge. North had campaigned in Europe, visited Spa in Belgium, and was fully aware of the appearance and properties of mineral waters. The Tunbridge waters were sufficiently well known by 1630 for Queen Henrietta Maria to choose them in order to recuperate after the birth of her son, Charles. Two years later, they received further publicity in the writings of Dr. Lodwick Rowzee of Ashford who published *The Queen's Wells, that is, a Treatise on the Nature and Vertues of Tunbridge Water.* Early visitors to Tunbridge Wells had to be lovers of exercise, or be prepared to suffer discomfort, for there was no settlement in the vicinity of the well. They had the choice of camping out, as the Queen had done, staying at Tonbridge five miles distant, or at a country house of a friend or relative. With the advent of the Civil War in 1641 the trickle of visitors virtually ceased, and during the Commonwealth period the County Committee discouraged attendance, fearing that the taking of the waters might be used as an excuse for the assembling of forces hostile to Parliament.[2]

It was the period following the restoration of Charles II in 1660 that saw the expansion and exploitation of most British spa towns. In 1663, Tunbridge Wells was once again graced with the patronage of an English queen, Catherine of Braganza, and other members of the royal family, and the fashionable and great followed. Even before 1660, a marble cistern appears to have been installed at the well and the area around it paved, but as late as 1680 little more had been added, except two or three public rooms and some traders' booths. Visitors were still expected to lodge in surrounding villages and hamlets. From 1680 to the end of the century, however, a building boom occurred and by the beginning of the eighteenth century the settlement could boast about 150 houses, 20 to 25 shops bordering the colonnaded walks adjacent to the well, public rooms for the amusement of the company and a chapel. The season lasted from May to October, and at most a few hundred fashionable visitors would take up residence during the entire period. Tunbridge Wells, although smaller and less fashionable than Bath, did not involve such a long and exhausting journey from London. At the same time, it was not so close to the capital as to attract tradesmen as visitors, a 'problem' which had been the cause of Epsom's fall from grace amongst the fashionable.[3] By the last decade of the seventeenth century Tunbridge Wells could boast another attraction to divert the pleasure-seeking visitors. They were now offered, from booths and shops that fringed the Walks, decorative woodwares which had the name Tunbridge ware applied to them. At exactly what date did this industry commence, however?

Prior to 1680, the size of the settlement and the number of visitors was clearly insufficient to support a local industry producing wooden souvenir wares. Despite this, however, some writers have placed the genesis of the Tunbridge ware industry as far as as the reign of Elizabeth I.[4] As late as 1924, the Tunbridge Wells Manufacturing Co., the last commercial producer in Tunbridge Wells, came to the conclusion that the words 'famous since 1629' should be included in its publicity material, though why this particular date is chosen is unclear. Significantly, John Evelyn, the diarist and author of *Sylva, or a Discourse of Forest Trees* (1664), does not mention Tunbridge ware. He visited Tunbridge Wells twice to take the waters, the first time in June and July 1652, and subsequently in August 1661. It is inconceivable that a person who so faithfully recorded in detail, and had such an immediate interest in trees and their commercial exploitation, should fail to mention this industry if it had existed.[5] Attempts to place an early date on the manufacture of wooden souvenir ware at Tunbridge Wells are often based on the belief that woodworking, and especially wood turning, were trades with a long history in the region because of the forest resources of the High Weald. Forest crafts such as coppicing to provide charcoal for the important iron industries were practised, while larger oak timber found a ready market in the Thames shipyards. No evidence of the art of turning, however, exists, and an analysis of the occupations of 143 tradesmen who lived in the parish of Tunbridge between 1661 and 1671 found only eight people associated with woodworking. Two of these were joiners and six were carpenters whose work would have been in house construction and fitting. The population of the parish, which included at this date most of the present area of Tunbridge Wells, was in total only 600–800.[6]

In the 1830s a number of Tunbridge ware makers put forward claims of early establishment. Two dates in particular were used. Humphrey Burrows Jnr. of Jordan House, Tunbridge Wells claimed that the business had been founded in 1685, while William Fenner, John Talbot Ubsdell, Edmund Nye and Thomas Barton all claimed at various dates in the nineteenth century that their businesses had been founded in 1720. In the case of the latter group there is a common factor, in that they all at one time or another maintained associated manufactories on Mount Ephraim in Tunbridge Wells. No documentary evidence survives to enable us to trace the predecessors of these firms beyond the middle of the eighteenth century and in many cases not even that far back.[7] The date 1685 was also attached to the business of George Wise of Tonbridge, an early producer of Tunbridge ware. This date was given to the Tonbridge historian, Beauchamp Wadmore, by members of the Wise family in the early years of the present century and has not been challenged subsequently. For the town of Tonbridge, however, a better degree of documentation survives than for Tunbridge Wells, the site of which was split between the Kentish parishes of Speldhurst and Tunbridge and the Sussex parish of Frant. George Wise's business was founded in 1746. During the period when the business was active, no claim for such an early date as 1685 was put forward, and an advertisement of 1847 merely stated that they had been 'established upwards of seventy years'. This suggests that claims made for the dates of establishment of individual Tunbridge ware makers must be treated with caution.[8]

Although the date of 1685 for the establishment of the Burrows business cannot be supported from independent evidence, it is likely that the sale of decorative woodwares at Tunbridge Wells did not originate much before this date. The earliest evidence of its sale at Tunbridge Wells comes from the diary of Celia Fiennes, who toured the country on horseback sampling the various spa waters. She arrived in Tunbridge Wells in 1697 and on the Walks near the well discovered:

> 'shopps full of all sorts of toys, silver, china, milliners and all sorts of curious wooden ware, which this place is noted for the delicate, neate and thin ware of wood both white and Lignum Vitae.'[9]

The Tunbridge wares were probably being offered as part of the stock of traders whose main interest was in other fields, for a survey of the businesses conducted on the Walks at the end of the century, although it includes a number of traders offering fashionable goods, mentions no specialist maker or seller of woodwares.[10]

The Walks, which extended westward from the well, became the focus for Tunbridge ware sellers and other trades aimed at the fashionable visitors. By the end of the seventeenth century, a long range of 20 to 25 shops with colonnaded fronts extended the full length of the Upper Walks on the north-west side, facing a line of trees which provided shade for the visitors. The public rooms were also centred on this area. At another level, the Lower Walks provided about 20 further shops. The Walks had been paved in 1698 at the expense of Queen Anne, and another great improvement was effected in 1739 when the public rooms on the Upper Walks were enlarged to cope with the greatly increased number of visitors, calculated in 1736 as around 900 in the first six weeks of July and August. These included substantial numbers of the aristocracy, gentry, Members of Parliament and senior military officers. By this date a member of the Burrows family, probably a Tunbridge ware maker or seller, was renting one of the shops and the names of Frances Burrows (1741–46) and William Burrows (from 1752) are recorded in the lists of tenants. By 1772, no fewer than five 'toy shops', a substantial part of whose trade would have been in Tunbridge ware, are recorded on the Walks. These were Dorcas Baker, Mary Burrows, Mary Fry, Jane Mercer and Sarah Upton. They represented the most numerous group of traders in this area, even exceeding the number of victuallers by one. Nine years later, however, the number was reduced to two, though there were several other fashionable trades represented, such as perfumers and booksellers who might also have stocked the products of the industry. This pattern of three or four specialist makers with showrooms on the Walks supported by retailers selling similar goods became the common pattern from this period onward. John Evans, who visited Tunbridge Wells in 1820, commented that 'the intermediate space between the libraries is occupied by shops chiefly stored with Tunbridge ware'. By the nineteenth century, however, the number of visitors in the season was in decline; little more than half as many as had visited the town at its peak in the

1. Print published by Edmund Nye of the Parade showing the Bath House containing the Chalybeate Spring. Such prints were used for the decoration of whitewood Tunbridge wares. 1827.

1730s and 40s. The younger and more vivacious had been lured away by the appeal of the seaside spas. This was, however, compensated for by the growing number of residents, especially retired people, who found it cheaper than living in London. The town had begun expanding rapidly in the early nineteenth century, not only by the establishment of the new town on Mount Pleasant, but also due to improvements and extensions in existing areas of development. This and the exploitation of markets in other parts of Kent and the adjoining counties maintained the Tunbridge ware trade. The Walks were usually referred to as the Parade by the beginning of the nineteenth century, and towards the end of the century the name changed once more to its present designation, the Pantiles.[11]

Workshops were not in general situated on the Walks, as rents were high and manufacturing inappropriate in such a fashionable area. Not until the 1830s did the prospect of visiting the workshops attract society. The earliest reference to a workshop in the Tunbridge Wells area is contained in a deed of 1713 concerning a 'turner's shop where Richard Pett formerly lived' and to Pett's will dated

29 January 1706. The workshop was in the parish of Speldhurst next to a 'rockhouse' suggesting a location on the Common or Mount Ephraim where rock outcrops occur. A number of turners, some specialising in particular types of turnery, are recorded in this parish in the first four decades of the eighteenth century. Those taking apprentices included Richard Vintiman 'hollow turner' (1713–20), John Willington (1720), Richard Brooker 'hollow ware turner' (1737) and John Groombridge 'spoon maker and round tuner' (1737). John Willington's apprentice was Darino Latter, a surname shared with Dorcas Latter who maintained a toy shop on the Parade (1781–3) and James Latter, a Tunbridge ware manufacturer of Culverden Gate (c1795). A further deed of 1737 concerned with properties in the parishes of Speldhurst and Tunbridge mentioned several workshops, some at Mount Ephraim House, and the names of John Rider, a turner, and Simon Wise who rented a workshop and may have been related to George Wise of Tonbridge. The number of turners, and their specialist nature in some cases, suggests that they may well have been manufacturing decorative turnery rather than the usual domestic products such as buckets, bowls, plates and country chairs. At Tunbridge Wells, the edge of the Common or Mount Ephraim continued as a favoured locality for workshops to the end of the nineteenth century, though others sought a nearer proximity to the Walks. In Tonbridge, George Wise and subsequent makers occupied premises in the High Street.[12]

As late as the end of the eighteenth century, some of the sellers – and possibly makers – of Tunbridge ware were not local residents, but came into town for the summer season only. In 1801 the residential population of Tunbridge Wells was only about 1,000[13], and for much of the preceeding century, a few hundred. A number of London traders were already established for the season by 1700, and although the number of local traders tended to increase as the town grew, the fashionable luxury trades retained this seasonal pattern until the end of the eighteenth century as winter demand would have been small. As late as 1796, G. Gardiner, a linen draper, was advertising his intention of closing and leaving the town on 1 November as 'the present season was drawing near a conclusion'. John Robinson, a London perfumer and Tunbridge ware maker, had a number of handbills printed for him by Jasper Sprange, the Tunbridge Wells printer, between 1795 and 1801, offering a wide range of elegant wares. He was probably trading in the town as early as 1792, for in that year a John Robinson was one of the subscribers to the paving of the Walks along with other traders whose shops fronted them. He appears to have ceased trading at Tunbridge Wells in 1809. Clearly, he regarded his London trade as important for the London addresses in Piccadilly are included on the Tunbridge Wells handbills and his claim to be Tunbridge ware manufacturer to the Princess of Wales and perfumer to both the Prince and Princess of Wales must have been through the London trade, as neither of them ever visited Tunbridge Wells. The address of the London business was changed to Margaret Street, Cavdendish Square in 1812 and Robinson opened a shop in Brighton in 1801. The business closed in 1822. It would seem unlikely that he would have kept a business in operation at Tunbridge Wells in the winter months if his main base of operations and manufacture was in London. He is, however, the only London Tunbridge ware maker known for certain to have traded in Tunbridge Wells.[14]

2. Whitewood Tunbridge ware hand screen and stand, the screen decorated with a coloured print of the Parade (Pantiles), Tunbridge Wells. The screen and stand additionally painted with foliage and vine borders. c1810. h: 43cm w of screen: 22cm. (Tunbridge Wells Museum).

The seasonal nature of the Tunbridge Wells industry made it necessary to exploit to the full the earnings from the visitors in the spring and summer months, as income for the remainder of the year would have been much diminished. In addition to their range of woodwares, other objects would have been stocked that would appeal to the fashionable society. In the period from about 1780 to 1830 topographical prints were published by a number of Tunbridge ware makers such as Fenner & Nye, Edmund Nye (fig. 1) and J.J. & A. Sharp of Tunbridge Wells and Thomas and George Wise of Tonbridge, to use in the decoration of their wares. These also found a ready sale to the visitors. They might also publish comic or satirical prints and buy work from other publishers or act as their agents. Fancy stationery decorated with local engravings was a logical extension to this trade and one maker added a circulating library to his business. Most manufacturers could find room in their houses to provide lodgings for visitors. Jordan House, the home and business centre of Humphrey Burrows and his son of the same name, had 15 rooms in 1837 and was advertising 'Genteel Apartments facing the Common'. For the winter months repair work, a limited trade from residents and the build-up of stock in anticipation of the coming season had to suffice.[15]

That Tunbridge ware was bought by visitors in considerable quantities there can be no doubt. Throughout the eighteenth century and into the nineteenth, visitors commented on their purchases in correspondence and diaries, and authors referred to their characters using or possessing such wares. In 1727, Mary Granville, Mrs Delany ('Mrs Pendarves') in correspondence with her sister mentions a Tunbridge ware jewellery box sent as a present from Mrs Tiller and two 'Tunbridge voiders', probably trays, for her mother. In 1745, Elizabeth Montagu sent items of the ware as a present to the Duchess of Portland after a visit to Tunbridge Wells. Samuel Derek, appointed Master of Ceremonies at both Bath and Tunbridge Wells in 1761, records in a letter in the following year the despatch from the latter town as a gift of 'a dressing glass, and a set of boxes for your daughter's toilette, together with the prettiest tea chest I could lay my hands upon'. The authoress, Fanny Burney, was a visitor in October 1779 in company with Mrs Thrale, and records the purchase on the Walks of 'a very beautiful inkstand' which was presented to the ten-year-old Miss Birch as reward for singing to them. In fiction, the ware was sufficiently well known by 1706 to be referred to in Thomas Baker's *Hampstead Heath* and is mentioned by a succession of later writers including the poet, John Gay (1720 – *The Funeral – A Town Ecologue*), and the novelists Fanny Burney (*Camilla* 1796) and Jane Austen (*Emma* 1816). By the closing years of the eighteenth century and the first decades of the nineteenth, Tunbridge wares had become eminently fashionable on almost a national scale, and production had spread well beyond the towns of Tunbridge Wells and Tonbridge.[16]

Chapter 2

THE LONDON TUNBRIDGE
WARE INDUSTRY

London capital was important in the development of Tunbridge Wells during the boom that occurred after 1680. It was Thomas Ashenhurst of Lambeth who was responsible for the building of several amusement rooms and at least 17 of the shops on the Walks, while Sir Thomas Janson of St. Martin-in-the-Fields was occupied with house development.[1] London traders took shops on the Walks, and the fashionable society that frequented the spa came to a large degree from London. It is therefore not surprising that London craftsmen became engaged in the manufacture of Tunbridge ware at an early date. Although the industry may possibly have had its origin in the productions of local Kentish craftsmen, it is unlikely that initially they would have had skill and design sense sufficient to satisfy the tastes of persons familiar with London standards. Celia Fiennes in 1697 noted the sale of lignum vitae turnery and this American tropical hardwood was not a timber likely to be used by country turners. It is likely that some of the Tunbridge ware displayed on the Walks at this date and on into the eighteenth century was produced in London.

Certainly, makers of Tunbridge ware were practising their art in London by the late seventeenth century. In 1686, a Mary Ferguson, probably the wife of John Ferguson, who supplied furniture to Kensington Palace in the early 1690s, petitioned the Customs who had impounded some 'white wood boxes, Tunbridge deskes, which had been sent by her to Holland to be lacquered there'. These wares must have been similar to those produced at Spa in this period and may even have been sent to that town for lacquering. Tunbridge turnery was also produced at an early date in London. The handbill of John Jackson 'at the Unicorn the corner of Woodstreet, Cheapside' lists 'Lignum Vitae and Ivory Toys, Tunbridge ware, and all sorts of Toys' as products that he stocked. This handbill, in the Banks Collection, was used as a receipt for goods supplied and is dated 24 February 1710. The head of the bill includes an engraving of the trade sign which bears the date 1699, possibly when the business was founded (fig 3).[2] Further evidence comes from a print of the Frost Fair held on the ice covering the River

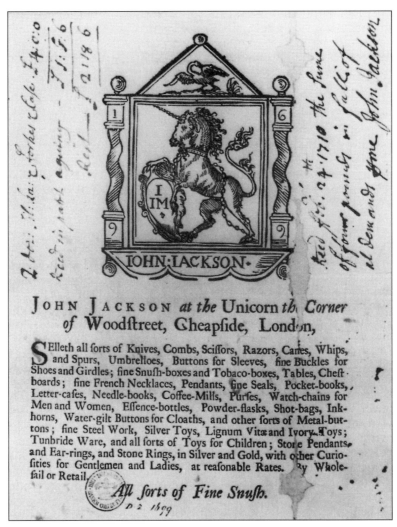

3. Trade card of John Jackson, a London toyman, offering Tunbridge ware. The card is used as a receipt for goods paid for on 24 February 1710, but the date figures in the surround of the trade sign suggest that the business may have been established in 1699. (British Museum Department of Prints).

Thames in 1716, on which one of the booths is identified as 'ye Hand in hand Tunbridge wareshop'.[3] Throughout the eighteenth century, a growing number of London businesses offered Tunbridge wares as part of their stock, and although a few of these were retailers, the great majority were turners and had facilities to produce the wares they advertised. None called themselves Tunbridge ware makers and they dealt in other goods as well, but this also appears to have been the practice in Tunbridge Wells at this period when the words 'toyman' and 'turner' were used to describe such enterprises.

The survival of trade cards for London businesses, coupled with the regular publication of directories from the mid eighteenth century, mean that much more is known about the London trade in the period up to c1790 than that of Tunbridge Wells. The items produced and described as Tunbridge ware appear in the main to have been decorative and fancy turnery, and lignum vitae and ivory are regularly mentioned in connection with them. An invoice in the Heal Collection of Richard Tomkins, turner of Savile Row, dated 29 May 1783 records the sale of '1 sett Best Tunbridge Casters, Silver Mounted' at £1 6s (£1.30) while below it '1 sett Common do.' cost only 3s (£0.15). This seems to indicate that 'Tunbridge' implied that goods were fashionable and of quality as opposed to items that were merely serviceable. Small cabinet wares were offered in London through toymen rather than turners though Willerton & Roberts of Old Bond Street, who traded as both turners and toymen, invoiced to the Earl of Atholl on 4 June 1775 a 'Tunbridge Work box Compleat' at £1 11s 6d (£1.57½). Businesses offering and making Tunbridge wares were scattered widely across London; some, often the most fashionable, were in the West End, and there were many in the Strand, Holborn or the City and a few in Clerkenwell.[4]

From about 1790, a change occurred which was also reflected in the Tunbridge Wells industry. Turnery was declining in importance and small cabinet wares such as workboxes, tea caddies, and even small pieces of furniture such as work-tables and teapoys were becoming more important. By the beginning of the nineteenth century, the number of retail outlets selling Tunbridge ware in London was considerable. *Johnstone's Directory* for 1817 lists no fewer than 44 'toy and Tunbridge warehouses' at least five which were manufacturers, 23 'turners and toymen' and 95 perfumers, many of whom no doubt stocked Tunbridge wares. A number of boxes of early nineteenth-century date, which may have been manufactured in London, are known decorated with London scenes. Some London businesses were also using simple whitewood boxes, similar to those made by Tunbridge ware makers, to market their products. One example has the label of E. Williams, a stationer of 11 Strand.

The nature of the trade of two of the largest retail sellers of Tunbridge ware in London is fortunately known through their regular advertising campaigns. One was William Vale of 62, Fleet Street who set up as a perfumer and Tunbridge ware repository in 1794. Initially, the perfumery side of the business may have predominated but by 1803 Tunbridge ware was the main line advertised. In January of that year Vale was announcing that in addition to his shop he had 'filled up a spacious Ware Room, where every article in Tunbridge Ware is constantly displayed'. He claimed to have the 'most complete assortment of these fashionable articles ever seen in London' which included:

'tables and desks for work, writing, drawing &c. on an entirely new principle, Boxes and Baskets, elegantly finished and fitted up with every requisite for work and netting, Caddies and Chests for tea and sugar, manufactured in various kinds of curious wood which change of climate cannot injure.'

Such wares were sold 'wholesale and retail on the same terms as at Tunbridge Wells' and he also offered to repair and revarnish old Tunbridge ware or take it in part exchange. In 1809, he stated that his ware rooms contained 'the most elegant and extensive display of real TUNBRIDGE WARE ever seen in the kingdom'. William Vale's business flourished on the basis of fashionable patronage until April 1822, when he announced his retirement from the trade after 'upwards of 30 years' and the selling off of his stock 'under manufacturers' prices'. The business may have survived for a year or two further, however, as it is still listed in *Kent's Directory* as late as 1825.[5] Vale's greatest rival was probably Malcolm Dunnett who traded from 154, Cheapside from 1799 to 1803 and then from 3, Cheapside. Initially he advertised his trade as perfumer and toyman, but the sale of Tunbridge ware soon became a major feature of the business. Already by 1804 he was describing his business as a 'toy and Tunbridge ware repository' and in February 1806 was announcing that 'his rooms are stored for the season with a complete Collection of real Tunbridge Ware, which, for beauty and elegance, are not to be equalled'. The range of articles offered was similar to that of his rival William Vale and like him he offered to repair old ware and to supply 'Merchants, Captains of Ships and Shopkeepers ... on the lowest terms'. Dunnett also offered a range of children's toys, puzzles and games both English and imported. The business featured both of these ranges until the late 1820s when Tunbridge ware declined in favour of children's toys. In 1828, the business was described for the first time merely as an 'importer of Dutch toys' and this designation was continued until 1846, when trading ceased.[6]

Fashionable sellers of artists' materials and prints also included Tunbridge ware in their stocks. The most famous of such businesses was that set up by Rudolph Ackermann. He was born at Stolberg, Germany in 1764 and subsequently settled in London where in 1783 he established himself as a designer of carriages and soon after, additionally, as an instructor in drawing. Book publishing was added from 1790, and in 1796 he moved from 96 to 101, Strand where he opened his print gallery. The business developed as a 'General Repository of Arts' capable of supplying a wide range of artists' materials and decorative items. By about 1810, he was offering to the public 'Tunbridge Ware in a variety of Boxes for Colours, Work, Netting, Tea Chests and Caddies &c. ornamented with handsome Medallions, highly varnished and polished'. A contemporary rhyming broadsheet issued by Ackermann to advertise his wares lists amongst other stock:

'his fam'd wares, which for Beauty envies
They're fit for the Toilet and presents for Princes.'

There is no evidence to suggest that Ackermann had facilities to manufacture small cabinet wares and these must have been furnished by Tunbridge ware manufacturers. London makers would seem the obvious source of supply but Ackermann also enjoyed a long-standing trade relationship with George Wise of Tonbridge. In the first four months of 1812 alone, Ackermann paid sums amounting to £436 9s 10d (£436.49) to George Wise and such substantial payments could only be in respect of Tunbridge ware in considerable quantities. It is unlikely that this trade was one way. Ackermann produced a wide range of prints, medallions, borders, inks, colouring materials and varnish which would have been needed by a Tunbridge ware maker. Ackermann prints have been recorded as used on Tunbridge ware made by Wise (fig. 16).[7] In 1827, the business moved back to extended premises at 96, Strand and then continued under the direction of his younger son until 1856, when trading ceased. His eldest son, Rudolph Ackermann Jnr. established a similar type of business at 191, Regent Street in 1826, and also dealt in Tunbridge ware to some extent, for in the 1833 edition of *Forget Me Not*, an annual literary anthology aimed at a feminine gift market, he advertised jointly with the Strand business panoramic views of Regent's Park which could be supplied 'in a circular Tunbridge case'. The enterprise, however, was eventually to concentrate on the publication of sporting and military prints. Next to the establishments operated by the Ackermanns, one of the most fashionable businesses was that of S. & J. Fuller, print sellers and stationers at 'The Temple of Fancy', 34, Rathbone Place (fig. 4). This business was established in 1809 and at an early date stocked Tunbridge ware. Like Ackermann, it issued a rhyming broadsheet advertising its wares:

*'There the Ladies will beautiful **Work Tables** find*
*Or **Plateaus** or **Cabinets** form'd to the mind,*
*Bedeck'd with **Medalions**, or furnish'd with **Borders**,*

4. *The showrooms of a London Tunbridge ware retailer, S. & J. Fuller of 34, Rathbone Place. The Tunbridge ware is displayed in the large cabinet on the left hand side wall. c1820.*

5a. Water-colour box retailed by George Blackman of 362, Oxford Street, London, showing lid decorated with an uncoloured engraving of Astley Castle, Warwickshire, almost identical to that in Vol. xv of The Beauties of England and Wales *(1814). w:16cm d:8cm h:6cm.*

> *And varnish'd and polish'd according to orders,*
> **Writing Desks, Netting Boxes,** *Tunbridge Tea Caddies,*
> *For the Beaux pretty Housewives, and Screens for the Ladies.'*

Fuller's published as part of their publicity an engraving of their showrooms which illustrates clearly display cases of Tunbridge ware. Other London suppliers of artists' colours were not slow to see the public demand for Tunbridge wares and offered their products in such decorated boxes. G. Blackman of 362, Oxford Street advertised c1805 that he had for sale 'A fashionable Assortment of Toys & Tunbridge Wares' and print-decorated Tunbridge ware colour boxes bearing his label are known (fig. 5). Blackman's rival, Reeves & Inwood, were also able to supply such print-decorated boxes and one exists in the Reeves collection at the Museum of London.[8]

The evidence of Ackermann's purchases from Wise is not the only sign that Tonbridge and Tunbridge Wells makers were interested in the London market. This would have been most attractive to them, not only because it would have been many times the size of their local market, but also because it did not suffer so seriously from seasonal fluctuations in demand. Goods were certainly being

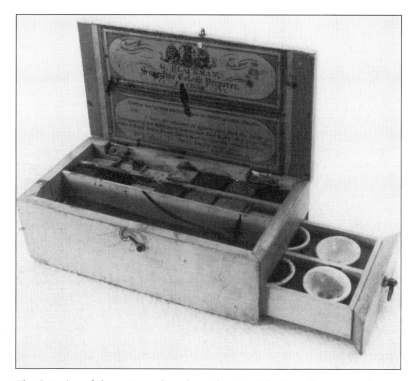

5b. *Interior of the water-colour box, showing Blackman's name and a*
testimonial from the Royal Society of Arts.

produced for the London market in the 1790s, for a label inscribed
'A TRIFLE FROM LONDON' is amongst the samples of Jasper
Sprange, a Tunbridge Wells printer. Only a few years later, Thomas
Wise of Tonbridge, was producing a circular map inscribed 'Five
Miles Round London' for box decoration. Wares manufactured in
west Kent could no doubt compete in price with London-made
items for although the additional costs of carriage had to be met,
these would be offset by the lower cost of skilled labour outside the
capital. The Kent makers do not at this stage appear to have thought
in terms of direct retailing in London. Only one instance of this is
known, and that was in May 1837 when William Fenner displayed
his wares at the Cosmorama, 209, Regent Street. This was a
fashionable public exhibition hall, the main feature of which was 14
panoramas which could be viewed through lenses to magnify the
image. The arrangements of exhibitions of art was a regular
occurrence here.[9]

Some trade also flowed in the opposite direction. John Bastard of
Blandford, a cabinet maker, was stocking Tunbridge wares as early
as the 1730s and in the great fire that consumed the town on 4 June
1731 lost amongst his stock 'about 12 doz of Tunbridge things as
pin (or pen) cases, tooth pick cases, Dogg calls and other little
things' which he valued at 8s (£0.40) per dozen. It is likely that these

were derived from a London source. In October 1770, William Waller, a Newbury cabinet-maker, advertised that he could offer 'All Sorts of Tunbridge Wares in the newest and genteelist Taste, from one of the most opulent Manufactories in London'. Mention has already been made of J. Robinson of Piccadilly who retailed his goods at Tunbridge Wells from the early 1790s and Brighton from 1801, and a similar enterprise was that of Samuel Bettison (1758?–1855) of 17, Theobalds Row, Bloomsbury Square, a perfumer and toyman, who maintained a shop next to Philpott's Bathing Rooms, High Street, Margate, in which he offered a wide range of Tunbridge wares. He is recorded at the London address in the early to mid-1790s, but his period of activity in London may have been short. He is the Samuel Bettison who a few years later was the proprietor of the subscription library operating in Hawley Square, Margate until the late 1830s, and in March 1816 purchased Henney's Library in Cheltenham. At both establishments he stocked Tunbridge ware. It is significant that both of these latter businesses were operating in the 1790s, and the sale of London-made Tunbridge ware outside the capital appears to have been in decline soon after.[10]

By the 1830s, Tunbridge ware designs began to change. The Tunbridge Wells industry developed the new mosaic techniques, but no comparable developments occurred in London. As the earlier print-decorated and painted wares declined in popularity, the makers and sellers either ceased business or diverted their efforts into allied products and trades that offered a better reward. Thomas Axtell of Bunhill Row, Chiswell Street was describing himself in the 1820s as a Tunbridge ware manufacturer, but in 1832 this changed to merely a box-turner and, from 1838, a tooth powder box-maker. Thomas and John Jacques of Leather Lane who had advertised as Tunbridge ware makers since the early 1790s had dropped all reference to such wares by the mid-1830s but had not fundamentally changed the nature of the business which was that of an ivory and hardwood turner, and desk, dressing-case and workbox manufacturer. A number of other makers made similar modifications to their business descriptions. The production of fancy and useful cabinet wares in London did not cease, and probably increased, but it was no longer a commercial advantage to use the name Tunbridge to describe such products.[11]

Chapter 3

THE BRIGHTON TUNBRIDGE WARE INDUSTRY

The development of the Tunbridge ware industry in Brighton in the first half of the nineteenth century is closely connected with the rise of the town as the leading sea-bathing resort. Tunbridge wares were also sold at other resorts, especially along the East Kent and Sussex coasts, but none of these developed an important manufacturing sector and were content to retail wares that had been made elsewhere. Thus the unique character of the Brighton industry, its extent, and the rapidity of its development all contribute to its interest and significance.

Following the success of the medical profession in popularising the use of mineral waters at inland spas, there developed an interest in the medicinal properties of sea water. Sea bathing had been recommended for gout by Dr Robert Wittie in his *Scarborough Spaw* (1667) and later Sir John Floyer the author of a *History of Cold Bathing* (1702) saw its virtues in promoting health and curing many diseases. However, the earliest evidence of sea bathing does not occur until the 1730s when it was known to have been practised at Scarborough. By 1750, bathing was also known at Deal, Margate, Eastbourne, Brighton, Portsmouth and Exmouth.[1]

Before the eighteenth century, Brighton had depended for its livelihood jointly upon fishing, coastal trade and agriculture. However, in common with other northern European towns, it suffered from a general decline in the fishing grounds at the end of the seventeenth century, and by 1750 the population was probably only half what it had been a century earlier. By this date, though, visitors were beginning to trickle into the town, and the first reference to sea bathing for pleasure is made in 1736. A great boost to the town's fortunes was administered by a local physician, Dr Robert Russell of Lewes. He is noted for his *Dissertation on the Use of Sea Water* (1750) which was to enjoy great popularity, as it arrived at a critical period when public interest in sea bathing had been sufficiently aroused to provide a receptive audience. Even before 1750, Russell had been sending patients to Brighton for the cure, and in 1753 he bought land and built himself a house facing the town's beach, where he concentrated much of his attention on the sea cure. At first, visitors to Brighton had found few facilities, and a lack of comforts, but the town was within a day's journey of London, and therefore one of the most convenient coastal towns to the capital. With the increasing numbers of visitors, facilities began to be provided that would meet the requirements of the society patronising the town, including an Assembly Room at the Castle Inn by 1754, the first subscription library by 1760, Assembly Rooms at the Ship Inn (1761) and a Master of Ceremonies (1767). Edmund Baker, proprietor of the first Brighton library, had been established as a bookseller and publisher at Tunbridge Wells since 1754 and continued to operate both establishments until his death in 1774. Royal patronage came – in the form of the Duke of Gloucester – as early as 1765, and his brother the Duke of Cumberland followed in 1771. More important, however, was the first visit of the Prince of Wales in September 1783 and the subsequent building of the Royal Pavilion. By 1800, the town had expanded well beyond its original boundaries into adjoining farmland and had a population of 7,300. Yet, it was not until the first decades of the nineteenth century that the greatest expansion occurred. Between 1801 and 1811, the population rose by 63 per cent and in the next decade by an astounding 67 per cent, the highest growth rate of any English town, exceeding even those of the booming industrial Midlands and the North. It was during this period of growth that many of the facilities were established to serve the fashionable visitors, one of these being the Brighton Tunbridge ware industry, both the establishment of manufactories in the town and the expansion of retail outlets.[2]

Tunbridge Wells was a mere 31 miles from Brighton and it is therefore not surprising that it was to this inland spa that in the second half of the eighteenth century the infant sea-bathing resort looked for guidance. In the use of the Steine as a place of promenade, the building of assembly rooms, the appointment of a Master of Ceremonies and the establishment of businesses to cater for the visitor, Brighton initially followed the pattern set by Tunbridge Wells. As late as the mid-1760s, Tunbridge Wells saw no threat from the marine upstart. Admittedly, two routes between the towns had been improved under the terms of a Turnpike Act of 1752 but it was judged that this would favour Tunbridge Wells 'as it will be an inducement to the company going and returning from Brighthelmstone to pass two or three days or a week by the way at Tunbridge'. Benge Burr, the Tunbridge Wells historian, dismissed the idea of a threat:

> *'if indeed Brighthelmstone was the superior place where pleasures abounded in greater perfection than at the Wells it might be bad policy to open an easier communication between them; but, as Tunbridge has confessedly the advantage of her rival in every respect, she cannot suffer.'*

Burr had, of course, failed to read the trend of the times correctly. Fashionable society more and more favoured the sea, especially after the strong endorsement of royalty, and increasingly Tunbridge Wells was regarded with disfavour by the young in spirit.[3]

6. *Whitewood wares of Brighton manufacture. The tray on the left and the box on the right show prints of the Chain Pier and Marine Parade, Brighton, while the workbox and small box in the centre are decorated with prints of the Royal Pavilion. The two turned objects to the left shaped in the form of the domes of the Royal Pavilion are a spice grater and box, and a sewing companion. c1825–35. (Graves, Son & Pilcher).*

In one respect, however, Tunbridge Wells and Tonbridge gained from the meteoric rise of Brighton. Visitors to the town sought fashionable souvenirs, gifts and trifles, none of which were initially manufactured there. The makers of the two Kent towns were not slow to see how their Tunbridge wares might help to meet this demand, nor were they blind to the need to modify the decoration to make them appropriate for sale in the new location. Libraries, from their first establishment about 1760, played a major part in the sale of Tunbridge ware in Brighton, for almost immediately they started to stock gift wares. A rhyming guide of 1770 comments:

> 'By way of appendage to this shop of books,
> With loungers e'er filled as some trees are with rooks,
> Is a shop stock'd with china and little gay toys,
> For fops, women, children and amusement of boys.'

By 1800, the number of libraries was three: the two original ones now managed by Gregory and Fisher respectively, and the recently established Marine Library of Donaldson & Wilkes. Their stocks were said to include 'Jewellery, Stationery, Perfumery, Tunbridge-Ware, Canes, Gloves, Toys &c.'. One of the first of the Tunbridge ware makers to sell his products in Brighton was Thomas Wise of Tonbridge and a small whitewood box in a private collection decorated with a print of 'HOVE CHURCH NEAR BRIGHTON' and a circular map of 'THE ENVIRONS of BRIGHTHELMSTONE' bears the legend 'Published Sept 12 1800'. Other boxes and prints of

Brighton views by Thomas Wise or his successor George Wise dated in the first decade of the nineteenth century exist in some numbers, and it seems certain that the Wise family were the major suppliers of the Brighton market at this time. Some of the boxes bear a view of Donaldson's Library in the Steine suggesting that he was one of Wise's stockists (colour pl. 4). The Tunbridge Wells makers, Fenner & Nye, may also have produced for the Brighton market, for although no labelled items have been recorded, two Brighton prints dated March and April 1808 with the firm's imprint and of a size suitable for box decoration, are known.[4] London-made Tunbridge ware also sold at Brighton and John Robinson, already trading in London and Tunbridge Wells, opened a shop in North Street in 1801.

By about 1810, Brighton, because of its growth and the number of visitors, represented a larger market for Tunbridge wares than Tunbridge Wells itself and was ripe for local manufacture. In its early stages, the Brighton industry no doubt relied on that of Tunbridge Wells for its techniques and designs, and craftsmen from

7. Whitewood boxes of Brighton manufacture. Front left: *the lid decorated with a print of the Royal Pavilion has a pencilled date on the base '27 Dec 1832'. w:18cm d:11cm h:5cm.* Right: *decorated with a print of the 'ROYAL MEWS' (The Dome) published by 'S.W. Morris, Manufacturer'. c1815. w:13cm d:8.5cm h:4.5cm.* Rear: *workbox with a print of Marine Parade and the Chain Pier published by W. Upton, Tunbridge Ware Manufacturer, 26, East Street. c1825. w:24cm d:18.5cm h:7cm.*

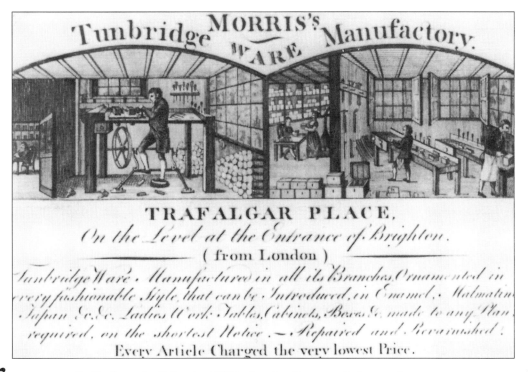

8. Trade card of Morris, c1815, showing the manufacture and decoration of whitewood turnery and cabinet goods. (British Museum Department of Prints).

west Kent were attracted to the Sussex coast. One of the main manufacturers to establish himself in the town was William Upton[5] (figs. 7, 85) who had been born in Speldhurst parish, which at that time included substantial parts of Tunbridge Wells, and he almost certainly learnt the trade there. Sarah Upton, possibly a relative, maintained a Tunbridge ware shop on the Walks in Tunbridge Wells from 1774. William Upton was living in Brighton by 1815 and was certainly an independent producer within a short while after this date. The involvement of the Upton family in the manufacture and sale of Tunbridge ware was to extend to the mid-1860s. A number of workmen may have been lured from Tunbridge Wells also, and it may be significant that a Henry Hollamby was working as a Tunbridge ware maker at Brighton in the 1830s and 40s. This man is not, of course, the noted Tunbridge Wells manufacturer of the same name, but may perhaps be identified with another Henry Hollamby, a Tunbridge ware maker, whose sons, James and Stephen, were baptised in Tunbridge parish in 1813 and 1815. A Thomas Hollamby and a Stephen Hollamby were also working in the trade at Brighton in 1847.[6] Apart from Upton, however, the principal manufacturers do not appear to have had Tunbridge Wells connections. An important manufactory was established by the Morris family[7] in 1808 and their business was operating in Trafalgar

Place by 1814, moving a few years later to Richmond Place (figs. 7, 8, 84). Here, an important repository for the sale of Tunbridge ware and other fashionable goods was maintained until the late 1840s. John Izard of St. James's Street also appears to have been a very substantial producer of Tunbridge ware and a print publisher. His business is first recorded in 1822 but continued until the mid-1850s.[8] The wares of Upton, Morris, Izard, John Hunt of Castle Square, William Saunders of St James's Street and R. Payne of North Street can be identified. Their wares were not often labelled, but all published Brighton topographical prints for the decoration of their productions and a number of these have been recorded with the imprint of the publisher, and can be related to boxes and other items decorated by them.[9] Much of the Brighton production at this period is of whitewood wares painted or decorated with prints, (figs. 6, 7, colour pl. 3) though some Brighton manufacturers, such as William Upton from the New Street address and Cheesman of 9, Cranbourn Street, West Street, produced veneered items (fig. 26, colour pl. 10).[10] As with the Tunbridge Wells industry, a number of makers are recorded in directories whose products cannot be identified. A date just before 1810 is suggested for the establishment of the industry in Brighton on the basis of the earliest recorded activity of the Upton and Morris businesses, and this is confirmed by the author of an 1818 guide to the town, who declared:

> *'The manufacture of Tunbridge ware is becoming an object of importance here. The manufactories established are yet in their infancy, but are likely to receive a fair proportion of public encouragement.'*

The industry was to develop in size and scale through the 1820s and 1830s and one guide of 1838, commenting on Brighton's trade, declared that 'Brighton is not a manufacturing or commercial town: the principal manufacture is that of Tunbridge ware.' There were probably never more than about eight to ten manufacturers, large and small, at any one time in Brighton in the first half of the nineteenth century, but there were substantially more than this number of retail outlets. A local trade directory, published in 1822, listed 21 sellers of toys and fancy ware and one, published in 1832, has 16 entries under this heading. Most of these would have stocked Tunbridge wares as would also the libraries and booksellers.[11]

Chapter 4

TUNBRIDGE WARE PRODUCTION AND SALE AT OTHER CENTRES

The success of the industry in decorative woodwares at Tunbridge Wells does not appear to have been emulated at other inland spa centres. Only one seller is known at Bath, a John Brabant who, in 1791, was running a Tunbridge and toy warehouse at Trim Bridge. A whitewood box, finished in simulated rosewood and with an uncoloured view of the Royal Crescent at Bath is known,[1] and others with coloured prints of Bath Abbey Church and All Saints Chapel. Some items must have been supplied from Tunbridge Wells or Tonbridge as a roundel inscribed 'A TRIFLE FROM BATH' is included in the Sprange printer's samples.[2] Cheltenham had one seller of Tunbridge ware, Samuel Bettison, who operated a library at 384, High Street in the 1820s and 30s. Print-decorated boxes made by Wise illustrating the old Montpelier Pump Room and the Well Walk, Cheltenham are known. No evidence exists of Tunbridge ware being sold at other inland spas, though it is likely that small items of cabinet or turnery ware were sold.[3]

In the case of seaside spas, sales up to about 1830 appear, in the main, to have been confined to the stretch of Kent and Sussex coasts from Gravesend to Bognor and at Southend in Essex. A number of Tunbridge ware items had printed paper labels attached to them with mottoes or indications of the place of sale. This may have resulted from the successful sale of Bilston enamel boxes at Tunbridge Wells, a lid from one is known inscribed 'A GIFT FROM TUNBRIDGE WELLS'. To satisfy demand, Tunbridge ware makers purchased enamel plaques, probably from Bilston, to add to their wooden manufactures. A turned whitewood box is known with a plaque on the lid inscribed 'A TUNBRIDGE PRESENT' and an oval cribbage board exists incorporating a plaque which reads 'A TRIFLE FROM ROCHESTER'. Contemporary with these are the paper roundels of the 1790s in the Sprange Collection, one inscribed 'A PRESENT from GRAVESEND' and the other 'A TRIFLE FROM GRAVESEND' while a box c1845 with a view of Greenwich Naval Hospital is known with a label 'A Present from TULLEY'S Bazaar, Gravesend'. They serve as a reminder that in the late Georgian and early Victorian periods the town had pretensions to being the nearest sea-bathing spa to the capital. Outside Brighton, Margate represented the largest market for Tunbridge ware. As a sea-bathing resort, it was one of the earliest to develop because of the ease and cheapness of access from London by sailing hoy along the north Kent coast. As early as 1769, it had an Assembly Room which could attract a subscription list of 930. With the development of steamships, the resort became even more popular. By the 1820s, fares from London averaged 4s (20p) but at times of fierce competition between vessel owners could fall to as little as 1s 6d (7½p) or 2s (10p). In the year 1820–21 nearly 44,000 people landed at the pier, a total that was to more than double by the beginning of the next decade. Samuel Bettison, with addresses both in London and Margate, was combining the sale of Tunbridge ware with perfumery as early as 1794. Later he opened a library at the north-west corner of Hawley Square, which also played a major role in retailing Tunbridge ware. Another early seller was Silver's Library on the east side of Cecil Square, which was selling Tunbridge ware in 1797. *The Margate Guide* of that year described Silver's as being:

'So well contriv'd for pastime and for ease,
It cannot fail the visitant to please.
The shop, which first we enter, is well stor'd
With trinkets, such as Tunbridge-wells afford.'

9a. Whitewood box finished in simulated rosewood, penwork borders and an engraving of 'UPTON COTTAGE near BROADSTAIRS'. Seller's label inside the lid of W.G. Bettison, Margate. Box attributable to George Wise, Tonbridge. c1830. w:15cm d:11cm h:5cm.

9b. *Seller's label from inside the lid of the whitewood box on page 36.*

Silver's successor, Bousfield and Pallister, and later other librarians such as William George Bettison and George Witherden, carried on the tradition of stocking such wares. The evidence suggests that the Wise business played a major role in supplying the resort (fig. 9). A circular map entitled 'Essay on the Isle of Thanet' exists with a Thomas Wise imprint, while later boxes with topographical views of the resort bear prints labelled or attributable to Thomas or George Wise. This Tonbridge maker was probably also the main supplier to libraries and stationers of Ramsgate and Folkestone.[4]

Hastings, on the East Sussex coast, had a number of active traders in Tunbridge ware, and the products of George Wise are known to have been on sale here too (fig. 10). The position of Tonbridge on the main London to Hastings road facilitated this trade. Edmund Nye, the Tunbridge Wells maker, also sought to exploit this market and set up a branch from the mid-1820s. One seller is known at Eastbourne and at Worthing a number of libraries were active in selling the ware. Stafford's Marine Library at the corner of the Steyne obtained some of its supplies from George Wise, but the nearness of the resort to Brighton meant that items also came from this source. The Sprange collection contains several roundels of the mid-1790s inscribed 'Presents', 'Gifts' or 'Trifles' from Hothamton, the name used at this date for Bognor. Richard Hotham, a wealthy Southwark hatter, employed considerable sums of money from the 1780s in an effort to develop the resort.[5] Some sale is recorded at coastal resorts in Dorset and Devon.

The stocking of Tunbridge wares by libraries in spa and resort towns is, in part, explained by the establishment of these businesses at an early stage in the development of the towns concerned, before

10a. Whitewood workbox decorated with amboyna veneer, penwork borders and a coloured engraving of 'THE PROMENADE, HASTINGS'. Published at Wise's Manufactory, Tonbridge Town, May 1 1813'. The centre building on the print is Barry's Marine Library. w:27cm d:22cm h:15cm.

10b. Label from inside the lid of the whitewood box above.

specialist traders in such wares had a sufficient market to be attracted to them. Libraries were more than just providers of books. They acted as a focal point in the well-established routine of spa life, and an assembly point for fashionable society. Initially, they were often the sole providers of the fancy goods, stationery and music that fashionable society demanded. Tunbridge ware provided more than just an additional line for retail sale, however. In libraries, much of it was distributed as prizes in games of chance, which proved a great attraction to the fashionable visitor. Facilities for gambling were one of the early developments at spas and Celia Fiennes when she visited Tunbridge Wells in 1697 noted the 'two rooms for the Lottery and Hazard board'. It is likely that the ware was used for prizes in games of chance at Tunbridge Wells, though no evidence of this has been discovered. Libraries, however, played a less central role in the disposal of ware at Tunbridge Wells because of direct sale by the makers and retailers on the Walks. Evidence of the use of Tunbridge ware as prizes by libraries comes from Brighton, Margate, Dover and Worthing, however. Raffling for prizes, the winner identified by the throwing of dice, is recorded at a Brighton library in 1770 and at Margate in 1797, when it was described in verse:

'To see how eagerly they throw the dice,
One would conceive the stake of wond'rous price;
Whereas a whip, a caddy, or some toy,
Creates the loser's chagrin, winner's joy,
Trifling as these appear, doubt not my friends,
They answer many salutary ends;
The guests they please, the owner's profits raise,
And spread afar the artist's well-earned praise.'

An explanatory prose footnote to the poem states that:

'The raffles or as they are politely called, the subscriptions, generally for some article in jewellery, Tunbridge Ware, toys, muslins &c. are so numerous that many goods are disposed of in an evening by this means.'[6]

Not all approved of such activities, however. The writer of one Worthing guide of 1813 claimed that many of the younger visitors to the resort were suffering 'great injury to their morals and health' by indulging in such games at the libraries in the town:

'The species of gambling is introduced, nay almost forced, upon the visitor, by persons who are either hired or feel an interest in the concern; under the specious appearance of being gentlemen and ladies, with a pleasing address, they invite your support of the library, requesting you to chance your shilling or half-crown, to raffle for an article, which should **you** win, is very short of the value laid upon it. It is a well-known fact that last season one **gentleman** and his **friends** were so very **fortunate** as to take away nearly all the principal articles.'[7]

Such activities were either illegal or verging on the illegal, and a number of prosecutions were taken out against librarians who organised them. Librarians attempted to protect themselves by introducing new activities such as trinket auctions or the card game known as 'Loo' or 'Pam', also of dubious legality. A complaint laid before the Brighton magistrates in 1817 was successful and the writer of one guide in 1818 mourned the fact that they 'thought *Pam* was an unwelcome resident, and by their mandate, supported by an obsolete law of Henry VIII, he was excommunicated from the libraries without benefit of appeal'. Such legal decisions were usually only temporary setbacks, and the games resumed in Brighton after a suitable time had elapsed. Worthing, too, knew the game and at the Colonnade Library in 1824 was to be seen 'a magnificent display of jewellery, Tunbridge ware, &c.' exhibited 'for sale or disposed of by that species of Lottery denominated "Loo".' Although by the mid-1820s there was a growing moral feeling against such games, the prelude to the Victorian 'age of cant', raffling appears to have survived at Margate libraries and bazaars as late as 1848. The number of Tunbridge ware items decorated with prints showing views of libraries or bearing the seller's label of libraries is explained by the considerable role they played in the disposal of such wares (figs. 9, 16, colour pl. 4).[8]

Outside of London and south-eastern England, there were few important centres for the production and sale of Tunbridge wares. A label in the Sprange collection inscribed 'A TRIFLE FROM OXFORD', a painted whitewood box (c1820) in the Tunbridge Wells Museum labelled 'A Present from Oxford' and a small workbox of similar date with a view of High Street (fig. 14) suggest sales in this university town. There is, however, little evidence of sale at the coastal resorts of south and south-western England, south and west Wales or East Anglia, though a whitewood box labelled 'A GIFT FROM SOUTHPORT' indicates that it was not unknown on the Lancashire coast. The growing industrial and commercial towns yield one maker at Birmingham and a seller at Coventry, so their inhabitants do not appear to have developed any great taste for Tunbridge wares. Two major centres, which developed as provincial capitals with roles in the social, administrative and legal fields, attracting gentry unwilling to face the long journey to London, did develop production of Tunbridge ware, however. One of these was York, where an industry, based initially on turnery wares, existed in the mid-1780s and continued until c1820. The earliest mention is found in an advertisement by Marshall & Doughty of February 1795, stating that they had opened a shop in Coney Street and manufactured and sold 'all kinds of Toys, Tunbridge and Turnery articles viz. small Cabinet Boxes, Tea Caddies, Writing Desks, Umbrellas, Trinkets'. The Doughty part of the partnership was Joseph Doughty, who was born in York in 1755, and, as early as March 1790, had a shop in Minstergate whose stock included 'bone and wooden toys'. Joseph died in December 1801 and his wife, Martha, continued the business; in March 1807 she described it as a 'Toy, Tunbridge and Cabinet Manufactory'. Martha Doughty married her husband's former partner and in an advertisement which appeared in 1814 refers to herself as M. Marshall. In March of that year she was advertising 'Lady's Work and Dressing Boxes, Gentleman's Dressing Cases &c.' but the word

Tunbridge does not appear in the advertisement. Another York maker of Tunbridge ware was George Stones, whose shop was in Spurriergate. He first appears in directories in 1798, described as a toyman. By 1809, however, his trade was listed as turner and Tunbridge ware manufacturer and in 1816 he was offering 'turnery and Fancy Cabinet Ware of every Description'. He was also dealing in foreign timbers and his stock contained 'Black and White King, and Tulip Wood'. No mention of Tunbridge ware is made after 1818, and George Stones died in May 1823, aged 59. His widow, Dorothy, continued the business but by now it appears to have been more concerned with the manufacture and retailing of furniture. Several other 'toymen' are recorded in York at this period. A workbox decorated in penwork and displaying a print of a Regency lady holding doves is displayed in the Royal Pavilion at Brighton and contains in the interior a label with an engraved view identified as 'Cliff Bridge Scarborough' (opened 1827). This could be of York manufacture, as could also a penwork workbox (c1830) decorated with a picture of York Minster in the Castle Museum, York collection. One important product of the Doughty business and other York turners was an elegant spinning wheel designed to enable fashionable ladies to spin the thread needed for sewing or embroidery. Such wheels achieved a considerable reputation and were sold in London and the south of England amongst other places. John Robinson, the London and Tunbridge Wells maker, advertised in the 1790s 'YORK and other Spinning Wheels' as part of his stock and William Vale kept them in his London showrooms and listed them in an advertisement of 1803.[9]

Dublin, a centre of attraction for the Anglo-Irish gentry, also developed trades to satisfy fashionable caprice. Here, Tunbridge wares were advertised for sale during the first four decades of the nineteenth century. No manufacturer has yet been identified, but six Tunbridge ware repositories are listed in Dublin directories. The city had established cabinet-making concerns and was fully capable of producing such wares. They might, however, have been brought in from another centre of production and if this was the case London would appear not unlikely. No items of certain Dublin origin have to date been identified but a fitted rectangular whitewood box decorated with a map of Ireland, very similar in style to George Wise items of the early nineteenth century is known, and is likely to have been made for the Irish market. This suggests that those sold may well have been indistinguishable from others produced elsewhere. Painted, pen-work and print-decorated whitewood wares and those veneered in parquetry patterns would seem most likely to have been on sale.[10] The popularity of such items would have been affected by changes in fashion from the 1830s, as well as increasing sales of bog oak and possibly arbutus wares, which would also have appealed to the rising national identity within Ireland, and the consequent interest in its culture and history.[11]

Chapter 5

THE NATURE OF TUNBRIDGE WARES PRIOR TO c1830

The mosaic and inlaid Tunbridge wares produced from the 1830s are instantly recognisable to collectors because of their distinctive patterns and designs. Of the products of the industry before this date much less is known, despite the fact that these wares were produced for around 150 years and several centres of production were involved. Attempts have been made by a number of writers to draw up a sequence for the development of Tunbridge wares over the period to 1830, but these tend to rely as much on speculation as on evidence.[1] One thing is certain, the items manufactured must still exist, but are often unrecognised as products of the Tunbridge ware industry. A good example of this is an oval harewood tea caddy of c1790 with simple floral marquetry, which bears the label of Joseph Knight, 'Tunbridge Ware Maker to Her Majesty, Tunbridge Wells' (fig. 11). Unlabelled caddies of a similar nature have never been associated with Tunbridge ware in the past. A Tunbridge ware maker named Connard, working in Tonbridge around the turn of the eighteenth century, was even producing *verre églomisé* panels for incorporation into boxes.[2] Initially, the industry confined itself mainly to turnery but small cabinet wares appeared as early as the late seventeenth century. In some cases these were veneered, but often they were of whitewood and by the late eighteenth century were being decorated with paint, prints or penwork. They remained popular until the end of the Georgian period. From c1800, a wide range of veneered wares decorated with parquetry developed as important rivals to the whitewood items and it is from this decorative tradition that the line of development to the post-1830 productions can be traced.

Turnery Wares

Celia Fiennes, in an early reference to Tunbridge wares (1697), noted on sale 'delicate neate and thin ware of wood both white and lignum vitae'. In London in the first half of the eighteenth century, lignum vitae is frequently mentioned in connection with Tunbridge

*11. Oval harewood tea caddy with floral marquetry on top and sides.
c1790. The interior bears the maker's label of 'Joseph Knight,
Tunbridge Ware Maker to Her Majesty, Tunbridge Wells'.
w:15cm, d:8.5cm, h:8.5cm.*

wares which were almost exclusively the products of turners.
Lignum vitae is a timber from the West Indies and the mainland of
tropical America, first imported into England early in the sixteenth
century when it was valued for the medicinal qualities of the resin
as a remedy for gout, rheumatism and other illnesses. When the
timber became popular with turners in the late seventeenth century
its earlier medicinal role was not entirely forgotten, and it would
seem likely that cups for the taking of spa waters in this timber
might be favoured (fig. 12). Other brown native timbers were also
used for turnery by Tunbridge ware makers and Benge Burr in 1766
named cherry, plum and yew as in use. The fruit woods were
readily available in a county which by the late seventeenth century
was already noted for its orchards, which supplied London
markets. The main whitewoods used were holly and sycamore.[3]
Apart from goblets, bowls and cups, a wide range of other turnery
might be offered as Tunbridge ware. The London turner, Robert
Horne (c1770), offered on his trade card 'Pepper Boxes and other
Tunbridge Ware' and pepper and spice mills, graters and storage
boxes were to remain popular in the industry until at least the
middle of the nineteenth century. A local guide lists amongst other

items on offer at Tunbridge Wells in 1780, snuff boxes and punch ladles. Turners producing fashionable Tunbridge wares were regarded as craftsmen with a skill superior to the common turner whose main trade was in utilitarian household wares. In London, such craftsmen were clearly distinguished, but in Tunbridge Wells, with the more seasonal nature of the trade in fashionable goods, the distinction may not have been so clear. As late as the first decades of the nineteenth century, turnery wares played a significant role in the industry. New items were developed to meet the changing needs and tastes of visitors, such as cylinders to hold the panoramic views of Regent's Park, Brighton seafront, etc. favoured by Regency society, and the wheels used in connection with the card games of Matrimony and Pope Joan. On Barrow's map of Tunbridge Wells published in 1808 'Fenner & Nye's Turnery' is listed at Mount

12. Goblet, lignum vitae wood of the type produced by turners in west Kent and London and referred to as Tunbridge ware. c1700. (A. & E. Foster Antiques).

13. Satinwood workbox, the front and sides decorated with floral and leaf swags and ribbons. The verre églomisé top with a central panel depicting a thatched cottage in a rural setting in gold and black and signed 'J. Connard'. Interior with lidded compartments and signed 'Jn. McEwen'. c1790. (Christopher Buck Antiques).

Ephraim and 'Fenner's Turnery' on Mount Sion. By this date, however, small cabinet wares were the major items produced in both Tunbridge Wells and the London trades. The late date of the commencement of the Brighton trade meant that turnery never occupied the same important role as it did elsewhere. A number of turned items were produced in Brighton, however, including pin cushions and sewing clamps, but the most interesting were sewing companions and spice graters and containers shaped like the 'Hindoo' domes of the recently rebuilt and extended Royal Pavilion, with painted detail, which appeared from c1820 (fig. 6). Perfumers and other tradesmen required simple turned boxes for their preparations, and these continued to be made well into the Victorian period.[4]

Whitewood Wares

Cabinet wares developed in parallel with turnery. In 1727, a Tunbridge jewel box was sent as a gift to Mrs Mary Granville and may have been of this nature. It is possible, however, that at this date it was turned. 'The Tunbridge, Powder, Patch, Washball and Snuff Boxes' offered by a London toyman called Bellamy in 1762 also seem likely to have been the work of the turners.[5] By the late eighteenth century, however, cabinet work started to gain the ascendancy. Boxes for writing, sewing, dressing, games and storage

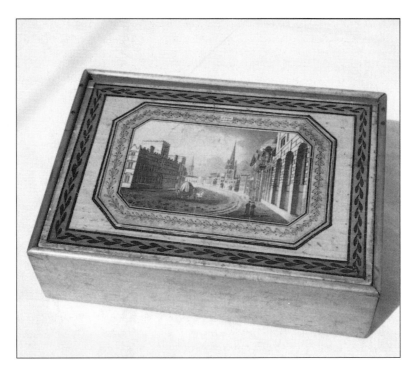

14. *Whitewood workbox, the top with a print identified as 'A View in Oxford', painted stylised leaf border, fitted interior lined in red paper. The print published in J.N. Brewer,* The Beauties of England and Wales *Vol. XII Pt II (1813). c1815. l:18.5cm, d:12.5cm, h:5cm.*

of tea, cosmetics and smelling salts were offered in great profusion by Tunbridge ware makers and sellers. Whitewood wares produced in holly, sycamore, beech and chestnut were particularly favoured, for these allowed for elaborate decoration in a variety of different mediums and forms at a much lower cost than the utilisation of marquetry. Since by the beginning of the nineteenth century a number of makers were marking their wares with printed labels, we can identify items produced by Tunbridge ware makers with certainty, and attribute related but unlabelled items to them.

One of the most common ways of decorating whitewood wares, and also some veneered items, was with prints. These had already been used as a means of decorating harpsichord and clock cases by the mid-eighteenth century and their use soon became a fashionable craze. Late Georgian print-decorated rooms still survive at The Vyne and Stratfield Saye (Hampshire), Blickling (Norfolk), Kew (Surrey), Heveningham (Suffolk), Uppark (West Sussex), Woodhall Park (Hertfordshire), Rokeby (Yorkshire) and Castletown (Co. Kildare). Tunbridge ware makers were certainly using prints for box decoration by the 1790s, producing wares which in appearance and function competed with the much more expensive enamelled goods then popular. In 1795, John Robinson of London and Tunbridge Wells offered a wide range of print-decorated wares, while in the following year William Fenner announced that he could supply his range of goods 'inlaid with all kinds of French and English Prints in as elegant a style as any yet manufactured'. Print publishers could provide a large variety of small prints and medallions to meet the needs of the public at large and also manufacturers of Tunbridge ware. Makers seeking local topographical prints of a suitable size for box decoration might find those used in contemporary guide books and local histories of use, but often engaged artists and published their own products for local sale as well as box decoration.[6]

Initially, boxes decorated with classical figures attracted the attention of a public influenced by the prevailing neo-classical ideals. Josiah Wedgwood had profitably satisfied a public demand with his ranges of jasper-ware medallions of classical subjects in imitation of cameos, and Rudolph Ackermann attempted to emulate the example in the cheaper medium of paper, ink and paint. He was able to offer 'upwards of 150 sheets of Medallions in Colours, plain or in Bronze, mostly engraved after Burney and Westall from Heathen Mythology, Greek, Roman and Modern History, allegorical and emblematical figures'. These he suggested were 'calculated for Ornamenting all kinds of Fancy Work such as Screens, Card Racks, Flower Stands, Vases, Card Boxes, Desert Stands &c. in imitation of Wedgwood's Ware, now quite in fashion'. The range of prints offered by John Robinson must have been of a similar nature. In a handbill published in connection with his Tunbridge Wells business in 1797 he offered 'PRINTS and MEDALLIONS of all Sizes … by M[R] Bartolozzi, and other Eminent Artists from Antique Gems'. There were, no doubt, many other print sellers who could provide similar items. The style was quickly taken up by Tunbridge ware dealers and in January 1806, William Vale was offering from his London showrooms wares in the Roman and Etruscan styles. Throughout the whole of the Regency period this style of decoration retained some popularity (fig. 15).[7]

Many Tunbridge ware items were aimed at a female clientele and print publishers found it to their commercial advantage to produce subjects which reflected this. Engravings of young ladies in costume influenced by the Greek revival partaking in genteel activities were thought to be suitable (colour pl. 2). George Wise used prints published by Rudolph Ackermann in box decoration, including those from a book entitled *Healthful Sports for Young Ladies*, which he issued in English translation in 1822 (fig. 16). The young ladies partaking in these decorous sports reflect well the spirit of the age of Jane Austen and could well be heroines of her novels. Such prints were suited to the decoration of a wide range of boxes and cabinets, including card boxes. It was, however, thought appropriate for card boxes to have lids decorated with a display of playing cards, and a number of manufacturers produced ink drawings for this purpose. The Tunbridge Wells makers, John, James & Ann Sharp, offered boxes so decorated (fig. 76, colour pl. 6). George Wise produced card boxes, some in the popular hexagonal shape, and one labelled box, apart from the display of cards, has the added inscription 'Presented to his wife by W.T. Hall, Hope Mill, Goudhurst', a

15. *Tea caddy, harewood with stringing of other woods, decorated with prints of classical subjects, the background painted in maroon. Interior contains two tea boxes and a cut-glass bowl. A similar caddy is in the collection of Temple Newsam, Leeds. c1790. w:30.5cm d:15cm h:15cm.*

specially commissioned item for a resident of this west Kent village. A favourite device from the 1790s into the next decade was to affix a roundel containing a motto or verse on the Tunbridge ware. Jasper Sprange's sample book contains large numbers of these ranging from the simple 'Remember Me' to one designed for a box fitted with a mirror and reading 'Within this Box You there may see/The face of one That's dear to me'.[8]

Articles of early nineteenth century date decorated with topographical prints have been recognised as Tunbridge ware though other print-decorated wares have tended to be denied such recognition. This is because the views are of Tunbridge Wells, Brighton and other resorts, the views are often identified, and the print publisher and maker are named on a label stuck inside the box (cut from beneath the print used). Topographical prints of rectangular shape or medallions were used in considerable quantities by Brighton, Tonbridge and Tunbridge Wells makers, as they were a convenient way of identifying objects with particular resorts in which they were sold (figs. 1, 2, 6, 7, 9, 10, 13, 16, 86, colour pls. 1, 3, 4, 7). It also eliminated the need to provide special labels indicating in which town the item was purchased, though these are occasionally found. Uncoloured prints, sometimes on coloured paper, were used initially, but from c1805 hand colouring was

16. *Three-drawer cabinet enclosed by doors below a sewing compartment. Whitewood with simulated rosewood finish. Top decorated with a coloured engraving of Stafford's Marine Library, Worthing and the doors with prints from the English edition of St. Sernin,* Healthful Sports for Young Ladies *published by Ackermann in 1822. Attributable to George Wise, Tonbridge. c1825. w:24cm d:15.5cm h:25.5cm.*

added in most cases. Topographical prints were particularly valuable to the Wise business at Tonbridge with its widespread trade contacts. Thomas Wise used such prints as early as 1800, as well as a series of circular maps of the country surrounding the resorts in which he had custom. George Wise followed the same practice of publishing most of his own topographical prints. Artists were commissioned to produce paintings and drawings for the Wise business and the work of T.R. Smith, P.W. Tompkins, Shawle and Sponberry has been identified. I. Buck and S. Rawle were employed to engrave some of the copper printing plates. A collection of 23 original water colours commissioned by George Wise between 1806 and 1814 is known.[9]

The term 'transfer print' has been applied to these print-decorated wares and one writer has asserted that the pictures were printed directly on to the wood by a method patented by Stephen Bedford of Birmingham in 1759.[10] Bedford's patent (No. 737) certainly referred to the decoration of snuff boxes amongst other items, but the process was little used in connection with Tunbridge ware. Transfer printing enabled cheap and instant decoration but only in a single colour, multi-colour transferring not being developed successfully until the work of Charles Valentine of Birmingham in 1809. Rudolph Ackermann marketed a 'caustic varnish' for 'Transferring Plain and Coloured Prints upon White Wood'. Ordinary prints could be used with this process. In most Tunbridge ware of this period, however, the print was fixed to the wood with an adhesive and then varnished to protect it. Only in the mid to late nineteenth century did transfer printing directly from copper and, later, steel plates on to wood become common, in connection with the ubiquitous Mauchline wares produced mainly by the firm of William & Andrew Smith. By this period, the print-decorated Tunbridge wares had long been superseded by the new mosaic.[11]

Additionally, many pieces of whitewood Tunbridge ware of the early nineteenth century were decorated with penwork borders. These were drawn or painted in dense black ink on the white wood (figs. 9, 10). This was a technique closely associated with the Regency period, and was also used to entirely decorate small cabinet wares, and occasionally more substantial pieces of furniture such as tables and chiffoniers. It is highly likely that Tunbridge ware makers were responsible for items completely decorated in penwork (colour pl. 5). The subjects used for such items are sometimes classical and often in the Chinese taste (colour pl. 1), which once more came to the fore in the early nineteenth century, inspired by the example of George IV when Prince of Wales and Prince Regent. The Chinese taste could also be well conveyed by the use of japanning, the European imitation of oriental lacquer. In January 1807, William Vale was offering in his London showrooms an assortment of wares finished in the Chinese taste, while Morris at Brighton c1815 included japanning amongst the finishes available for his Tunbridge wares. The collection in the Tunbridge Wells Museum includes a penwork box and tea caddy c1810 which came through a member of the Wise family and are believed to be products of this Tonbridge manufactory. Labelled items with penwork borders by George Wise from the Regency period are known.[12]

Borders were required to surround prints and finish the top and sides of Tunbridge ware boxes. A number of techniques in addition to penwork could be used for this purpose. Parquetry borders of contrasting woods set in a geometrical pattern were used by George Wise on many of his pieces made in the first two decades of the nineteenth century and probably later. William Upton of Brighton also used this technique (fig. 7). As an alternative, fancy gilt borders might be employed (fig. 10, colour pl. 4). George Wise was particularly fond of using these to surround the central print or medallion. His supplies may have come from Rudolph Ackermann who c1810 offered 'a great Variety of Borders, on plain or coloured Paper from 9d to 5s per dozen'.

Much whitewood Tunbridge ware had painted decoration, and this might either complement a coloured print or constitute the entire decoration of the box. Much of the painted work was of floral character, sometimes consisting of profuse bouquets of roses, though often of ill-defined but exotic blossoms, figments of an artist's imagination (fig. 17). Rustic cottages and rural scenes, Chinese subjects, exotic birds and borders of stylised motifs are also encountered. There has been a reluctance to recognise items decorated in this manner as Tunbridge ware, but the writer of a Tunbridge Wells guide of 1883, reminiscing on the nature of earlier Tunbridge wares, had no doubts:

> *'Painting on wood – holly wood to begin with, then sycamore and chestnut – was at an early date a peculiar industry practised in Tunbridge Wells, and later in Brighton. The boxes, hand-screens and similar objects made of white wood, painted in a peculiar and attractive style with flowers must be familiar to many of our older readers.'*[13]

The method of decoration was relatively cheap to execute, highly colourful and widely practised. Specialist artists were employed, no doubt in most cases women, but in September 1822 Charles Carter of Brighton declared his trade as Tunbridge ware painter, suggesting the employment of men also. This type of decoration was particularly prevalent in the Brighton trade and as early as *c*1815 Morris was advertising from his Trafalgar Place address wares decorated in 'enamel, Malmatint, Japan &c.'. A box painted with exotic tulips to complement a print of Tonbridge Bridge and Castle with a Wise label confirms the use of this style of finish by the major producer in the town. Tunbridge Wells makers also used painted decoration and an unusual watch stand in the form of a

17. *Whitewood workbox, the top printed with sprays of roses and the sides with roses, fuchsias and exotic birds. Brass feet decorated with rococo scrolls. c1830. w:25cm d:19.5cm h:11cm.*

Gothic tower with painted detail is known bearing the label of James Friend and dating from *c*1820. This tradition, although much less favoured after *c*1830, did continue in Tunbridge Wells; a hand screen and stand decorated with chaffinches, flowers and foliage and bearing the maker's mark of Thomas Barton (c1870) is a late example (fig. 40). Cylinders designed to hold panoramas were often painted, and as many of these were printed and published in London, this suggests that this style of decoration was also practised there.[14]

Tunbridge ware makers produced a number of simulated wood finishes that could be used on whitewood boxes (figs. 9, 16). Rosewood was frequently imitated on items, paralleling its simulation on fashionable light Trafalgar chairs, while imitation of more exotic timbers, such as amboyna, was attempted. George Wise was a frequent user of this form of finish. Another alternative was to imitate tortoiseshell, which in the late Georgian period was frequently used as a veneer on small cabinet wares, especially tea caddies. Sophisticated attempts to counterfeit tortoiseshell date back to the late seventeenth century, but for whitewood Tunbridge wares, the method adopted was merely to scorch the wood with hot sand. The practice was certainly used in the Brighton trade and probably by Wise at Tonbridge. No matter what form of decoration was employed, it had to be protected by a number of coats of clear varnish. This was the weakness of these wares, for the varnish became scratched and tended to go opaque with the passage of time, and therefore most Tunbridge ware makers advertised a service for the repair and re-varnishing of older items.[15]

The creation of decorated whitewood Tunbridge wares was not the monopoly of commercial manufacturers. The finishing of such wares was considered an appropriately genteel occupation for ladies who were encouraged to undertake this work. Rudolph Ackermann published designs for the decoration of such wares commenting that:

'Among the many pleasing recreations of the fair sex, is that of painting and ornamenting Tunbridge and fancy ware, which at once becomes an elegant and useful amusement.'[16]

There was a long tradition of amateurs decorating woodwares, extending back to the end of the seventeenth century, when a craze for japanning by ladies led to the publication of manuals and the proliferation of teachers of the art. This interest was revived in the mid-eighteenth century. From the end of the century, a number of Tunbridge ware makers and sellers were offering materials for the amateur decorator. In 1795, John Robinson advertised 'PRINTS and MEDALLIONS of all sizes both ENGLISH and FRENCH in a great variety (for Inlaying Boxes &c.)', and many others followed suit. Undecorated whitewood wares were also available, and both William Vale and Malcolm Dunnett offered boxes 'for ladies' own painting' in the first decade of the nineteenth century. As late as the 1830s, these were still available from Charles Ingall, a Reading bookseller who offered:

'Prints, Varnish and all Materials for Transferring, together with a Collection of White Wood Screens, Work Boxes, Card Cases, Watch Stands &c.'[17]

S. & J. Fuller at their Temple of Fancy in Rathbone Place and Rudolph Ackermann at his Repository of Arts in the Strand were in the forefront of those in London offering materials for the amateur. Although suppliers must have drawn undecorated whitewood boxes from commerical makers of small cabinet wares, most Tunbridge ware makers do not appear to have advertised the sale of such items to the public, possibly considering such a trade detrimental to the sale of finished products.[18]

Veneered and Parquetry Wares

In Britain, the art of veneering was little known before the Restoration of Charles II, but was widely practised in the capital and important provincial centres within a decade or two following 1660. As the Tunbridge Wells area kept in close contact with London developments and fashions through its annual influx of visitors, it is likely that the skill of veneering would have been absorbed here at an early date if it had fulfilled a need. As has already been indicated, however, the earliest types of Tunbridge wares were turnery, with boxes of lesser importance not developing until the early eighteenth century and even then often being made of turned wood. By the 1760s, however, veneered wares were on sale in Tunbridge Wells and in 1762 Samuel Derrick, the Master of Ceremonies, was able to comment on the beautiful 'inlaying and veneering'. Four years later, Thomas Benge Burr referred to the recent popularity of yew in the production of Tunbridge ware, adding that 'the goods fineered with it are certainly excessively pretty'. He too commented on 'ornamental inlays' which in most circumstances would be interpreted as marquetry. However, as he appears to be commenting about wares made from holly and adds that the inlays are so excellent 'that it is hard to believe they are not assisted by the pencil' it is far from certain that these were marquetry wares. The term 'inlay', as has been seen, was used loosely in the late Georgian period, and even included the addition of prints to whitewood boxes. Thus, all that can be said is that there were veneered wares at Tunbridge Wells by the mid-eighteenth century but their nature is uncertain and none have so far been identified.[19]

From the 1790s, however, we are on much more certain ground. A small sycamore-veneered table dating from this period is known with a parquetry border to the top and an applied print in the centre. The table bears the trade label of John Fry of Tunbridge Wells.[20] Veneered boxes exist, decorated with prints, a number of these having printed labels that identify them as the work of Thomas or George Wise of Tonbridge. Many print-decorated wares are of whitewood, however, as it was found to be easier to simulate a hardwood finish when desired than to resort to veneering. Parallel

18. Early examples of perspective cube parquetry. Rear: *mahogany box with large cube work (sides 3cm) completely covering the top (always a sign of early work). c1825. w:19cm d:13.5cm h:6.5cm.* Front left: *rosewood box, perspective cube work bordered with miniature parquetry. c1835. w:20.5cm d:10cm h:5cm.* Right: *box with perspective cube work on top, vandykes on all sides. c1825. w:20.5cm d:8cm h:6cm.*

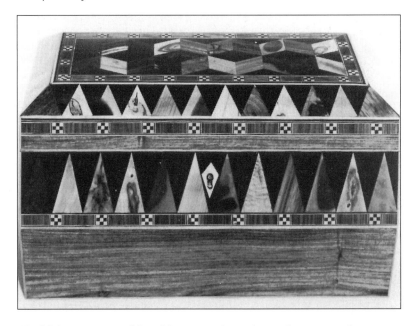

19. Mahogany tea caddy with perspective cube work on top and vandykes on chamfered edges of top and sides of alternate ebony and fruitwoods. Perspective cube work on the interior of the lid and tops of the tea compartments. c1830. w30.5cm h:16.5cm. (Sotheby's).

with the whitewood wares, however, was the development of a range of items decorated with parquetry, utilising small geometrically shaped pieces of wood which contrasted in colour and grain and were arranged in patterns. Of those used, the two most popular were an arrangement of diamonds and triangular-shaped pieces to give the illusion of perspective cubes, and elongated triangular shapes in contrasting dark and light wood which were known as vandykes (figs. 18, 19, 20, 21, 22, colour pls. 8, 9, 10).

The perspective cube work already had a long history before it appeared in Tunbridge wares around the end of the eighteenth century. It originated, no doubt, in the craze for perspective work inspired by the Renaissance. Its earliest recorded use in connection with furniture is in a chest dated *c*1540 in the Historisches Museum, Basle. Although no English examples are known this early, perspective marble table tops of a different pattern were imported from Italy in the late sixteenth century, one of which is now

20. *Rosewood tea caddy, the top decorated with three diamonds of small parquetry work and the sides with demi-rosettes of various parquetry woods. The tops of the tea compartments feature single perspective cubes. c1820. w:33.5cm d:17.5cm h:17cm.*

21. *Octagonal workbox, the top decorated with a rosette of fruitwoods on a coromandel ground, the sides decorated with vandykes in fruitwoods and ebony. The diamond-shaped keyhole escutcheon is common on late Georgian small cabinet wares. c1820. dia:21.5cm h:9.5cm.*

displayed at Aston Hall, Birmingham. It is in the late seventeenth century that the first published designs for perspective cube work emerge in connection with the laying of stone and marble floors, and these continued in popularity into the first half of the eighteenth century. Such designs were equally applicable to wooden parquetry floors, which first made their appearance in Britain in the reign of Charles I and became popular after the Restoration. No English examples of perspective cube work in wood are known, but the pattern was chosen for a parquetry floor installed in the Hotel d'Hare-Skenluyse, Ghent (1776–81) and from c1760 it was extensively used in furniture on the Continent, especially commodes of the Louis XVI period. The pattern was much favoured by the workshop of the maître ébéniste J-F. Oeben (d. 1793).[21] It is probably from French cabinet-making practice that this type of parquetry came into Tunbridge ware. The date of introduction must have been close to 1800. Henry W. Wolff, in his book *Sussex Industries* (1883) claimed that 'mosaic' [cube and diamond work] was introduced by a Mr Burrows of Tonbridge in 1797 but fails to indicate the source of this information. A small harewood veneered cabinet of five graduated drawers enclosed by two doors, these and the top being decorated with mosaic panels of diamond shape incorporating similarly shaped pieces of wood selected for their striking figure and variety, is known. It bears the label 'From Robinson's MANUFACTORY, No. 53 Piccadilly AND Tunbridge Wells' and must date from c1800. The earliest firmly dated record of the sale of such wares was in April 1806 when Malcolm Dunnett advertised that he had in his London showrooms 'a great variety finished in the mosaic style'. If the style had come from France, which at this period was exerting a strong influence in the furnishing trades, it would be expected that the first wares would have been of London manufacture. There can, however, be little doubt that the style would have quickly been adopted at Tunbridge Wells and at a slightly later date, Brighton.[22]

Perspective cube work was to be one of the most enduring designs introduced into Tunbridge ware, surviving until the closure of commercial production with the onset of the Second World War. It was known in the period immediately following its introduction as 'mosaic', but this term was dropped soon after 1830 when it was transferred to the new types of ware then under development, and a writer in 1844 used the term 'square work' as a replacement.

22a. *Work- and reading-table, rosewood with perspective cube and vandyke parquetry of various woods, well under top for writing materials, fitted drawer for needlework equipment and sliding bag of pleated silk for needlework in hand. c1810. w:58cm d:47cm h:76cm. (W. R. Harvey & Co. (Antiques) Ltd.).*

22b. *The same table, opened.*

Almost from its introduction, perspective cube work was used as a means of displaying a wide range of contrasting timbers and grain effects. No dyeing or treatment of the wood was resorted to. The range of effects was extended by cutting timbers transversely, longitudinally, and on the splay. The late eighteenth century had seen the introduction of decorative table tops displaying specimens of a large range of marbles or alabaster, often accompanied by a chart listing their names. This practice was followed for the larger pieces of perspective cube Tunbridge ware, such as work-tables and teapoys. A manuscript chart accompanying a work-table of *c*1800 lists 21 different timbers of which nine were native (thorn, laburnum, broom, plum, mulberry, lilac, chestnut, box and holly) and 12 foreign (green and black ebony, coromandel, zebra, barberry, partridge, tulip, canary, madagascar, keng, rose and palmyra). The wide range of foreign timbers needed by the beginning of the nineteenth century was available through specialist suppliers in London, a number of whom also produced Tunbridge ware. John Lowe, a hardwood turner and Tunbridge ware maker of White Cross Street, Savile Row (fl. 1700–91) listed on his trade card 21 timbers, mostly foreign, that he was able to supply. By the 1830s, supplies could alternatively be obtained from Brighton, and Edmund Nye appears to have had business contacts with James Atkins of Portland Street, Brighton (fl. 1832–48) a mahogany and foreign wood merchant. By 1840, the range of woods available to the Tunbridge ware maker was more extensive and included 'upwards of forty varieties of native wood besides foreign'. These early perspective cube wares can be identified by such details as keyhole escutcheons in wood, ivory or bone of diamond or shield shape and the use of plain red, pink, blue or green lining papers. Some early cube work is much larger than that used later, the diamonds having sides about 3cm in length (fig. 18). Fruitwoods and certain strongly marked timbers such as zebra and partridge, beloved by the Regency, are less likely to appear in Victorian and twentieth-century pieces.[23] Perspective cube work was used by cabinet makers who made no claim to be producers of Tunbridge ware. A large rectangular workbox so decorated with the label of 'W. BARKER, Cabinet Maker, 7 LADY LANE, LEEDS' dating from the 1840s, is representative of such items.

Another parquetry pattern very characteristic of early Tunbridge ware is the elongated triangles of alternate light and dark wood placed base to apex, known as vandykes. The name, no doubt, derives from the shape of the beards seen in the early seventeenth-century portraits of this artist, but it is not known when the term was first applied to this form of decoration, though a reference dated 1842 has been discovered. The design is clearly derived from the markings on backgammon boards. This game was popular in the medieval period, and a number of boards survive from the late seventeenth century, displaying the characteristic triangles. One dated *c*1670 incorporating oyster veneer in lignum vitae was at one time said to have been made in Tunbridge Wells to the designs of the Comte de Grammont (1621–1707) for Mary Kirk, Maid of Honour to Catherine of Braganza, but it is now considered very unlikely to be of Tunbridge Wells manufacture. Nevertheless, backgammon boards were one of the items manufactured and sold by Tunbridge ware makers and dealers. Samuel Jarvis, a turner and Tunbridge ware maker of Snow Hill, London (fl.1740–84) offered 'Backgammon Tables', and these were also included in the stock of John Robinson of London and Tunbridge Wells, Marshall & Doughty of York, and Malcolm Dunnett of London. Vandyke work was frequently used to decorate the sides of boxes or as a border for the top of small decorative tables, and was often executed in fruitwood and ebony (figs. 19, 21, 39, 53, colour pl. 9). It was less frequent after *c*1840 though George Wise and Thomas Barton did favour its use in the second half of the century. Other parquetry designs found were associated with perspective cube work such as stars, quartered diamonds and sunburst motifs but these are less common (figs. 20, 21).[24]

These parquetry designs, utilising a wide range of timbers of striking grain or colour, take on a particularly attractive form when used on small pieces of decorative furniture such as elegantly fitted work- and writing-tables and teapoys. When a committee of Tunbridge Wells residents was formed in 1826 to raise a subscription to provide the young Princess Victoria with a present, it was just such a piece of furniture that was considered appropriate. Princess Victoria, in the company of her mother, the Duchess of Kent, was a frequent visitor to the town, staying there five times between 1822 and 1835. A print of 1822 shows the Princess returning from a morning ride passing Jordan House, the Tunbridge ware manufactory of Humphrey Burrows, and from the numerous claims to royal patronage made by the manufacturers, it would seem that the Princess and her mother took an interest in the ware. The committee managed to raise 25 guineas (£26.25), and commissioned William Fenner to manufacture a combined work- and writing-table in kingwood which was presented in September 1826. This was:

> *'veneered with party-coloured woods from every part of the globe. It was lined with gold tufted satin, and comprised a complete writing and reading desk, covered with purple embossed velvet fitted up with cut glasses mounted in massive silver. A side drawer exhibited a complete workbox, with appropriate instruments of richly chased silver, the reels, runners &c. being of sandal wood and the silk winders fine specimens of native and foreign woods; the whole lined throughout with gold coloured embossed satin. A drawer on the opposite side was furnished with a drawing box, comprising the necessary colours, pencils, palette, sandal wood rulers &c. From the lower part of the top a workbox of rich gold-coloured silk appropriately ornamented fell in graceful folds. The whole was supported by a finely-worked tripod of solid kingwood.'*

The present whereabouts of this piece is unknown but its nature can be judged from a number of less elaborate but still distinguished pieces of Tunbridge ware furniture of this period reflecting the Sheraton and Regency styles favoured in the first three decades of the nineteenth century (figs. 22, 67).[25]

Apart from these easily identified parquetry wares, in a number of cases Tunbridge ware makers produced small decorative cabinet items which have no features to distinguish them from other veneered wares of the period. James Friend of Tunbridge Wells produced such items and his label is known on a two-door Regency table cabinet of four drawers made in mahogany and banded with satinwood. It is not known whether such pieces were common items of stock and production, or special commissions made to customers' requirements.

Mosaic
Tunbridge Ware
c1830–1939

Chapter 6

THE NEW MOSAIC WARES

About 1830, a number of developments in design and production techniques occurred, resulting in Tunbridge wares which are of particular interest to collectors today. It is often assumed that these wares are of one type, floral bouquets, views, animals, butterflies, birds, etc., composed of minute square tesserae which form veneers to adorn a wide range of useful and decorative household objects. This type of work has been generally known as *end-grain mosaic ware*, but close examination has revealed that cross-grain tesserae are as frequently used as those displaying end-grain. Very few pieces consist entirely of end-grain tesserae and some are entirely cross-grain; most are a mixture.[1] For this reason, the term *tessellated mosaic ware* is used here for this technique, the most commonly used in the Victorian period and thereafter. There was also another type of veneer, a clear development from the parquetry of the Regency period. The geometrical forms, predominantly diamonds and triangles of various contrasting woods, were miniaturised to produce intricate patterns useful for borders, and the name *miniature parquetry* can be given to this work (figs. 18, 24, 25, 30, 31, colour pls. 11, 12, 13). It was a form of decoration very popular in the 1830s and 40s but thereafter went largely out of fashion. To these two types of decorative veneer must be added yet a further development, *inlaid turnery*. This was produced by fixing triangular or other shaped segments of various contrasting woods together, or on to a core of an inferior timber, and then working it on a lathe, to produce intricate turned wares which could either be used in their own right as pin cushions, napkin rings, etc. or could be incorporated as handles, rests or feet into veneered mosaic pieces (fig. 32, colour pl. 15). All of these developments occurred within a few years of one another, though the exact dates of introduction are not known. Also continuing into the Victorian period were the perspective cube and vandyke patterns, which might be used in conjunction with tessellated mosaic or miniature parquetry from the 1830s. A large proportion of items from this period are veneered, and whitewood wares rapidly lost favour.

Inlaid Turnery Wares

The earliest of the new wares to be developed may have been inlaid turnery, though this is not certain. Its inventor was probably James Burrows, and an account of the background to this new development appears in the 1840 edition of *Colbran's New Guide for Tunbridge Wells*. It is related that he was attracted by a row of beads worn by a lady which did not correspond to the colour of her dress and he felt that something of this kind might be effected in Tunbridge ware of different woods. A mosaic necklace was produced which sold for two guineas (£2.10) to a lady residing in Cumberland Terrace, who promptly ordered another. It is unlikely however that many such sets of beads were produced, as today they are uncommon (fig. 23). The date of this initial order is not recorded, but it is significant that as early as 1832 James Burrows was proudly recording in a national directory that he was the 'inventor of inlaid turnery', a claim not made in the previous 1828 edition.[2]

23. *A necklace of inlaid turnery consisting of 34 oval, circular or oblong components. c1840. (Sotheby's).*

Miniature Parquetry Wares

Miniature parquetry must also date from the late 1820s and was in use prior to the introduction of the tessellated mosaic wares. Charles Holtzapfel in the second volume (1846) of his comprehensive work on turning and working materials, chiefly wood, shows himself to have been very conversant with the Tunbridge ware industry. In this work he declared that 'the square wood mosaics, called also Berlin mosaics … are more recent than the triangular'. Holtzapfel also records that James Burrows had informed him that 'he was the first to introduce this work in Tonbridge-ware turnery, boxes and toys'.[3]

It would therefore seem likely that we must seek the origin of the inlaid turnery and miniature parquetry wares in the late 1820s and that the enterprising James Burrows was probably responsible for pioneering both of them, though they were promptly copied by rivals.

Tessellated Mosaic Woodwares

Much more important to the development of the Tunbridge ware industry in the nineteenth century, however, were the mosaic wares utilising square tesserae. This form of marquetry must have developed within a few years of the other two, and by the late 1830s it had achieved a considerable degree of sophistication. The

24. *Rosewood workbox with central tessellated mosaic panel featuring a bird and bandings of miniature parquetry. c1840. w:24cm d:11.5cm. (Sotheby's).*

65

author of a guide published in 1837 could declare that the Tunbridge ware most admired was:

'*entirely of Mosaic work, (a late invention), ... brought to that perfection, that even birds, dogs, butterflies &c. are correctly delineated in beautiful coloured woods, both English and foreign, of which there is a great variety.'*

This would suggest a date in the early 1830s as a likely one for the genesis of this technique. The Pintos believed that James Burrows was also the inventor of tessellated mosaic. There is little doubt that he was one of the earliest makers of this ware and a guide of 1840 stated that he was the first to introduce 'butterflies and birds into this description of manufacture'. He was also advertising in the same guide that he and his partner George Burrows were the 'Inventors of the Mosaic Inlaid ware'.[4] The term 'mosaic', however, could equally have been applied to miniature parquetry. There is also a possible rival to James Burrows as the inventor of the new mosaic. To coincide with the opening of his new Tunbridge Wells

25. *Tea caddy, rosewood, the top of the lid decorated with a tessellated block of Eridge Castle, the front with Holy Trinity Church, Tunbridge Wells. Butterfly blocks on the front and the tops of the tea boxes, miniature parquetry bandings. c1840. l:36cm d:18cm h:17.5cm. (Bracketts).*

showrooms at 11, Calverley Parade in 1832, George Wise issued a handbill stating that he was 'The Original Manufacturer of the Fashionable Mosaic and Inland Tunbridge Ware'. Again, it is difficult to know what interpretation to place on the terms 'mosaic' and 'inlaid' but Wise, if not the inventor of such wares, must be regarded as a pioneer in their development. He certainly appears to have been well to the fore in the use of tessellated mosaic blocks of topographical views to replace the wide range of prints used on his earlier wares, and to satisfy his extensive trade contacts away from the Tunbridge Wells area. His mosaic view of the Round Tower, Windsor Castle shows it in its pre-1832 form before it was heightened and altered by Sir Jeffrey Wyattville, and almost certainly originated in the 1830s (fig. 30), as must also his block of Tonbridge Priory which was already being demolished in March 1840 to clear the site for the South Eastern Railway. These early Wise pieces feature tessellated mosaic panels as their major decorative emphasis but have miniature parquetry bandings and side decoration.[5]

Most of the other Tunbridge ware makers quickly adopted the new techniques. The family connection made it likely that Humphrey Burrows at Jordan House would adopt the new wares. This is confirmed by a block of Eridge Castle in the Tunbridge Wells Museum collection which bears on the reverse a contemporary inscription stating, 'This was the last work made by Mr. Humphrey Burrows the Elder at Jordan Place, Tunbridge Wells in the year 1844'. This view, like a number of early topographical blocks, is a composite of tessellated mosaic and conventional cross-grain marquetry. It has been asserted that William Fenner was an early user of the new techniques on the basis of an advertisement in 1840 in which he announced that he was selling a range of 'Mosaic and Inlaid Wood Work … at very much reduced prices, owing to the introduction of new Machinery'. Fenner had advertised 'mosaic wares' for sale three years earlier and these were in all probability items decorated with perspective cube, vandyke and other parquetry designs. The 1840 advertisement may well refer to an intention to change production to the newer wares, hence the sale of old stock, but as his business appears to have closed in this year, he may well have had second thoughts about the necessary investment and transition to the new techniques and designs. His former partner, Edmund Nye, adopted all the new techniques, however, and a design for mosaic work in the firm's pattern book, now in Birmingham Museum and dated 1843, suggests an early changeover. Henry Hollamby appears to have used tessellated mosaic techniques from the start, which is hardly surprising, as he was apprenticed to George and James Burrows.[6]

Russell Marquetry

After the rapid development of the new techniques and designs in the late 1820s and 1830s, there was a sad lack of enterprise in the industry in promoting developments, which was ultimately to prove fatal. Only one maker pioneered a major new design development, and this was Robert Russell. He appears to have established his business in Tunbridge Wells in 1841. At times, he carried out work entirely in the conventional Tunbridge ware techniques and designs, but by the early 1850s he was pioneering new ground. His exhibit for the Great Exhibition in 1851 was described as a 'Tunbridge ware marquetrie inlaid lady's workbox' and from about this time he insisted on describing his productions as 'Tunbridge Wells Marquetrie' which although 'analagous' was also distinct from Tunbridge ware.

He developed a form of cross-grain marquetry, using finely and distinctively marked woods. These were cut into intricately lobed forms, segments of which might be jointed together to form centre blocks for the lids of square or rectangular boxes. They might also be placed side by side to form veneers for the lids of long, narrow boxes or for side bandings. These distinctive Russell designs were at times used in conjunction with perspective cube and tessellated mosaic decoration (fig. 75). No other maker appears to have attempted to use Russell's designs commercially though their success is apparent from the fact that he produced them for over 30 years. One Russell 'marquetrie' box is, however, known with a Barton label. This may have been a specially commissioned item made by Thomas Barton for a client after Russell's death, as the shape of the stationery cabinet in question is characteristic of Nye and Barton work. A less likely explanation is that it was a Russell-made box brought in by Barton to meet an order. A writing slope of Henry Hollamby manufacture has also been noted incorporating Russell marquetry.[7]

Chapter 7

THE VICTORIAN TUNBRIDGE WARE INDUSTRY 1830–75

By 1830, the production of Tunbridge ware in London was past its peak and was to go into immediate decline. At Brighton, too, the zenith had been reached by 1830, and although production was to continue for another three decades or so, it was a declining trade especially from the late 1840s. This left the Tunbridge Wells and Tonbridge area as the major base for the industry, and by the 1860s, almost the sole centre of production. Tunbridge Wells itself was, however, changing. In the late seventeenth century and for most of the eighteenth century, it was maintained by the fashionable visitors who paraded on its walks, partook of the spa water and patronised the shops and amusements for a few months each spring and summer. By the end of the eighteenth century, many of these visitors had deserted Tunbridge Wells for the burgeoning seaside spas. To some extent, the fashionable still came in the early years of the century, including the Duchess of Kent and her daughter Princess Victoria. Some improvements to the spa facilities were undertaken in the nineteenth century, such as the portico over the spring provided by public subscription in 1847, and even a new pump room in the late 1870s. The habit of patronising the spa was, however, on the wane, and by the second half of the century those who had faith in such water cures were often taking advantage of the ease of rail travel to convey them to major continental spas. Visitors still came, perhaps in greater numbers than ever before, but the day tripper by train was unlikely to be a patron of the more prestigious manufactures of the Tunbridge ware maker.[1]

The residential population of Tunbridge Wells was only around 1,000 in 1800 but the town benefited, like other inland spas, from a boom in building in the early nineteenth century. The largest and most elegant development took place from 1825, when a new town was created on the 56-acre Calverley Estate providing 90 houses, shops, two hotels and a market building. Many of the houses were large detached dwellings in extensive grounds aimed at the wealthy, and they set the pattern for much further high-class development throughout the nineteenth century. Supporting working-class areas arose in the adjoining Camden Road and St.

Peters (Windmill Field) areas while Grosvenor, Hanover and Rock Villa Roads provided dwellings suited to middle-class residents. By 1831, the population had risen to 5,929 and four years later, an adequate local government to replace the parish vestries of Tonbridge and Speldhurst was established under the terms of the Tunbridge Wells Improvement Act. The coming of the railway enhanced Tunbridge Wells' attraction and introduced the commuter to the area. Population continued to rise, reaching 8,032 by 1841, 24,309 by 1881, and 33,373 by 1901. Tonbridge also expanded from a population of about 3,400 in 1801 to 12,736 in 1901 but its position in the damp Medway valley and its more commercial aspect meant that it never attracted the wealthy and leisured in the same way as its neighbour. This growth in population provided a larger potential clientele for Tunbridge ware makers and, in the case of Tunbridge Wells, there were people of wealth prepared to provide local industry with patronage on a considerable scale. Nineteenth-century residents of the town included Queen Marie-Amélie of France, wife of Louis-Philippe, the Marquess of Lorne and F.G. Molyneux, son of the second Earl of Sefton, amongst others. The ease of communication afforded by rail also gave opportunities for selling on a wider basis, thought the high value relative to weight of Tunbridge ware had enabled the ware to be widely marketed earlier than this.[2]

Commercial directories provide the means by which the prosperity of the industry can be traced, for from these the number of makers at any one time can be ascertained. These figures show a relatively stable position from the beginning of the nineteenth century until the mid-1850s, but from then on there was a continuous decline.

Number of Tunbridge ware manufacturers in the Tonbridge/Tunbridge Wells area 1803–1878

	1803	1824	1832	1840	1851	1859	1870	1878
Tunbridge Wells manufacturers	8	5	8	9	9	5	4	4
Tunbridge Wells specialist sellers	–	–	–	–		1	–	–
Tonbridge manufacturers	1	3	1	1	1	1	1	1
Total	9	8	9	10	10	7	5	5

Note: only specialist retailers are listed; many others would stock Tunbridge ware as part of a much wider stock.
Sources: 1803 W. Finch, *An Historical Sketch of the County of Kent.* 1824, 1832, 1840; *Pigot.* 1851, 1859, 1870, 1878 *PO Directory.*

The makers varied in size from one-man businesses to enterprises employing numbers of craftsmen, but the size of unit in the industry was never large. Grossly exaggerated estimates of the numbers of persons employed have been published in the past, with one writer claiming that 300 people were engaged in the industry in Tunbridge Wells in the mid-nineteenth century. The number of persons residing in Tunbridge Wells and engaged in the manufacture of Tunbridge ware, taken from the census returns, is:

1831	22
1841	23
1851	32
1861	26
1871	29

It is possible that these numbers underestimate the labour force for they do not include workmen who lived in surrounding villages and workers who declared a trade that was not apparently concerned with the industry. However, this is clear evidence that the units of production must have been small. George Wise, the sole manufacturer in Tonbridge in 1851, was employing nine men, and in 1861, three men and a boy. Thomas Barton, at the height of his career in 1871 was employing 14 men, and in the same year Robert Russell was assisted only by his sister and four women, and James Brown by four men and a girl. Henry Hollamby, who built up a substantial wholesale business, was in 1883 stated to be employing about 20 persons at his works.[3]

The zenith of the industry appears to have been in the middle years of the nineteenth century, when a sufficient passage of time had elapsed to enable the new techniques developed 20 or so years earlier to be fully absorbed, and before the fund of design possibilities had been exhausted. The industry, proud of its products, was seeking national, and in the case of a few more enterprising businesses, international markets for the products. The way to attract attention was seen to be through the agency of international exhibitions, and leading manufacturers were not slow to submit suitable items. The 1851 Exhibition saw Edmund Nye, Robert Russell and Henry Hollamby taking part. Nye produced the largest assembly of exhibits, four in number, a table with a mosaic picture of a ship in full sail (110,800 pieces of marquetry wood), a chromatrope table decorated with two North American birds (129,000 pieces), a book stand with a drawer decorated with panels of two tropical butterflies, and a workbox displaying a view of the ruins of Bayham Abbey. For these exhibits he received the reward of an honourable mention from the jury, the only award made to a Tunbridge ware maker. Additional publicity for Nye's business was achieved by the display of these items in his Tunbridge Wells showrooms, prior to their despatch to London. Robert Russell displayed a workbox in his characteristic 'marquetrie' described as being in the Gothic style, while Henry Hollamby provided a workbox and writing desk, both being described as 'specimens of mosaic inlaid Tunbridge ware'. Two years later it was New York that staged an international exhibition in emulation of the British success. Hollamby once more submitted exhibits which were described as:

> *'an inlaid chess-table, containing 200,000 pieces of naturally coloured woods, writing desk with 80,000 pieces, work box with 100,000 pieces, tea caddy; knitting box &c.'*

George Wise also participated in this exhibition with 'many varieties of inlaid and mosaic Tunbridge ware; table, stands, boxes, desks and fancy articles'. Both makers were rewarded with bronze medals. It is, however, significant that after this flurry of activity in the early 1850s, Tunbridge ware makers took little further interest in the international exhibition scene. Henry Hollamby submitted exhibits for the 1862 International Exhibition held in London which were vaguely described in the catalogue as 'mosaics in natural coloured woods'.[4] Neither Edmund Nye nor his successor, Thomas Barton, attempted to exhibit at international level after 1851, but Barton did play an active part in an exhibition held at Tunbridge Wells in September 1864. It was described as an industrial exhibition, a surprising description in a town that had little industry to boast of. Even the Tunbridge ware makers, with the exception of Barton, appear to have ignored the event. Manufacturers and retailers from outside the town helped to swell the number of trade exhibitors, while many of the items on display consisted of amateur craftwork, curiosities from other lands, and even antiquities. Barton, who had only recently taken over Edmund Nye's business, displayed a range of Tunbridge ware including a much-admired perspective view of Battle Abbey gatehouse (fig. 64), and was awarded first prize for skilled craftsmanship. Thereafter, with the exception of an exhibition held in October 1899 in the optimistic hope that the fortunes of the Tunbridge ware industry might be revived, makers appear to have given up using exhibitions for publicity purposes.[5]

Tunbridge ware found a ready sale in Tunbridge Wells in the nineteenth century and a considerable number of retailers who stocked the ware can be identified from directories and advertisements (see appendix 4, pp. 248–64. The use of topographical views of castles, houses, churches and abbey ruins in West Kent, East Sussex, also Dover, Netley, Windsor and Eton, Warwick, Stratford-upon-Avon, the Malvern area, South Wales, the Scottish Borders and the south-west of Ireland suggests an extensive sale outside the immediate area of production. In some cases these views date from the late 1830s and the height of their popularity appears to have been reached during the next three decades. After *c*1870 the range of views in use seems to decline and in the main was concentrated on east Sussex and west Kent, no doubt reflecting a decline in patronage in a number of former markets. Advertisements by sellers help in the identification of a number of retailers away from Tunbridge Wells. William Tiffen (1785?–1855), a Folkestone bookseller and librarian, listed a wide range of goods manufactured by George Wise of Tonbridge in advertisements added to the back of guide books that he published in the late 1840s and early 1850s. East Kent coastal resorts had provided valuable markets for the print-decorated wares that Wise had manufactured earlier in the century. Sellers in the Isle of Wight are known from their advertisements. Other stockists have been identified by the labels that they attached to the base or inside the lid of wares they sold. The Liverpool jewellers, Frederick Hausburg (1845–59), and his successor, William Tooke (1860–65), are examples, (fig. 71c) but all too few stockists followed this practice. Evidence from various sources is, however, sufficient to be able to state that marketing of Tunbridge ware was carried on very widely in the mid-Victorian period, mainly, but not exclusively, at resort centres.[6] There is also some evidence of exportation to the United States and France. The interest of Wise and Hollamby in the 1853 New York Exhibition, and the existence of a mosaic view of the Capitol, Washington, are clear evidence of an attempt to exploit markets in the eastern United States. The exportation of veneers or finished items to France or the importation of French materials is suggested by the use of a mosaic butterfly panel in a papier mâché box impressed 'Made in France' and a Tunbridge ware workbox with ormoulu mounts by Alph. Giroux & Co. Paris. Such items are, however, rare and the export trade probably small.[7]

In Brighton, the new developments in mosaic and inlay techniques were not adopted with the same speed and enthusiasm as in the Tunbridge Wells and Tonbridge area. By the end of the 1830s, the Tunbridge ware industry at the resort was already in a state of decline, and retailers seemed content in the main to draw supplies from west Kent rather than aid the development of the native industry. Why this should have been so is difficult to analyse. Admittedly, Brighton suffered to some degree in the eyes of fashionable society once the railway from London had opened in 1841 spewing tradesmen, clerks, and even working-class day-trippers into the town. It also lost the favour of Queen Victoria after 1845. Fashionable society did not, however, desert the town, but merely retreated in the face of the summer invasion and moved the season into the autumn, continuing as late as early December. The grand estates of Brighton and Hove planned in the late Regency period, such as Kemp Town and Adelaide Crescent, continued to grow, and were not complete until about 1860, while substantial villa development proceeded on the Montpelier Estate and other parts of the town. The population increased at an even more rapid rate than at Tunbridge Wells. In 1801, the town had 7,339 inhabitants but by 1851, this had swelled to a remarkable 65,569. It would thus seem at first sight that the opportunities to develop the production of Tunbridge ware were more propitious at Brighton than at Tunbridge Wells. The Brighton industry was, however, of recent growth, and had to compete for labour and resources in this thrusting, booming town to a much greater extent than in Tunbridge Wells. Its industry was also heavily involved in the production of print-decorated and painted whitewood wares, and when these declined in favour, the change to techniques of veneering and parquetry and marquetry decoration produced strains. The number of manufacturers was fewer than at Tunbridge Wells and the expiry of one major manufacturer was of much

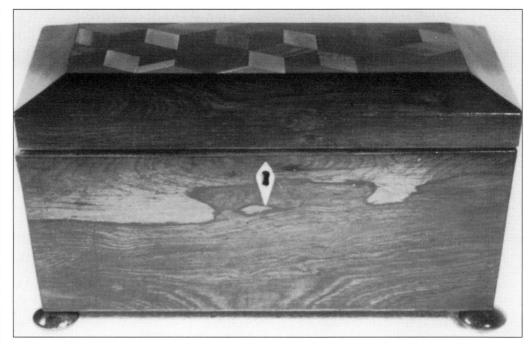

26. *Tea caddy, sarcophagus shape on bun feet, the top decorated with perspective cube work, ivory keyhole escutcheon. The interior has two tea compartments, whose lids are decorated with cube parquetry, and there is a central glass bowl. The base bears the label 'CHEESEMAN, from Morris's, Turner, and Tunbridge Ware MANUFACTURER ... No 9 CRANBOURN STREET, West Street, Brighton'. c 1830. w:30.5cm d:15cm h:16.5cm.*

greater significance to the health of the industry as a whole than at the Kentish spa. Thus, although the industry in Brighton did attempt to adapt to the new wares it was not to survive beyond the 1860s.[8]

Print-decorated whitewood wares continued to be made in Brighton well into the 1830s, but there is evidence to suggest that perspective cube parquetry was also being produced in the town from the 1820s. A tea caddy, and a workbox decorated in the manner are known bearing the label of Cheeseman, 9, Cranbourn Street (fig. 26, colour pl. 10). Cheeseman claimed to be a former employee at Morris, who may also have used this type of decoration. Unfortunately, he does not appear in any directories at this address, though a Thomas Cheeseman is listed in *Pigot's* 1832 directory in Riding School Lane. In style, the caddy and workbox in question would suggest a date *c*1830. There is, however, no evidence of inlaid turnery or miniature parquetry being used in Brighton, though some pieces of tessellated mosaic may have been produced in the town.

A number of items with tessellated mosaic, often on the front, bear either the label or stamp of William Upton at 5, Kings Road, the address which he occupied from 1851–64 (figs. 26, 72a, 72c) or more rarely inscribed 'From Upton's' at a Gloucester Lane address which was occupied by William and John Upton from 1838. Articles so marked include pin cushions, stationery boxes, tea caddies and book slides. Some of these are quite distinctive in style, using light maplewood-veneered bodies, decorated with a number of small square or rectangular mosaic panels of floral design, or pictures of dogs or birds. Bandings of floral or geometrical work were also used. It would seem likely that Upton produced the boxes and basic veneers, and may well have produced some of the mosaic panels. The existence of a box decorated with a view of St. Helena Cottage, Tunbridge Wells bearing a William Upton stamp must, however, indicate a policy of buying in items for stock from Tunbridge Wells manufacturers from whom Upton might also have obtained veneers for items of his own manufacture. Many items bearing Upton labels also incorporate perspective cube work.[9]

Morris's Royal Repository also appears to have produced mosaic wares, though at what date is uncertain. A billhead used by this firm in October 1840 includes details of the wide range of items stocked, but makes no mention of mosaic Tunbridge ware which would probably feature as a new development if it had been in production. However, a small rectangular box with a Morris label and a very distinctive complex tessellated mosaic lid exists in a private collection. The sides are decorated with a cross-grain

27. *Rosewood stationery box, the lid decorated with a mosaic view of a boy in a kilt (compares with the larger and more sophisticated version of the same subject in fig. 43). The front is adorned with perspective cube work; the box also incorporates mosaic borders. Label on base 'WM UPTON Tunbridge Ware Manufacturer No 5 KINGS ROAD BRIGHTON' (as plate 71). c1855. w:20.5cm d:11.5cm h:(back) 12.5cm. (Tunbridge Wells Museum).*

parquetry design of inter-connecting lozenges. The label is identical to the trade card in the Banks collection of *c*1815 showing the processes of manufacture (fig. 8), but the address has been changed to 'Richmond Place opposite the New Church' and the word 'Mosaic' replaces 'Malmatint' in the description. The uniqueness of this item may indicate a late introduction of such wares possibly in the mid-1840s and point to Abraham Morris as the manufacturer. However, Morris's Repository seldom marked any of its products. A label is known on a box with a tessellated view of Tonbridge Castle, a subject unlikely to be of local production. If the introduction of the ware was post-1840 its scarcity would be explained, for the business closed in 1848, and the demise of probably the major manufacturer in this line in the town must have been a considerable blow to an industry already struggling to adapt to change.[10]

The business operated by William Childs Snr. and Jnr. sold mosaic Tunbridge ware in Brighton. It appears to have been established some time before 1830, and in 1832 was at 3, East Cliff moving to 53, Kings Road in 1839 (renumbered 51, Kings Road in 1844). It is from this latter address, which the firm occupied until its sale in 1873, that labelled pieces of Tunbridge ware came. The business, initially described as a toy dealer, appears to have developed into a substantial and prosperous enterprise. It claimed the patronage of George IV, William IV and Queen Victoria. The business probably manufactured some of the goods it sold including desks and dressing-cases, but it never described itself as a Tunbridge ware manufacturer, and frequently used the words

28. *Box, veneered with maple and decorated with a mosaic view of Eridge Castle, with wide mosaic bandings of floral and leaf patterns. On the inside of the lid is attached the seller's label 'W CHILDS Fancy Repository, 51 KING'S ROAD, corner of Middle St, BRIGHTON'. c1850. w:21.5cm d:12.5cm h:7cm.*

'fancy repository' or 'warehouse' in describing the business. It dealt in a wide range of fancy goods, papier mâché, cutlery, brushes, combs, glass and gilt wares 'and toys and games'. The items of Tunbridge ware with Childs' labels appear to be in no way distinctive in style and the appearance of a label on a box bearing a block of Eridge Castle would seem to confirm the Tunbridge Wells origin of the items sold (figs. 28, 71a, 71d). R.H. Perry bought the business in 1873 and traded from the same address and in the same line of business until 1884. Two of Childs' employees, Burville & Littlewood, set up on their own at 39, Western Road, Brighton as fancy goods dealers when the business was sold, and their label is found on pieces of Tunbridge ware bought in from Tunbridge Wells.[11]

Three other Brighton makers survived into the mid-Victorian period. The label of Benjamin Whittaker of 1a, Hampton Place has been recorded on Tunbridge ware. He worked from this address from 1855–59 and described himself as a Tunbridge ware and fancy cabinet manufacturer, but known items are mainly of Tunbridge Wells manufacture. William Camfield of 76, St. James' Street traded as a Tunbridge ware and brush manufacturer from 1851–9 but this combination of trades suggests that his main interest was probably in whitewood turnery wares. A stamp box marked with his label is unlikely to be of his manufacture. He continued trading after 1859, but no longer mentioned Tunbridge ware amongst his products. Another Brighton maker working into the 1840s – and possibly later – was Edward Saunders of 3 and 4, Western Road. His father William Saunders operated as a juvenile bookseller, print dealer, fancy goods retailer and Tunbridge ware manufacturer from 112, St. James' Street from 1826. A considerable number of engravings of Brighton with his imprint are known. The son appears to have taken over the business in the late 1830s, moving to the Western Road address in 1839. He described himself as a 'Tunbridge ware Manufacturer, ivory, bone and hardwood turner' and declared that workboxes and other articles were 'made, repaired, re-varnished or altered'. This advertisement was repeated in 1843, and the wording suggests print-decorated whitewood wares. Edward Saunders was to remain in business at the Western Road address until 1878 but directories record him as a toy and fancy repository and stationer and he may have ceased production in the 1840s, though mosaic wares from Tunbridge Wells may have featured in his stock.[12]

It would therefore seem likely that Tunbridge ware production in Brighton had stopped by the early 1860s. Although Upton's business did not close until 1864, in the latter years it was carried on by a Miss Upton, possibly a daughter of William Upton, and it is unlikely that production continued, for the business was described as a 'Tunbridge warehouse'. Thus, within the course of about 50 years the Brighton industry witnessed a dramatic growth to meet the demands of its Regency patrons, rivalling Tunbridge Wells and largely driving out the latter's wares, only to succumb just as rapidly because of its failure to adjust to changes of fashion and the new techniques and designs developed in the trade.[13]

Labels of Brighton retailers and others inscribed 'Present from

BRIGHTON' were applied to Tunbridge Wells manufactured inlaid turnery and small cabinet wares.

Makers emerged at other south-coast resorts in the Victorian period. The best known of these was James Medhurst, whose businesses in Maiden Street, Weymouth and West Buildings, Worthing were opened in 1839. He appears to have learnt his trade in Tunbridge Wells and some of the wares that he produced at Weymouth, which utilise timber from vessels wrecked on the south coast, are fully in the Tunbridge Wells tradition both in design and construction (fig. 29). From the early 1850s, he occupied premises on the Esplanade at 9, Chesterfield Place, Weymouth where he maintained a museum of antiquities. Members of the Medhurst family were active in Sussex at the same period. Worthing libraries had been sellers of Tunbridge ware in the late Georgian period taking their cue from the larger and more prestigious resort of Brighton a mere 12 miles to the east. These libraries are known to have been supplied by George Wise of Tonbridge and possibly by other Tunbridge Wells and Brighton makers. The town was, however, to have its own manufactory by the late 1830s. One was established by James Medhurst from premises at 11, West Buildings, Worthing where he sold 'his own manufactured goods in the turnery line with views of Worthing … where families may see the articles made on the premises'. One of his brothers, George Medhurst, initially manufactured from an address in the upper part

29a. Glove box, the top decorated with a mosaic panel of roses, surrounded by a mosaic geometrical border. The base bears the label of James Medhurst of Weymouth, and a statement that the box was made from wood salvaged from the wreck of the Abergavenny. *Medhurst labels are also known in French. c1855. w:14.5cm d:9cm h:5.5cm.*

of the High Street in Lewes from 1832. He was still in Lewes in August 1841 but in 1843 may have moved to Worthing, where a George Medhurst maintained a Tunbridge ware and turnery manufactory at 14 (later 12), Prospect Row. He also sold his wares on the Parade. James Medhurst, however, also had a son named George, born at Brighton in January 1819, and the Worthing business may from the start have been maintained by him. He was certainly in charge of the Prospect Row business by March 1845. He was also the executor of his father's will in 1877 and the business was still listed as a turner in directories as late as 1892. Another son of James Medhurst was Robert. He worked in his father's business before setting up in the late 1850s in Montague Street. He died on 2 June 1869, aged 38, but the business appears to have continued to operate from Montague Street.[15] Pieces have been recorded with the label of R. Medhurst, 3, Montague Street, one bearing the information that it was made from timbers salvaged from the naval sail training vessel, H.M.S. *Eurydice*, which sank off Ventnor in a squall on 24 March 1878.[16]

Only one maker set up business in East Kent, though this appears to have been a fruitful market for both the whitewood and the new tessellated mosaic wares from Tonbridge and Tunbridge Wells. This maker was Robert Licence (1824?–1913) who is first mentioned in trade directories in 1855. At this date, he was operating from an address in Woolcomber Street, Dover and declaring his trade to be a hardwood turner. Three years later, in an advertisement, he expanded on this brief description stating that he was an 'ivory, hard wood turner and Tunbridge ware Manufacturer'. In the 1861

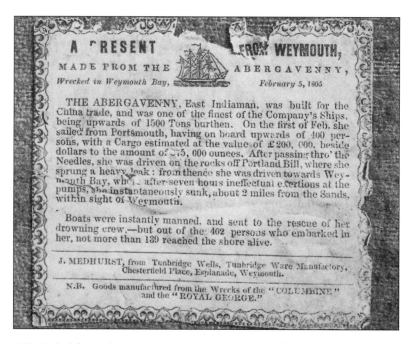

29b. *Label from glove box, explaining the origin of the wood.*

census, his dwelling was described as a Tunbridge ware factory. By 1865, he was additionally occupying premises on Marine Parade in which he opened a library. This may well have become the main part of his business, for in 1871 he declared his trade simply as 'librarian' and soon gave up the Woolcomber Street premises and presumably manufacturing. In 1882, he was describing the business as the 'Marine Library, stationer & Tunbridge ware repository'. Another member of the Licence family was in trade in Dover. In 1878 James Licence was conducting business as a wood turner from 80, St. James' Street and he continued in this trade as late as 1890. He never declared himself to be a Tunbridge ware maker, however. Little is known of the wares produced by Robert Licence. He was born in 1822 at Redgrave in Suffolk and presumably spent all of his youth in that region, for his wife came from Godmanchester in Cambridgeshire. Where he acquired his knowledge of Tunbridge

30. Rosewood blotter cover with central mosaic representation of the Round Tower, Windsor Castle, enclosed with bandings of miniature parquetry. The other side shows a mosaic view of the Eastern Range, Upper Ward, Windsor Castle. Attributable to George Wise, Tonbridge, and possibly one of the items supplied to Princess Victoria through Rudolph Ackermann of the Strand, London. c1835. w:34cm h:26.5cm. (Museum of London).

1. Whitewood boxes. Top: *decorated with an engraving on green paper identified as "SELDEN COTTAGE" (Salvington, Worthing). An almost identical engraving was included in J. Mackcoull,* A Sketch of Worthing *(1813). Additionally painted with leaf sprays and bandings. w:20.5cm d:8.5cm h:5cm.* Front left: *box bears label of "PALMER & SONS, Royal Pen Manufactory, East Grinstead" w:12.5cm d:6cm h:3cm.* Right: *decorated with Chinese figure in a boat fishing with a cormorant, pagoda in background. w:9cm d:5cm h:4.5cm. All c1810–20.*

2. Workbox, sarcophagus shape, veneered in yew wood, the top decorated with a print of a mother holding a bunch of grapes and a child reaching for them, additional chevron bandings, Pressed brass feet and handle mounts. The fitted interior lined with green paper. c1810. w:23.5cm h:13cm.

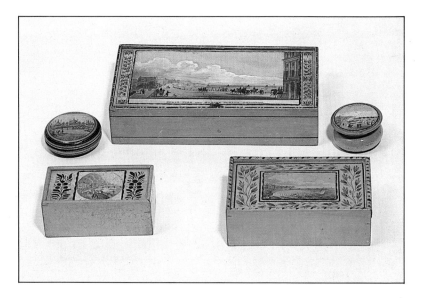

3. *Whitewood wares probably of Brighton manufacture. All are decorated with prints of the Chain Pier and Marine Parade with the exception of the screw-top box on the right which displays a view of the Royal Pavilion. Items additionally decorated with painted floral designs and bandings. c1830. Top row: rectangular box w:23cm d:11.5cm h:5cm. Front row: (left) w:11cm d:6cm h:4.5cm, (right) w:14.5cm d:9.5cm h:5cm. Turned circular boxes (left) dia:6cm (right) dia:5.5cm.*

4. *Octagonal satinwood card box, the top decorated with a print of Donaldson's Library, the Steine, Brighton. The use of gilt borders is characteristic of the work of George Wise, Tonbridge. c1815. w:20cm d:17cm h:6cm.*

ware production is not known.[17] His trade appears to have been that of a hardwood turner and turnery wares would seem to be his most likely products. This is confirmed by a labelled turned ring-stand in the Pinto collection, Birmingham Museum. It has been suggested[18] that Robert Licence was responsible for the production of Tunbridge ware decorated with photographic views, a number of pieces of which are known (fig. 51). The attribution of these wares to this maker is, however, considered unlikely.

There is no evidence that wares similar to those developed at Tunbridge Wells from the late 1820s were ever made by the London trade. By the 1830s interest in the production of Tunbridge wares in the capital was already in decline. *Robson's Directory* could list five Tunbridge ware makers as late as 1835, but soon thereafter separate listings of this trade in London directories were discontinued. Some subsequent utilisation of Tunbridge Wells-made veneers by London makers is known. A workbox incorporating Tunbridge ware panels in its decoration and dating from *c*1870–80 made by Cormack Brothers of 37, Ludgate Hill is in the Guildhall Museum, Rochester, collection (fig. 49). There is good evidence, however, for the retailing of the new mosaic and inlaid wares in London. Wadmore mentions the sale of Tunbridge ware made by George Wise and decorated with a view of Windsor Castle, to Princess Victoria through the agency of Rudolph Ackermann of the Strand. A blotter case with tessellated mosaic views of Windsor Castle and miniature parquetry borders, typical of the work of George Wise from the mid-1830s, was presented to the Museum of London by King George V, having been used by him when Prince of Wales. This may possibly be one of the pieces supplied through Ackermann's (fig. 30). Ackermann & Co. continued to stock Tunbridge ware, much no doubt supplied by George Wise, until business ceased in 1852. The inventories of stock taken after the closure of the business contain many listings of such wares. Other London fancy goods dealers no doubt stocked the new mosaic Tunbridge wares but no sellers' labels or advertisements have been traced to date.[20]

Chapter 8

METHODS OF PRODUCTION

The perspective cube, vandyke and other parquetry designs used during the Regency period involved geometrically shaped pieces of wood of a sufficiently large size for them to be fitted individually on to the piece of furniture or box that they were to decorate. As late as 1883, one Tunbridge Wells guide referred to the decoration of ware 'produced by inlaying in single pieces', a technique still employed to some extent by Thomas Barton in that year.

Miniature Parquetry Wares

The development of miniature parquetry in the late 1820s meant that this method would have been too laborious and expensive to employ for the new work, and the patterns required started to be assembled in blocks from which veneers could be cut. The most basic units in miniature parquetry were either triangles or rhombuses, and sticks of this cross-section could be produced by using saw-beds inclined at the required angle. Wood of an appropriate thickness and about six to seven inches (15 to 17.5cm) in length would be used. The process was fully explained and illustrated by Charles Hotzapfel in 1846 based upon information supplied by James Burrows (diagram i):

> '*Figure 743 shows that a bed of 45 degrees, will at one cut for each piece, convert the veneer into rhombuses figured separately at* **a**, *the acute angles of which measure 45, the obtuse 135 degrees each; and when the wood is turned between each cut, right-angled triangles* **b**, *are produced, with the same bed. When, as in the dotted line fig 743, the bed measures 22½ degrees and the work is also turned over, triangles are produced such as* **c**, *and from which three figures a,b,c, almost all the work is composed.*'[1]

The sticks of various woods had next to be assembled in the pattern required. The centre, especially of circular blocks, was usually constructed of an assembly of triangles or rhombuses which would be glued and bound tightly with string and allowed to dry. For

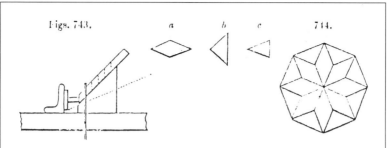

Dia. 743. - Method of cutting sticks of a diamond or triangular cross-section for miniature parquetry, using an inclined saw bed.

Dia. 744 - Initial assembly of the block, using sticks of diamond and triangular cross-section.

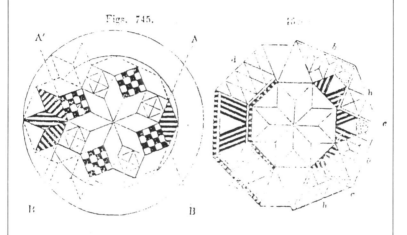

Dia. 745 & 746 - Assembly of more complex blocks, using dia. 744 as a core.

Diagram i. *Diagrams from Charles Holtzapfel,* Turning and Mechanical Manipulation *Vol II (1846) pp. 764–5, showing the method of cutting and assembling miniature marquetry (see pp. 82–3).*

larger circular or octagonal blocks, additional sticks of the appropriate shape and colour would be glued to the circumference of the first block, and in their turn clamped or bound up with string and allowed to dry. Apart from circular blocks, borders could be assembled from such shapes. After some weeks, the blocks were ready for use and veneers could be cut to decorate the wares as appropriate. Circular blocks could be used to veneer, or laid into the tops of lids, pin tables, snuff boxes and bases for taper holders. Circular blocks were also used occasionally as the central feature on boxes and book rests. Bandings of miniature parquetry were popular in the 1830s and early 1840s before the full potential of borders of tessellated mosaic were fully realised.[2]

31. *Two early examples of the use of miniature parquetry. Top: box with sides veneered in diamond pattern parquetry; the top has a similar pattern, but the diamonds are filled with miniature parquetry. c1830. w:30.5cm d:15cm. Bottom: rosewood workbox, the top inlaid with square panels of miniature parquetry, thin bandings on the sides. 'G.R. Patent' stamped on the lock, suggesting a date just prior to 1830. w:30.5cm d:14cm. (Sotheby's).*

Inlaid Turnery Wares

As an alternative to cutting into veneers, circular blocks of miniature parquetry of various diameters could be turned on a lathe to provide specimens of inlaid turnery, also utilised from the late 1820s. Supports for watch and thermometer stands, fancy handles, feet, knobs and taper holders could be produced in this manner. For objects of larger size, such as circular hat-pin or pin cushions, the laborious assembly for quantities of expensive timbers in decorative blocks was seen to be unnecessary, and a cheaper method adopted. This was to use a core of an inferior wood which would be notched and faceted so that a layer of sticks of triangular cross-sections of various colours, sometimes placed base to apex, could be glued firmly to the exterior providing a 'veneer'. Turning on a lathe would merely shape and cut into this outer layer, but would not extend deep enough to expose the core-wood, which would be disguised at the base by the application of a circle of lining paper or a trade label. For serviette rings, a similar core of a wood such as beech was used. This would be largely bored out once the turning had been completed. A number of recent writers on the subject of Tunbridge ware have used the term 'stickware' to describe this inlaid turnery. Although there is evidence that this term was used to describe certain Tunbridge turnery wares in the eighteenth century, no contemporary use is known for it in the nineteenth century. The term 'mosaic turnery' was, however, used in addition to 'inlaid turnery'. The great majority of Tunbridge ware makers had lathes in their workshops, and produced objects made of inlaid turnery or incorporating it.[3]

32. *Examples of inlaid turnery.* Rear row, left to right: *pair of taper holders h:9cm; rosewood rouge pot with screw top dia:4.5cm; rosewood ring stand h:7.5cm.* Front row, left to right: *rosewood matchstick holder in the form of a barrel h:4.5cm; thimble case with threaded top h:3cm; thread-winder in the form of a cross h:5cm; thread-waxer and pin cushion h:3cm; thimble case in the form of a barrel with a threaded top and two caddy spoons. All mid-nineteenth to early twentieth century. (Sotheby's).*

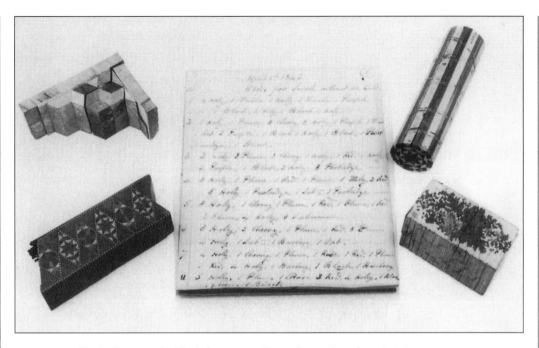

33. Left: *part of a block for perspective cube work and a miniature parquetry block probably from Humphrey Burrow's manufactory.* Centre: *manuscript chart dated 6 April 1842 for the assembly of tessellated mosaic block.* Right: *a block of parquetry sticks of diamonds and triangles and a floral tessellated mosaic block. Mid to late nineteenth century. (Tunbridge Wells Museum).*

Tessellated Mosaic Wares

As both miniature parquetry and inlaid turnery appear to be developments of the late 1820s, whereas tessellated mosaic marquetry does not appear much before the mid 1830s, this might suggest that the method of building up blocks from which veneers could be cut was already established before the popular tessellated mosaic wares were first devised. The exact date when this principle was first used is not clear. In some cases, examples of perspective cube and vandyke work may have been produced from blocks before the 1820s, and a part block of the former type of work is in the Tunbridge Wells Museum collection (fig. 33). As this design was in constant use in the industry well into the twentieth century, an early date cannot be assumed for this item. Examination of the borders on a wide range of late Georgian boxes, including a number of Tunbridge ware examples, shows irregularities of pattern match at points where separate sections join, suggesting that these borders were worked in long lengths allowing for the possibility that in some cases they were produced in blocks. This seems to be confirmed by a comment made by James Burrows to Charles

34. *Coloured design drawn and painted on graph paper for a mosaic block of the Solar and Buckingham Buildings, Penshurst Place attributable to Henry Hollamby. c1850. (Tunbridge Wells Museum).*

35. *Two workboxes by Henry Hollamby. Although both boxes use the same carcase they are differently veneered.* Left: *maple veneer, the top showing a view of Eridge Castle with a mosaic border of roses, with oak leaf bandings on the sides.* Right: *rosewood veneer, the top decorated with a view of Penshurst Place to the design shown in fig. 34 with flower and leaf bandings. c1870. w:24cm d:18.5cm h:10cm.*

Holtzapfel concerning miniature parquetry work, that 'striped, feathered and tessellated works somewhat of the same kind, were used long prior in the bandings and stringings of ornamental cabinet work'.

There is also the possibility that the earliest tessellated mosaic work developed as a by-product of miniature parquetry work. By the mid-1840s, some miniature parquetry blocks incorporated square segments made up from smaller square tesserae, often 16 to each segment, in contrasting dark and light woods to form a chequered design (diagram i). These were composed using the same methods as those adopted to produce tessellated mosaic work. Admittedly, by the mid-1840s, the method of producing the new mosaic was well developed and the chequer work, might have been recently introduced. It would, however, seem likely that it is of much earlier origin and possibly represents the genesis of the technique that was to revolutionise Tunbridge ware production.[4]

As tessellated work was the dominant form of decoration used in the industry from the 1830s, adequate space must be devoted to describing the technique. Fortunately a number of published accounts of the manufacture of this ware exist, ranging in date from 1846 to 1910. It is significant that they completely agree on the principal stages of manufacture and differ very little even in the detail, showing that once the method became established it underwent very few changes. Well before the 1830s, the Tunbridge ware industry, in common with the furniture trades in general, had developed an established division and hierarchy of skills, and in all but the smaller workshops the trades of sawyer, turner, bandmaker (or block-maker), box-maker and polisher (or finisher) were all recognised as peculiar to one worker or a group of workers who spent the whole of their time in this restricted occupation.

The starting point of the process was the design stage. A painting or pattern, often in colour, had at this stage to be interpreted so that its flowing lines could be translated into the form of wooden tesserae, without the whole concept appearing angular and artificial. Appropriate woods had to be identified so that their gradations of colour from black through a range of browns to white could be used to reproduce the much wider colour range of the original. The colour design, which was larger than the desired marquetry panel or border, was first covered with a grid of squares, and the appropriate wood identified for each of these, and recorded on a similarly squared piece of paper. From this, a manuscript sheet listing the woods required for each row would be prepared for the band-maker to work from. This resembled in many ways the instructions contained in a knitting pattern. One surviving sheet from Edmund Nye's workshop and dated 24 November 1843 reads:

1	3 holly	2 fustic	2 holly	1 green	2 holly	3 fustic	3 holly	
2	6 holly	3 green	6 holly					
3	4 holly	7 green	4 holly					

and so on for 18 rows.

The design stage of the work involved considerable skill and artistry and in many businesses was the work of the proprietor. A number of original designs for mosaic work from Edmund Nye's manufactory dating from the 1840s and 50s are in the Tunbridge Wells Museum and one book of designs is in the Pinto Collection at the Birmingham Museum. One design, for a table top of 110,800 pieces displaying 'a vessel sailing on an ocean', made and exhibited at the 1851 Hyde Park Exhibition is signed by Nye's foreman and successor Thomas Barton, as is another in Tunbridge Wells Museum. This seems to suggest that Barton had a considerable involvement in the design of Nye's products in the later years of the business. A series of squared paintings of topographical designs including Eridge Castle, Tonbridge Castle, Penshurst Place, Battle Abbey, Herstmonceux Castle, Dover Castle, and St. Mary's Church also exist in the Tunbridge Wells Museum. Although their exact source is unknown, they are identical to views used in Tunbridge ware and are probably from Henry Hollamby's workshop (fig. 34). George Wise produced designs for his earlier print-decorated wares and it cannot be doubted that he continued into the period when he initiated the production of topographical subjects in mosaic.[5]

Once the design stage had been completed, sufficient quantities of the woods required were prepared ready for assembly. The number of timbers available was potentially large, and in 1890, James Brown of Boyce, Brown & Kemp claimed that 150 different woods were in use. To hold guaranteed stock of, and to utilise regularly, such a wide range was unnecessary, and for most practical purposes around 30 to 40 were found to be sufficient. A printed sheet in Maidstone Museum produced by Edmund Nye describing specimens of timbers used in the Tunbridge cabinet and turnery trades lists 45 timbers. A number of native woods were utilised and as timber was not required in large sizes or quantities, local supplies could be used derived from the woods, commons, hedgerows and even large gardens of the area. Unusual species in small quantities could be obtained as fellings and branch prunings through gardeners of large houses, and put to use. The type and size of timbers assembled in this manner, caused one visitor to Boyce, Brown & Kemp's works to compare their timber stock in the basement to a 'fire-wood store'. Foreign woods bought from London or Liverpool timber merchants probably arrived in the form of boards.[6]

Most woods were used, without treatment, in their natural colours and a wide spectrum of effects could be obtained in this manner alone. One commentator in 1883 described the main colours available:

> 'Holly supplies a clean white wood, Ebony the well-known black, finely marked, in larger pieces, with lighter veins. The brightest red, such as may serve for tiles in pictures, is cut from Bar-wood blocks, but this is rather soft. Red ebony, supplied from Natal, is harder and more brilliant. Blood-wood gives, as its name implies, a deep red hue. Green ebony enters into the mixture of colours very freely, supplying an effective olive green, which does admirably for many kinds of foliage. Barberry-

wood polishes to a brilliant yellow. Laburnum gives a variety of shades according to its age, from a dark brown to a light drab. Mulberry is yellow, Rosetta rosy brown, Kingwood a deep brown, approaching purple. Fustic is yellow, Tulip-wood gives a rich marbled red. Palmyra (Palm tree) is spotted and veined, according as it is cut, brown and drab and very effective. A very striking colour is that supplied by Purple wood (Copaifera rubiflora), from Guiana, namely a rich Mauve.[7]

Although the industry was proud to state that it only used timbers in their natural colours, some minor deviations were resorted to. Where a brighter green was required than was provided by green ebony, the limited supplies of fallen branches of oak and other timbers in the initial stages of decay, affected by a minute fungus

36. *A reconstruction of a Tunbridge ware workshop. Many of the tools including the treadle-operated circular saw (centre) and the hand-operated circular saw (right) were used by Edmund Nye in his workshops in the first half of the nineteenth century and were in the auction conducted by Brackett's of Tunbridge Wells on 24 February 1933. (Tunbridge Wells Museum).*

(*Chlorosplenium aeruginosum*) could be used. This fungus spreads its mycelium through decaying wood turning it green; such wood could be gathered from the locality, especially from parkland in the Eridge area.[8] Nye, and particularly his successor Thomas Barton, were attracted to the use of green woods and a report on Barton's exhibits at the 1864 Tunbridge Wells Industrial Exhibition seemed to imply that this colour was a recent introduction. To remove excess sap in holly and enhance its whiteness, it was boiled for four hours in a copper and seasoned away from the influence of sunlight. From about 1860, treated Hungarian ash, maple and holly were particularly favoured for veneering cabinet work and boxes. The veneers were immersed in chalybeate water obtained from the well on the Pantiles for ten days effecting a change in colour from a yellowish white to a soft grey, the figure of the wood appearing as a deeper shade (fig. 37). This idea was introduced from Spa in Belgium where it had been practised in connection with the wooden souvenirs manufactured in the town. Grey timber was also found useful in mosaic work for simulating blue, as no natural timber produced this colour.[9]

37. *Box veneered in burr maple treated with chalybeate water, the top incorporating a mosaic block of Muckross Abbey, Killarney with geometrical mosaic top and side bandings. Possibly by Henry Hollamby. c1870. w:23cm h:7cm. (Sotheby's).*

For tessellated mosaic work, timber was sawn in pieces usually but not invariably about 7in (17.8cm) or 3½in (8.9cm) long, 1in (2.5cm) in width and about ½in (0.8mm) in height, and it was from units of this size that the initial assembly commenced. Sizes varied slightly from maker to maker. The height represented the final size of the mosaic tesserae, and for very fine work this might be ¹⁄₆₄in (0.4mm). Fine work of this kind was suited to mosaic heads of Queen Victoria for stamp boxes and small floral or animal panels such as Henry Hollamby used on the plinths of obelisk-shaped ('Cleopatra's Needle') thermometer stands. Larger tesserae of ³⁄₆₄in (1.2mm) are found in the early work of both Edmund Nye and William Upton, and late productions of Thomas Barton and Boyce, Brown & Kemp and their successors. The pieces of different-coloured wood were assembled according to a chart and after one row was completed it was glued together, put under pressure and left to dry. The next row was then assembled and so on until separate blocks corresponding to each row of the pattern had been completed. The next stage was to saw lengthwise down each assembled block taking off a strip of the same size as the height of the unit from which it had been assembled i.e. usually ½in (0.8mm). This strip would show all the timbers from which the block had been composed. This unit which would measure ½in (0.8mm) by ½in (0.8mm) by 7 in (17.8cm) (or 3½in (8.9cm)). The strips obtained from each block were then assembled in order and glued together to form a further block, with the desired mosaic design exposed at both ends and running throughout its entirety. It was from this block that veneers could be cut to be used on the boxes or other objects being decorated (diagram ii). The two-stage operation used in assembly was adopted in order to avoid the need to work with minute sticks of wood which would have to be used if a single stage process had been adopted and also because cross-grain rods ½in (0.8mm) square would have been too fragile. Large blocks were usually assembled from six, nine or twelve smaller units, and could take weeks or even months from the time of commencement, because of the need to allow the glue to dry thoroughly at each stage before proceeding to the next. Larger production blocks, such as the view of the Pantiles used by Henry Hollamby and Boyce, Brown & Kemp could contain 25,000 tesserae (fig. 38). This two-stage nature of the process also meant that a seven-inch (17.8cm) block would produce around 70 to 80 identical veneers allowing for wastage in sawing. Larger blocks required saws with thicker blades to cut them, and therefore greater wastage in sawdust, and fewer veneers were cut per inch. The total number of veneers would, however, be substantially more than the 70 to 80 indicated, for about ten or eleven blocks would have resulted from this two-stage operation, giving a total of 700 to 800 veneers in all. The blocks would usually have been stored and used up over a period of time.[10]

Small blocks and borders and bandings, and some of the larger blocks, required no further treatment before use. Many mosaics however, including topographical, floral and other naturalistic subjects, needed to be inserted into a holly surround to protect

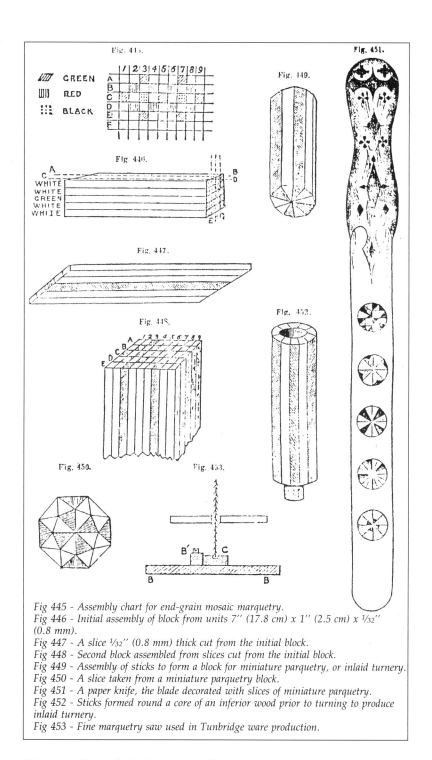

Fig 445 - Assembly chart for end-grain mosaic marquetry.
Fig 446 - Initial assembly of block from units 7'' (17.8 cm) x 1'' (2.5 cm) x 1/32'' (0.8 mm).
Fig 447 - A slice 1/32'' (0.8 mm) thick cut from the initial block.
Fig 448 - Second block assembled from slices cut from the initial block.
Fig 449 - Assembly of sticks to form a block for miniature parquetry, or inlaid turnery.
Fig 450 - A slice taken from a miniature parquetry block.
Fig 451 - A paper knife, the blade decorated with slices of miniature parquetry.
Fig 452 - Sticks formed round a core of an inferior wood prior to turning to produce inlaid turnery.
Fig 453 - Fine marquetry saw used in Tunbridge ware production.

Diagram ii. *Method of assembly of tessellated mosaic marquetry, miniature parquetry and inlaid turnery from Elias Taylor,* The Lathe and its Uses *(3rd edn 1871).*

38. *Blotter cover decorated with a mosaic picture of the Pantiles, Tunbridge Wells with broad mosaic rose bandings in a style attributable to Henry Hollamby. c1880. w:27cm d:23cm.*

delicate projections in the design and provide a rectangle or regular geometrical shape which could be more easily incorporated in the veneers covering the box or object to be decorated. Once the mosaic veneer had been cut from the block, a piece of backing paper was glued to it to provide strength. The holly veneer into which it was to be set was in its turn stuck to the underside of the paper and the 'sandwich' carefully sawn round with a buhl-saw, using the shape of the mosaic as a guide. By means of a knife the mosaic design and its surround were separated from the paper and then fitted together. Some later products of Boyce, Brown & Kemp and their successors dispensed with the solid surround and merely filled the spaces round floral designs with long tesserae of holly to build up rectangular or square blocks from which the veneers could be cut and fitted without further work being necessary.[11]

The introduction of tessellated mosaic in the early 1830s provided an exciting new medium for pictorial representation, but many makers, especially in the period to *c*1860, utilised additional conventional cross-grain marquetry from time to time. Edmund

Nye from time to time used conventional cross-grain marquetry for the colourful and lifelike representations of birds and butterflies, which are a particular feature of some of the finest work from his manufactory in the 1850s. This tradition appears to have been carried on by Thomas Barton after Nye's death, and it is probable that he may also have been responsible for the design of the Nye pieces (fig. 63). One Barton design which is particularly highly regarded is that of Battle Abbey gatehouse in which every piece of stonework is represented by an individually selected piece of wood with considerable regard for colour and shading (fig. 64). This view was very favourably commented upon when shown at the 1864 Industrial Exhibition at Tunbridge Wells. Several examples of this view are known and it is possible that, although the design uses conventional cross-grain techniques in its execution, a block might have been made to satisfy demand. Some of the earlier mosaic topographical blocks also incorporated foreground and detail in conventional marquetry, though the buildings were depicted in mosaic (fig. 46).[12] Robert Russell, as mentioned earlier, utilised and developed new designs for cross-grain marquetry which he marketed as 'Tunbridge Wells Marquetrie' (fig. 74).[13]

An important workman in any Tunbridge ware manufactory was the box-maker, who was responsible for preparing the boxes of various shapes and sizes in preparation for veneering. Carcase woods conventional to the cabinet-making trades such as pine, sycamore and occasionally cedar were used for this purpose. These were veneered with a range of fashionable timbers, usually tropical hardwoods. Brazilian rosewood retained its popularity from the Regency period through to the termination of the industry, and was the most widely used timber even in the last years of production, despite the fact that its popularity in the cabinet-making trade was on the wane from c1860. In the early decades of mosaic production the industry was also attracted to light-coloured veneer woods such as holly, satinwood, birch and maple, possibly a carryover from the whitewood wares of the Regency period (figs. 25, 28, 71). A number of early pieces with the Edmund Nye label are of this type, but he was certainly not the only maker to use light woods. His successor, Thomas Barton, on the other hand, was inclined to favour dark veneers and the lavish use of coromandel or ebony are often an indication of his work. Hungarian ash or maple stained grey as a veneer is a sign of post-1860 production in virtually all cases, and was much favoured by Henry Hollamby, Boyce, Brown & Kemp and their successors; George Wise Snr., and Thomas Barton are known to have used this type of veneer more rarely. One rather unusual wood used for decorative work has been given the name 'composite veneer'. In appearance, it bears some resemblance to marbling, and is said to have been formed from the compression and adhesion of a number of distorted veneers of contrasting timbers into a block from which fresh veneers could be cut (fig. 39). No contemporary account of its production is known and it appears on items ranging in date from about the mid-1830s to the mid-1850s. The makers using this technique cannot be identified as no labelled pieces are known, but Wadmore suggests that George Wise Snr.

39. *Rosewood table, octagonal stem and concave-sided base,the top decorated with a parquetry star surround with miniature parquetry bandings and vandyke work. The top also incorporates a wide band of 'composite veneer' resembling marbling. c1840. w:51cm h:7cm. (Sotheby's).*

5. (Above left) *Whitewood card box, sarcophagus shape, decorated with penwork. The top depicts a watermill built amidst ruins, the sides have a pine and lotus border. It is lined with red paper. The penwork cribbage board displayed in front fits in a compartment in the interior. c1820. w:24cm d:16.5cm h:12.5cm.*

6. (Above right) *Card box veneered in kingwood, the top decorated with a hand-drawn and coloured display of playing cards, the ace of spades bearing the inscription at the base "I J & A SHARP. TUNB WELLS" (i.e. I.J. & A. Sharp of Oldenburgh House, London Road, Tunbridge Wells). c1810. w:22.5cm d:12cm h:6.5cm.*

7. *Whitewood box, the lid decorated with a print of the Boulevard, Margate (also known as Levey's Bazaar). This establishment offered visitors "jewellery of all descriptions, trinkets of endless variety, bijoutry, foreign china of great beauty and excellence, toys for the amusement of children, perfumery from the best manufacturers, and cutlery and other goods". c1830. w:20.5cm d:12.5cm h:5cm.*

8. (Above left) *Workbox veneered in kingwood, the top decorated with fine quality large scale perspective cube work. c1800. w:23cm d:15.5cm h:8cm.*

9. (Above right) *Rosewood jewellery casket, sarcophagus shape, the top decorated with perspective cube work and sides with vandyke borders, wooden ring handles at ends, on bun feet, the interior fitted and lined in violet velvet, the inside lid with a mirror. c1830. w:28cm d:23cm h:15cm.*

10a. (Above left) *Rosewood workbox, the top decorated with perspective cube work, interior lined in green. The base bears the label of "CHEESMAN, Turner and Tunbridge Ware Manufacturer, No 9 CRANBOURN STREET, West Street, Brighton". c1830. w:25cm d:19cm h:11cm.*

10b. (Above right) *Label on base of Cheeseman workbox.*

made such veneers at his Tonbridge manufactory.[14] In addition to the basic veneer wood, decorative panels and bandings were applied.

Box-finishing was the final stage in production. This consisted firstly in polishing or varnishing the objects. French polishing was favoured for the finer or larger objects, the cheaper items being covered with a few coats of shellac or hard white spirit varnish. Practices may have varied from manufacturer to manufacturer. The next stage involved the lining of the interior, and the covering of the base with paper to mask the carcase wood. The papers used can provide an indication of the age of the object. In productions to *c*1840, plain papers coloured red, pink, green or blue were favoured for interior lining. The same paper might be used on the base or a marbled paper, though some boxes, particularly those made in Brighton, were left with the base uncovered. Through most of the Victorian period patterned papers were favoured for interiors, though imitation leather papers in black or dark red tended to be used for the base. Twentieth-century productions used both plain and patterned papers, but on smaller boxes there was a growing tendency to show the body wood of cedar or walnut, and leave them unlined. Workboxes were often lined with silk, satin or velvet. The final stage in finishing involved the fitting of feet, handles, knobs, etc., which might have been turned on a lathe and be examples of inlaid turnery. The completed items would then be ready for sale either direct to the public or to a retailer. Some makers such as George Wise, Henry Hollamby and Boyce, Brown & Kemp developed extensive wholesale connections; others, mostly small businesses, but including Thomas Barton, concentrated their efforts on direct sale to the public.[15]

There is some evidence that makers did not entirely desert the production of whitewood wares. A number of items marked with the stamp or label of Thomas Barton are known in this form (fig. 40). Transfer printing was available by this period and was used by some makers. One commentator in 1871 noted in his account of the Tunbridge ware trade that:

> *'A great number of articles, such as glove-boxes, fire-screens, card cases and baskets, manufactured at Tunbridge, are decorated with Decalcomanie, now pretty well known as a means of ornamentation.'*

This was a process of transferring a coloured image painted in reverse on paper to the wood. The wood was treated with a 'liquid cement', the transfer floated on water and, when the paper was dampened sufficiently, placed in position on the object. The paper could be removed after a few minutes, and the image which had been transferred to the wood was protected with varnish. A further account, written two years later, indicated the continuance of this process in the trade, but specified spirits of wine as the dampening agent for the transfer paper. Nevertheless, it is likely that the production of such objects at this date was small, and they would not be easily recognised as being of this late date unless marked with a manufacturer's stamp or label.[16]

40. *Whitewood face screen and stand decorated with a representation of chaffinches and their nest. Stamped 'Thomas Barton, Manufacturer of Tunbridge Wells'. Late nineteenth century. h:43cm d of base:14cm w of screen:24cm. (Tunbridge Wells Museum).*

Chapter 9

VICTORIAN TUNBRIDGE WARE DESIGNS AND THEIR SOURCES

Tessellated mosaic work was the greatest achievement and the most characteristic product of the Tunbridge ware industry, and it is important to try to trace the sources that inspired it. The use of inlay techniques in woodwork can be found in the Ancient World, and one Egyptian casket of the eighteenth dynasty has part of its top and sides decorated with around 47,000 thin strips of ivory and ebony. It is, however, in connection with stone mosaics that the technique was most widely known in the Ancient World and especially in Roman decorative art. These skills were transmitted through Byzantium and medieval Italy to the Renaissance when an interest in intarsia work in wood, including chequer work, became a major element in furniture decoration. Renaissance designs started to influence furniture and woodwork in Britain from the early decades of the sixteenth century and during the second half of the century inlay work was being widely practised. A number of designs used re-occur in Tunbridge parquetry of the Regency period, though apart from chequer work borders, mosaic elements are little in evidence. The art of marquetry did not develop in Britain until *c*1670, and by this date the Renaissance-inspired designs of the late sixteenth century had long been out of fashion. It is thus not possible to trace any continuous line of influence from the woodwork of the Ancient World, or even the Renaissance, which might have influenced nineteenth-century designers and craftsmen at Tunbridge Wells to adopt mosaic techniques.[1]

Various explanations have been offered in the past for the introduction of tessellated mosaic techniques in the early 1830s, and all look to Italy as the immediate source. One explanation claims that the technique was learnt by William Burrows from an Italian refugee working in a hut on the edge of Rusthall Common, Tunbridge Wells where the Spa Hotel now stands. This story does not appear in print, however, until 1882 and is not supported by local parish registers and directories of the first half of the nineteenth century which fail to list any persons with an Italian name working in the trade.[2] This story also presupposes that the wood mosaic techniques were being practised in Italy at this period

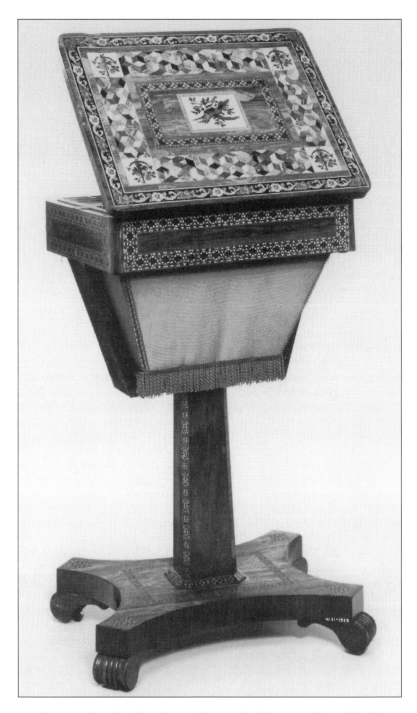

41. *Rosewood work-table, the top decorated with a central tessellated mosaic panel of a bird with additional perspective cube work, miniature parquetry bandings and tessellated mosaic bandings and panels. The front decorated with tessellated mosaic panels of butterflies. c1845. w:47cm d:37cm h:73.5cm. (Victoria & Albert Museum).*

and there appears to be no evidence for this. It has been assumed that the production of mosaic wares at Sorrento commenced in 1827 but recent research has shown that no mosaic work was produced in the town until 1871.[3] What then did inspire the production of the tessellated mosaic wares? As has been previously explained, the technique of assembling blocks from which veneers could be cut was established before 1830 and its application to a block consisting of square tesserae was a natural development. The English public were well aware of Roman stone mosaic floors. These had been seen by countless gentlemen on the grand tour and they had even been imported from Italy in the eighteenth century for use as table tops.[4] In England, Roman villa sites providing similar pavements were being discovered in increasing numbers in the late eighteenth and early nineteenth centuries and publicised in books on British antiquities. What more natural in an age whose art and design was

42. *Rosewood stationery cabinet, the top decorated with a mosaic representation of the Prince of Wales's feathers supported by a lion and a unicorn, and the motto 'Ich Dien', the top and sides with additional geometrical and leaf bandings. Possibly by James & George Burrows. c1845. w:16.5cm d:21cm. (Sotheby's).*

heavily influenced by classicism than that the technique should seem applicable to woodware?

Initially, the subjects used for production in tessellated mosaic were birds, butterflies, buildings or patterns worked in square or rectangular surrounds and used as the central feature of a box or other object. The bandings surrounding this panel were all of the miniature parquetry type. Boxes so-decorated often retain the sarcophagus shape popular in the Regency period, and can be dated to the decade following c1835. It is also on similar objects that the first naturalistic leaf and flower borders in tessellated mosaic are to be found in association with miniature parquetry ones. Wares of this type appear to have come from the manufactories of George and James Burrows and Edmund Nye, but may also have been produced by others. One range of objects from this early phase of mosaic wares can probably be dated with more certainty. These are items decorated with the three ostrich plumes and motto of the Prince of Wales. Two versions exist, one with the lion and unicorn supporters, and the other and more common without. James Burrows claimed to be the designer and maker of the block featuring 'the Prince of Wales's features, arms and motto' measuring 3½in (8.9cm) by 2½in (6.4cm) and containing 8–9,000 tesserae, but is is not known whether others produced blocks of this subject (fig. 42).[5] The event most likely to have inspired this exhibition of royalist fervour for Edward, Prince of Wales, was his birth in November 1841, though a continuing interest in the royal child no doubt maintained this design in production for a number of years. Another interesting subject known in Tunbridge ware shows a boy wearing a kilt reclining on the ground. He is accompanied by a dog and a parrot. This design was also the subject of a Berlin embroidery pattern and may well represent the Prince of Wales (fig. 43). If this is so, the design may date from the late 1840s or early 50s.[6]

The increasing use from the 1840s of floral centres and bandings, usually of roses, can be attributed to the popularity of Berlin woolwork designs of a similar nature. In Berlin woolwork, coloured designs were prepared on squared paper which corresponded to squares applied to the canvas or cloth being embroidered. The first patterns issued in connection with this technique were published in Germany in 1804 and designs were reaching England as early as the following year. The practice only enjoyed modest popularity until about 1830. The establishment of the business of Mr Wilkes in Regent Street, London in the following year, supplying patterns and materials imported direct from Berlin, was an important influence in popularising this technique, and by 1840 14,000 different patterns had been published or imported into England. The closeness in date of the introduction of the tessellated mosaic in the Tunbridge Wells industry and the rise in popularity of Berlin woolwork cannot be mere coincidence, and it may well have been an important factor in influencing its introduction. Tunbridge ware makers are known to have utilised Berlin woolwork patterns in their work. The small size of the unit of production in the Tunbridge ware industry precluded the employment of full-time professional designers on the staff, and

43. Above: *jewel case, the top decorated with a rare reproduction in tessellated mosaic of a boy (possibly Edward, Prince of Wales) wearing a kilt and holding a parrot in one hand and a dog in the other. c1850. w:20cm h:6.5cm. Below: a needlework box, the top covered in Berlin wool embroidery, showing an identical design. The design for the Tunbridge ware box was probably taken from a Berlin woolwork pattern. (Sotheby's).*

Berlin woolwork designs provided a ready source of new subjects. The patterns from the Edmund Nye hoard, now at the Tunbridge Wells and Birmingham Museums, contain such published designs, including German imports. Many of the designs from this source are dated, ranging from 1845 to 1853. The profuse roses, heavily shaded and standing out from a dark ground, favoured in Berlin woolwork of the mid-nineteenth century, are reproduced in the boldest form in the manufactures of Edmund Nye and Thomas Barton. Other makers, including Henry Hollamby and Thomas Waterman, worked in a similar style and another collection of Berlin woolwork patterns in the Tunbridge Wells Museum, including those of a hawk (colour pl. 15) and deer grazing (fig. 45) came mainly from the stock of Henry Hollamby when his works eventually closed. They passed successively through the hands of later makers, finally being owned by Albert Botton (see pp. 123, 128). Although in embroidery the virtual monopoly of Berlin woolwork was already under attack by the 1850s and the technique was soon to decline, its influence in Tunbridge ware designs was to survive well into the twentieth century. There are also other connections between Berlin wool embroidery and Tunbridge ware. Sellers of embroidery materials were also often stockists and, in one case, a manufacturer, of Tunbridge ware. The manufacturer was James Friend who by 1850 was already advertising his business as 'Tunbridge Ware Manufactory and Berlin Wool Repository'.[7] Briefly in the mid-nineteenth century Crossley's of Halifax, carpet manufacturers, used the Tunbridge ware technique to produce wool pictures resembling Berlin woolwork.

Of all the mosaic blocks designed, those displaying floral subjects were the most popular. They ranged from single blossoms to bouquets and were often entirely of roses, and the appeal of this flower to manufacturers of Tunbridge ware was maintained until the collapse of the Tunbridge Wells industry in the late 1920s. In Berlin woolwork, rose designs were also predominant, and the popularity of other flowers lasted a year or two at the most. In 1848 and 1849, the convolvulus was favoured and there were also hydrangeas and striped tulips. Large-headed flowers were popular through the 1850s, but in about 1855 more delicate subjects such as violets, heather and harebells began to be favoured, and in the late 1850s ferns came to the fore. It might be useful to keep such trends in mind when dating Tunbridge ware designs, but evidence of exact parallels do not exist and seem unlikely. Convolvulus featured in Tunbridge ware blocks in association with roses, and the pansy, fuchsia and arum lily also appeared (fig. 44). Wild flowers were not favoured, but borders based on the oak leaf and acorn and ferns were used. Animals were less popular in Tunbridge ware though dogs, which appeared as early as the late 1830s, and to a lesser extent cats, were representative of domestic animals. Among wild animals, the stag was a Victorian favourite, no doubt popularised by Sir Edwin Landseer's paintings and the Royal family's Scottish hunting forays (fig. 45). One rare block features a pair of mice. Butterflies, moths and birds carried out in mosaic were featured from the late 1830s when James Burrows was producing such

44. *Rosewood tea caddy containing four tea containers and two bowls, decorated inside the lid with a spray of fuchsia blooms and with wide mosaic rose bandings on the concave sides. Possibly by Henry Hollamby. c1860. w:42cm. (Christie's, South Kensington).*

designs, and carried on through the 1840s (colour pl. 12). The mosaic technique, however, often failed to achieve the delicate and lively effect desired, and many of Edmund Nye's panels of these subjects in the 1850s were conventional cross-grain marquetry, though the boxes or pieces of furniture were additionally decorated with mosaic bandings (fig. 63). These subjects became less common towards the end of the nineteenth century. The utilisation of motifs from nature was a trend in all forms of decorative art in the Victorian period, endorsed by leaders in the field of design, though neither John Ruskin nor William Morris would have wished to identify with the profuse artificiality of some of the more crowded, exuberant renderings of full-blown 'cabbage' roses found in Tunbridge ware.

The other main class of blocks used as major decorative elements were those displaying views. Topographical prints had been used

45. *Rosewood reading stand with mosaic representations of hawk and deer grazing, copied from Berlin woolwork designs, also mosaic leaf bandings. Attributable to Henry Hollamby. c1860. w:36cm h:28cm. (Sotheby's).*

extensively on earlier Tunbridge wares, and within a few years of the establishment of the tessellated mosaic technique attempts were being made to produce likenesses of buildings in the new material. James Burrows of Tunbridge Wells and George Wise of Tonbridge appear to have been the pioneers in this development, with blocks already in production by the late 1830s. Early makers would use conventional cross-grain marquetry in association with mosaic, especially for foreground and details and the resulting views show an interesting similarity in style to the prints used to illustrate *Clifford's Tunbridge Wells Guides* from the mid 1820s (fig. 46). One of the earliest and most persistently popular of the topographical blocks was that of Eridge Castle, the seat of the Marquis of Abergavenny who was a substantial owner of property in Tunbridge Wells. Most Tunbridge ware makers appear to have produced one or more blocks of this subject and it has been estimated that there are over 30 variations in style and size and that half of all objects decorated with views show Eridge Castle. As over 80 other views exist it follows that all the others range from uncommon to scarce.[9] Next to those of Eridge Castle, the most common subjects were houses, abbey ruins and castles of Kent and East Sussex which would have featured as places to visit in local guide books for the Tunbridge Wells area (figs. 35, 47, colour pl. 22). Views well outside south-east England exist, ranging from the south-west of Ireland to the border counties of Scotland, and there is even one of the Capitol building in Washington D.C., United States of America. Although some of these more distant views may have sold at Tunbridge Wells on their merits as attractive representations of ancient or stately buildings, in most cases they must indicate a local sale in the area depicted, emphasising the wide market for Tunbridge ware in tourist-orientated areas in the nineteenth century. James Burrows, Humphrey Burrows, Edmund

46. *Rosewood workbox decorated with a floral mosaic border and a central block of Eridge Castle, constructed partly in tessellated mosaic and partly in conventional marquetry (foreground, flag and part of building). The mixing of techniques in topographical blocks is usually a sign of an early date. The Eridge Castle view closely resembles that on a panel in the Tunbridge Wells Museum inscribed, 'This was the last work made by Mr. Humphrey Burrows the Elder at Jordan Place, Tonbridge Wells in the year 1844'. c1845. w:23.5cm d:18.5cm.*

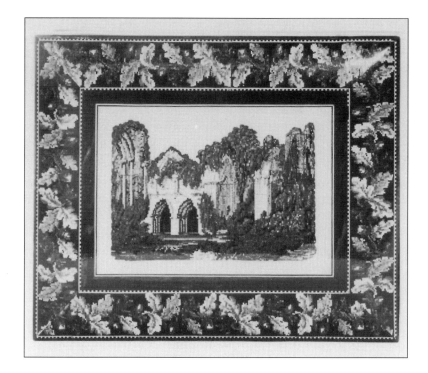

47. *Examples of topographical blocks used on Tunbridge ware. Above: View of Bayham Abbey on a coromandel games box, the view edged with a broad oak leaf and acorn border. In the manner of Henry Hollamby. c1870. w:25.5cm, h:7.5cm. Below: Ebony box with a view of Great Malvern Priory Church surrounded by an unusual patterned mosaic border. c1860. w:23.5cm h:10cm. (Sotheby's).*

Nye, Thomas Barton, George Wise, Alfred Talbot, Robert Russell and Henry Hollamby are all known to have used topographical blocks. Henry Hollamby appears to have been a particularly prolific producer and his designs were utilised by Boyce, Brown & Kemp and in turn were featured by the Tunbridge Wells Manufacturing Company as late as the 1920s.[10]

Floral and other subjects derived from nature, topographical views and perspective cube work provided the main repertoire of the Victorian Tunbridge ware maker. Designs associated with Edward, Prince of Wales have also been noted. A few other blocks were also produced. In the period prior to *c*1850, symmetrical abstract patterns were favoured by some makers and were produced in holly surrounds as important features (colour pl. 13). Edmund Nye certainly used such blocks and it is possible that G. & J. Burrows did so also. From this early period, and sometimes associated with such abstract designs, is a square block featuring St. George slaying the dragon (fig. 48). The famous table featuring a ship in full sail displayed by Edmund Nye at the 1851 Exhibition does not, however, appear to have spawned further nautical essays. Small blocks of a particular type were produced to meet special

48. *Rosewood tea caddy decorated with blocks of abstract patterns in mosaic. The design on the top is based on floral subjects; two of those on the front show stylised butterflies. The front also features a representation of St George and the Dragon in mosaic. There is additional floral and geometrical mosaic bandings, perspective cube work and 'composite veneer'. The interior contains two tea compartments and a bowl. c1845. w:30.5cm d:15cm. (Sotheby's).*

needs. It seemed appropriate that Victorian stamp boxes should be decorated with the head of the monarch, as featured in the issues of the period. A number of mosaic blocks were produced for this purpose, often utilising very small tesserae to facilitate the reproduction of the facial features of the Queen. A black background was used on some, influenced no doubt by the colour chosen for the first penny stamp of 1840. As a cheaper alternative, manufacturers could use a current unused definitive stamp or facsimile as the main feature, stuck on the top of the box and varnished (fig. 52, colour pl.16). The sides and remainder of the top could be decorated with Tunbridge bandings. Double- or triple-compartment stamp boxes provided space for additional Tunbridge ware decoration on the lid and on very late examples commemorative stamps might be used as part of the scheme (fig. 57). This practice of using current British stamps, which commercial producers continued until the 1930s, does help with the dating of such boxes, as the dates of issue of the stamps concerned can be located in standard stamp catalogues. Henry Hollamby and his successors also made up small rectangular blocks for trinket or other boxes which spelt out a brief message or advertisement in mosaic. These have been found with the names of tourist resorts such as 'PRESENT FROM WORTHING', 'A PRESENT FROM HASTINGS', 'KILLARNEY LAKES', 'A PRESENT FROM MALVERN' and 'A PRESENT FROM THE ISLE OF MAN', an interesting throwback to the late Georgian whitewood ware trifles. They are also known with the names of commercial firms, who used the boxes as an advertisement for their wares, such as 'FROM E. DURRANT' (a Tunbridge Wells grocer and wine merchant). Bézique and whist scorers are known inscribed 'DE LA RUE'S BEZIQUE BY CAVENDISH', 'CAVENDISH WHIST MARKER DE LA RUE & CO. PATENTEES' and 'CAVENDISH WHIST MARKER DE LA RUE AND Co.'. These were, no doubt, marketed by Thomas De La Rue & Co., playing card and security printers.[11]

The attribution of pieces of Tunbridge ware to particular makers presents problems. Only two makers, Edmund Nye and Thomas Barton, regularly marked their wares, and even with these two makers pieces, almost certainly from their manufactory, exist without labels or stamps. Other makers only used labels or stamps briefly or intermittently, and thus only a small percentage of items can be identified by this means. A further complication is caused by the designs of one manufacturer being taken over by another when trading ceased. Barton took over Nye's business in 1863, but had been its foreman and designer for many years previously. Thus, unlabelled pieces displaying characteristics that suggest that they come from this enterprise may be by one maker or the other. The stocks and designs of Henry Hollamby passed to Boyce, Brown & Kemp in 1891 when the former's business closed, so that the blocks were used by both and the range of wares is similar. This is particularly true of the topograhical blocks such as Battle Abbey gatehouse, Bayham Abbey, Eridge Castle, the Pantiles, Muckross Abbey and Shakespeare's Birthplace. There is also evidence that Henry Hollamby was supplying Boyce, Brown & Kemp with blocks

49a. *Workbox veneered in walnut and decorated with geometrical cross-grain marquetry bandings of various woods, labelled inside on an ivory panel 'CORMACK BROTHERS MAKERS 37 LUDGATE HILL LONDON'. The two small Tunbridge ware panels were probably supplied by Henry Hollamby. c1870–80. w:29.3cm h:13.2cm d:21.3cm. (Guildhall Museum, Rochester).*

49b. *Ivory label inside the workbox.*

or veneers before 1891. The successors of Boyce, Brown & Kemp also continued to use these designs. In this case, matters are complicated by the very limited number of items labelled by Hollamby or Boyce, Brown & Kemp. It is highly likely that these two instances of the use of earlier designs by a subsequent maker is only the tip of a very substantial iceberg, and that interchange and

50. *Walnut overmantle incorporating mosaic Tunbridge ware panels of butterflies (top) and dogs (bottom). Here is a clear case of a Tunbridge ware maker selling veneers to a cabinet-maker. c1875. w:104cm h:104cm. (Sotheby's).*

sale of bandings and blocks, and complete items within the industry may have been on a wide scale. A distinctive centre decoration featuring a spray of pansies, has been found in identical form on boxes bearing the labels of Thomas Barton and George Wise Jnr. It is also clear that Edmund Nye was in correspondence with James Burrows and George Wise which may suggest some degree of co-operation. Tunbridge ware makers are known to have supplied veneers to cabinet-makers. A mahogany glazed bookcase on a cupboard base in the Tunbridge Wells Museum collection incorporates blocks of Tonbridge and Dover Castles and is unlikely to be the work of a Tunbridge ware maker. Blocks and bandings have been seen on shop display cases, a writing-table, a chair, a long case, clock case with a movement by W^m. Marshall, Wishaw, banjos and a chimney overmantle (fig. 50). Barometer cases decorated with Tunbridge ware are known, the instruments bearing the names of

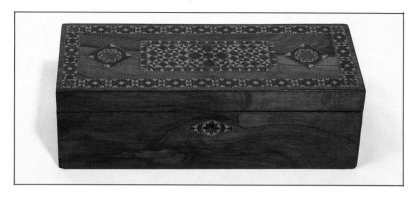

11. *Rosewood glove box, the top and keyhole escutcheon decorated with miniature parquetry patterns. The front of the box is hinged. c1830. w:27cm d:10.5cm h:8cm.*

12. *Domed rosewood glove box decorated with bandings and panels of miniature parquetry, the top with a mosaic veneer of a moth. An early example of tessellated mosaic work of c1835–40. w:24mm d:8.5mm h:7.5mm.*

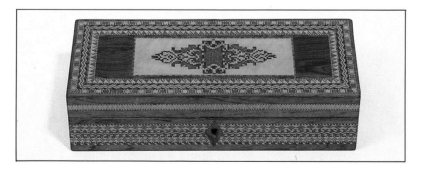

13. *Rosewood box with central abstract tessellated mosaic panel and various conventional marquetry bandings. An early example of tessellated mosaic. c1840. w:22cm d:9cm h:5cm.*

14. *A characteristic group of late nineteenth century Tunbridge ware. The domed stationey cabinet at the rear has the top decorated with a tessellated mosaic view of Muckross Abbey and is attributable to Henry Hollamby. w:25cm d:16cm h:14.5cm. Other items left to right are a thermometer mounted on an obilisk (Cleopatra's needle type), a turned box, a serviette ring, a stamp box, a tape measure and a ring-stand. (Worthing Museum & Art Gallery).*

15. *Examples of inlaid turnery. Centre: handscreen with mosaic veneer depicting an eagle attributable to Henry Hollamby l:33cm. Other objects include pin cushions, a serviette ring, turned rosewood boxes, a pin poppet (front right) and a scent bottle in a case with a screw top (top centre). Late nineteenth century.*

51. Top: *Rosewood box decorated with geometrical, leaf and floral mosaic tessellated bandings, the top displaying a photograph of Bonchurch Pond, Isle of Wight. c1870. 2:22cm d:15.5cm h:1.5cm.* Bottom: *Blotter case in rosewood with mosaic edge border, featuring a photograph of Shanklin Chine, Isle of Wight. c1870. w:14cm l:21cm. (Tunbridge Wells Museum).*

P. Rosapini, Tunbridge Wells and G. Kalabergo, Banbury. These cases were probably made in London or one of the large provincial towns and the veneers bought in. One London box maker at least used bought-in Tunbridge ware veneers. This was Cormack Brothers of 37, Ludgate Hill who traded at this address from 1866 to 1889 as 'dressing-case makers'. A labelled box of their manufacture

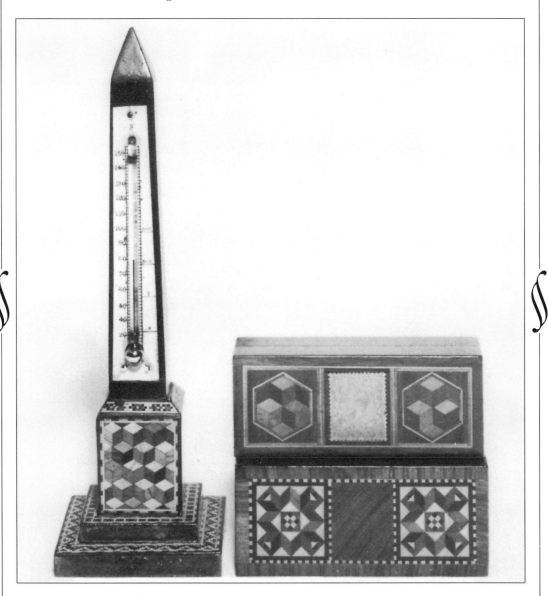

52. *Thermometer stand in the form of Cleopatra's Needle decorated with perspective cube work and bandings. c1890. h:19cm. Two triple-compartment stamp boxes decorated with parquetry designs, the top one decorated with a 1½d stamp of the 1912 issue. c1920. All attributable to Boyce, Brown & Kemp and their successors. (Sotheby's).*

decorated with cross-grain geometrical marquetry and two small mosaic Tunbridge ware panels is in the Guildhall Museum, Rochester (fig. 49). Papier mâché items, such as spectacle cases, are known veneered in Tunbridge ware. All these examples suggest a regular trade in the sale of veneers by some makers.[12]

Some Tunbridge ware of the late nineteenth century features photographs (fig. 51) instead of larger topographical mosaic blocks. These have been attributed to Robert Licence of Dover, for reasons that are unclear. His manufactures were mainly turnery wares, though he probably stocked items made in Tunbridge Wells, featuring the blocks of Dover Castle and St Mary's Church and the Pharos. There is no evidence that he produced the small cabinet wares on which the photographs are normally mounted. The views on these photographic Tunbridge ware pieces are not captioned, but many appear to be places in the Isle of Wight. A tea caddy, trinket boxes and a paperweight are known bearing the stamp of the seller, Stephen Knight & Son of Ventnor, dating from the 1870s. Knight's stamp is also to be found on a box showing a photograph of London Road from the Common, Tunbridge Wells and a photographic view of Muckross Abbey has been found on a needlecase. Mosaic bandings are used as a border for the photographs, ranging from thin and geometrical to wide and profuse oak-leaf designs. One box is known with a black and white lithographic print of the River Thames at Hampton, Middlesex instead of a photograph. This range may have been made by a Tunbridge Wells maker, probably Henry Hollamby, or he may have supplied just the mosaic bandings.[13]

The range of Tunbridge ware items produced in the Victorian period was very wide.[14] The most prestigious pieces were items of furniture, in the main tables designed for games, needlework or occasional use. These were made in small numbers throughout the nineteenth century by several makers and many of the later ones bear the stamp of Thomas Barton. Cabinet furniture does not appear to have been made, possibly because the workshops did not have the facilities for fabricating large structures. Chairs, too, are uncommon, though a fine set of five single and two armchairs and a matching loo table of c1835 in striking parquetry, exist at Buscot Park, Oxfordshire. The main trade of Tunbridge ware makers was, however, in smaller cabinet wares such as tea caddies, portable desks, stationery and sewing boxes. These were aimed at a discerning middle-class clientele. Cheaper ranges of trinket boxes and small turnery wares were in production throughout, but became of greater importance towards the end of the nineteenth century, and in these items novelty was often a greater selling attraction than utility. Some degree of topicality was sought, and the obelisk-shaped thermometer stands made by Henry Hollamby and Boyce, Brown & Kemp owe their inspiration to the so-called Cleopatra's Needle, an ancient obelisk brought from Egypt and erected on the Victoria Embankment in London in 1878 (fig. 52, colour pl. 14).[15]

Chapter 10

THE INDUSTRY IN DECLINE
1875–1939

Although by 1875 the perceptive could sense that the Tunbridge ware industry was past its prime, the casual observer would have noticed little change. Admittedly, in this decade Robert Russell had ceased manufacturing his delicate Tunbridge Wells marquetry, but a newcomer in the form of James Brown had taken his place, while at Tonbridge, the cessation of trading by George Wise Jnr had resulted in the establishment of the business of Thomas Burrows. The industry was still capable of generating new enterprises to take the place of those who had retired. However, the 1870s was to be the last decade in which this regeneration was to be witnessed, and from then on it was a story of continuous decline. Burrows, isolated from the main centre of production, ceased trading in 1883 ending a tradition of manufacturing in the town of Tonbridge extending back nearly a century and a half. The next decade was to see the closure of Henry Hollamby's works in Frant Road, Tunbridge Wells, though to some extent the wholesale business devolved on the partnership of Boyce, Brown & Kemp. A further blow fell in 1903 with the death of Thomas Barton. As early as March 1891, his advancing years had dictated the closure of his retail depot in the Pantiles, and a consequent cutback in production. Although attempts were made to carry on Barton's business on a limited scale after his death, these too had ended by *c*1910, leaving Boyce, Brown & Kemp as the sole survivor. Even the Royal borough, which had once been proud to publicise the ware, started to lose interest. A guide book published as early as 1888 fails to mention the industry, and by the turn of the century few thought it worthy of attention. The impending demise was sensed by Henry Wolff as early as 1882, when he wrote his account of the industry for the *Sussex Advertiser*, and over the next three decades several other detailed accounts were published, all the authors being determined to describe the expertise of a craft soon to disappear for ever.[1]

The industry was fully aware of its decline but seemed unable to take effective action to remedy the situation. A number of local councillors, especially those on the Tunbridge Wells Technical Institute Committee, no doubt prodded by Thomas Barton, were sufficiently concerned to attempt to reverse the trend. An exhibition was planned for October 1899 to be held in the Council Chamber of the Town Hall. This included not only items from Thomas Barton's manufactory (fig. 53), but those of former producers such as James

53. *Games table veneered in ebony and decorated with tessellated mosaic bandings and parquetry, including a vandyke border on the top. This table was made in 1895 by Thomas Barton for David Salomons of Broomhill, Southborough, Kent and exhibited at the 1899 Exhibition at Tunbridge Wells Town Hall. (Victoria & Albert Museum).*

Friend and William Foley. A range of 45 marquetry pieces showing various techniques dating from the Renaissance period onwards were loaned by the Victoria & Albert Museum, and two items were even lent by the Queen. The aim of these displays was 'to show typical examples of old and recent Tunbridge Ware: to stimulate the improvement of its artistic qualities by the production of new designs, and to suggest the use of such inlaid decoration in other ways than are customary at present'. A lecture, 'Inlay with Reference to Tunbridge Ware', was given in connection with the Exhibition by C. Tattershall Dodd. The speaker was critical of the usefulness of the mosaic techniques being employed and declared 'inlay of floral forms must be true inlay or "intarsia' of pictures shaped and arranged, and not be built up of little squares which gives the appearance of Berlin wool work'. A public competition to encourage design innovation was held but the entries were disappointing with 'almost an absence of local effort'. The entries were judged by Walter Crane, a leading figure in the Arts and Crafts movement, and at the time President of the Arts and Crafts Exhibition Society and Principal of the Royal College of Art. He passed a number of pertinent, but far from flattering, remarks on the state of the industry and the design talent shown. The Exhibition could hardly have been said to have been successful in its aims. There had been a similar attempt to revive the industry six or seven years earlier and some effort was expended through the Technical Education Committee to interest students in the industry and stimulate suitable designs.[2]

The truth was that the industry, which had shown such innovative energy both in techniques and design in the second quarter of the nineteenth century, was by 1870 drifting into a state of lethargy, with only Thomas Barton showing any originality. The same designs that had accorded well with the early and high Victorian taste, were in the last decades of the nineteenth century failing to adapt to the Arts and Crafts tradition, the revival of classicism or the images conjured up by the 'aesthetic' furnisher. Warnings had been given that change was necessary. As early as 1871, Elias Taylor had suggested that the skills of the Tunbridge ware craftsman in combining woods of various colours could be more widely applied in larger turnery objects and especially furniture where 'a demand would quickly arise for furniture of this rich and decorative character'. This was a plea repeated by Tattershall Dodd at the 1899 Exhibition. He explained that Tunbridge ware must not merely be used to decorate souvenirs but must be developed as a technique to be applied to fine quality furniture generally. Walter Crane had pointed out the paucity of new designs in the field declaring that 'mechanical skill has outstripped artistic endeavour in the arrangement and design. There is a somewhat stereotyped fashion and a desire to be ornamental without due regard to natural effect.' He did not mince his words when laying blame for the paucity of artistic talent. He noted that one workman was paid 5d (2.08p) an hour and added succinctly, 'Artists are expensive people'. By this date, however, the industry had neither the drive of youthful entrepreneurship nor the resources required to change.[3]

The industry in the period after *c*1875 was being progressively weakened by an influx of foreign goods, performing similar functions, but because of lower wage costs, selling much more cheaply. As early as 1882, Wolff commented upon 'the cheap foreign goods without wear or labour in them – painted articles of light make – which at present damages the more solid and unquestionably more lasting Tunbridge ware'. It was not only European wares which competed. Items deemed fashionable to the aesthetic taste, but at the same time inexpensive, were flowing in

54. Top: *A type 6 glove box, and* bottom: *a type 11 handkerchief box invoiced to the Royal Botanic Gardens, Kew on 5 July 1924 by the Tunbridge Wells Manufacturing Co. at 30s (£1.50) and 35s (£1.75) respectively. The coarse quality of this type of work is shown well in the mosaic used on these boxes, which is characteristic of this period. (Royal Botanic Gardens, Kew. Crown copyright).*

from Japan, China and India. Even some British-made goods offered competition, for the range of transfer-printed sycamore wares produced by the Smiths of Mauchline were proving popular. It is interesting to examine the catalogues of the major London retailers such as Harrods, the Army and Navy Stores, and Gamages for the decades immediately prior to the First World War. None of these major stores featured Tunbridge ware, but they did offer ranges of tea caddies, glove and trinket boxes, pin cushions and paper-knives, much imported from the Far East, in sandalwood, lacquer, ivory and silver. Japanese, Indian and Russian wares were prominent and prices attractive, often a half or a third of an equivalent Tunbridge item.[4]

In the face of such competition the Tunbridge Wells industry had two alternatives. It could either maintain quality and restrict its wares to a small but discerning market, or attempt to compete by cutting costs at every possible point. Boyce, Brown & Kemp, the major producer by this period, was, however, geared to the wholesale trade, with few direct retail sales. They relied upon small fancy goods retailers, often in seaside and resort centres, who were all too conscious of the cheap, attractive foreign wares on offer. Price was therefore a major consideration. The production of Tunbridge ware was labour intensive. By 1890, Boyce, Brown & Kemp had installed a small steam engine to drive the saws and lathes, but steam was never an efficient means of powering a small workshop which could not guarantee a continuous flow of work, and savings from this source could not have been large. There was only one way left to economise on labour, and that was to screw wages down to the lowest possible level and maintain long hours of working. This made the employment unattractive and those with initiative and skill were hardly likely to stop long. Apprenticeship ceased, and only the elderly seemed prepared to continue in employment. As a consequence, the labour force declined, until by 1910 only 11 remained. Further economies resulted from the use of long tesserae to replace several adjacent tesserae of the same colour, and the replacement of solid holly surrounds with long tesserae. When bandings were used to decorate the tops of boxes mitred joints were not matched with the care exercised previously. By a range of such stratagems production was cheapened but a limit was soon reached beyond which further economies could not be made.[5]

Despite its difficulties, the firm of Boyce, Brown & Kemp showed a remarkable resilience. As early as 1894, one commentator had declared that 'there seems every probability of the art practically dying out with the century's end', and in 1910, in an unguarded hour James Brown, then 67, had confided to a reporter that he was 'nearly sick of it. I shouldn't be surprised if this, the only factory, shuts down soon.' Despite this pessimism some investment continued and in March 1914 an electric motor was installed to supply power to the whole factory. The business did not close and survived to be sold into other hands in 1916.[6]

The buyer was John Thomas Ellis who was already proprietor of a shop in the Pantiles trading as Porter's Warehouse. This retail outlet had been opened about the turn of the century by Mrs

Rachael Porter as a Berlin wool repository, but from its early days carried extensive stocks of Tunbridge ware and fancy goods. It was probably one of Boyce, Brown & Kemp's largest retail outlets and it may possibly have been the threat to future supplies of Tunbridge ware, if the Camden Road manufactory closed down, that induced Ellis to take an interest in it. The business of Boyce, Brown & Kemp was already in a parlous state by 1914. One of the principals had died, the other two were elderly, and the business was in decline. The war brought difficulties in obtaining raw materials and labour, while the unsettled conditions prevailing reduced the number of visitors to the town and inhibited the public demand for fancy goods. In June 1916, soon after Ellis had taken control, a client enquiring about their range of Tunbridge ware was informed, 'We are not issuing a price list as many of our men have joined the colours and we are therefore unable to keep a full range of goods as we would like.' He was, however, offered three different small tables priced from £1 12s 6d (£1.62½) to eight guineas (£8.40). These may have been manufactured by Boyce, Brown & Kemp or be residual stocks from Barton's depot which was stated to have closed down only three years earlier. Of the two surviving partners of Boyce, Brown & Kemp, Amos Kemp died in 1917 but James Brown continued to supervise production and in 1920 demand was stated to be more than equal to supply. Brown's death in May 1922 was probably the reason for Ellis seeking to dispose of the business. Porter's, however, were to continue as retailers for several further years (colour pl. 26). They maintained substantial stocks of Tunbridge ware which, in October 1923, included octagonal tables, boxes, book slides, blotters, tea caddies, photo frames and inkstands. They also appear to have had on offer some second-hand items, including a desk with a view of Eridge Castle at four guineas (£4.20).[7]

The Tunbridge ware manufactory in Camden Road was bought by David H.E. King Ltd. of London in 1923. The firm was listed as a publisher of 13, Paternoster Row, EC4. They also produced indoor games, and at the 1923 Ideal Home Exhibition demonstrated their 'Table Lawn Tennis … played on miniature hard courts and is not to be confused with Table Tennis (Ping Pong)'. By early 1924 they had moved to larger premises at 46, Ufford Street, Blackfriars Road, SE1. It is evident that the takeover of Ellis must have been early in 1923, for King was advertising Tunbridge ware in June of that year and exhibited at the Fifth Annual London Fair and Market in the Agricultural Hall, Islington in July. Their prize exhibit was an octagonal-top occasional table veneered with a mosaic of a vessel in full sail on a tripod base (fig. 56a). This may not have been King's manufacture as Barton had produced a similar table, an example being known with his stamp. This table was offered by Porter's in October 1923 at ten guineas (£10.50). King no doubt hoped to use his connections with various London stores, including Gamages, to find a wider market for Tunbridge ware, and to use the manufacturing facilities for games production. The latter point is illustrated by the fact that the Camden Road works produced darts for a time. As Tunbridge ware manufacturers, the firm of David

55a. Tunbridge ware of the 1920s and 30s. Back: *Tunbridge Wells Manufacturing Co. type 126 cigarette box in walnut with floral mosaic centre panel and geometrical mosaic bandings. c1925. w:15.5cm d:9cm h:6cm.* Front left: *Tunbridge Wells Manufacturing Co. trinket box in mahogany, the top decorated with perspective cube work. c1925. w:8cm d:6cm h:3.5cm. Both of these items are stamped on the inside of the lid with the trade mark of the manufacturer.* Front right: *cigarette box, the top decorated with small perspective cube work within a mosaic banding by T.L. Green of Rye. c1935. w:16.5cm d:7.5cm h:4cm.*

55b. Trade mark of the Tunbridge Wells Manufacturing Co. Ltd.

H.E. King was short-lived, and by March 1924 a new company, the Tunbridge Wells Manufacturing Co. Ltd., had been formed. At the 1924 Ideal Home Exhibition the two concerns had totally separate stands and the relationship of one to the other, if any, is not clear. The Tunbridge Wells Manufacturing Co. Ltd. had a separate London address at 36, Rusholme Road, Putney Hill and the directors of the new concern did not include David H.E. King.[8]

Initially, the directors of the Tunbridge Wells Manufacturing Co. were Lady Capel Wolseley, Alfred E. Adams and Stanley Geary. They traded from the old Boyce, Brown & Kemp premises at 128 and 130, Camden Road, Tunbridge Wells, but the London address was a private house in Putney which none of the contemporary London directories show as being occupied by the company or any of its directors. Adams had ceased his association with the business by 1925 and Geary appears to have been the manager and leading figure. The company had stands at the Daily Mail Ideal Home Exhibitions from 1924 to 1926 and issued a comprehensive trade list of their products (fig. 56). Initially, these were small cabinet wares ranging from jewel cabinets and cases and domed tea caddies priced at six guineas (£6.30) each, to tie-pin, needle and stamp boxes at 2/6 (12½p). Pin cushions, napkin rings, book-markers, paper-knives, photo frames and inkstands were also featured. Mahogany, walnut, plane and cedar were commonly used in box construction. Blocks used included some of the views originally developed by Henry Hollamby, such as Tonbridge Castle, a range of floral designs, at least one bird design, blocks incorporating lettering and perspective cube work. Bandings tended to be narrower than on earlier Tunbridge ware pieces and were of floral or geometrical patterns. Small unlined boxes were usually stamped on the inside of the lid with the firm's trade mark, though not on larger boxes with lined interiors. Two boxes of this nature supplied to the Royal Botanic Gardens at Kew in 1924 feature large chromium-plated hinges and a chromium-plated lock marked 'SECURE LOCK', features that might help to identify other larger wares not stamped. The qualify of the work ranged from indifferent to poor with the use of coarse tesserae, somewhat irregular repeats of motifs in bandings, and poor mitring of bandings at the corners (figs. 54, 55, colour pl. 26). Initially, little turned work was produced but in the display at the 1926 Ideal Home Exhibition this was given some prominence. It is probable that little was manufactured, however. The company also appear to have made whitewood wares in the Mauchline tradition decorated with photographic prints. The company's hope of creating a wider market for their products was not to be realised and the business closed early in 1927. Apart from their new ware, the company offered a repair and repolishing service for earlier pieces and also dealt to some extent in second-hand Tunbridge ware.[9]

With the collapse of the Tunbridge Wells Manufacturing Co., the industry in Tunbridge Wells came to an end. Some of the workmen did attempt to produce on a limited scale. Albert Botton kept up some production of small boxes until his death in 1963. He acquired a stock of veneers and blocks from the Tunbridge Wells Manufacturing Co. and in the 1930s regularly purchased veneers, varnish and lining paper, evidence of continuing production. A double stamp box, displaying a 1951 Festival of Britain 2½d stamp against a mosaic background, is in the Tunbridge Wells Museum collection (fig. 57). Botton was employed as a caretaker to the Rose Hill Preparatory School in Tunbridge Wells and this suggests that the work was only part time. Another worker who obtained

ROYAL . . . .
TUNBRIDGE
WARE . . . .

FAMOUS SINCE 1629.

THE famous Royal Tunbridge Wells Ware Factories have produced this unique Ware for nearly 300 years.

The industry has been carried on through father to son for generations.

Three generations are employed at the Works to-day.

The Ware is an interesting Local Art of the Royal Borough of Tunbridge Wells; but although it has existed for nearly three centuries, it has only recently been offered to the public beyond the local traders.

Artistically designed mosaic of inlaid woods, varied and beautiful designs are fashioned from numerous and minute pieces of wood selected for their natural colour.

About 180 different woods are used in the mosaics.

Exclusively made at Tunbridge Wells.

All the woods are in their natural colours.

Permanent in colour and beauty.

Blending and fine workmanship unsurpassed.

All kinds of novelties and useful articles.

From "THE DAILY MIRROR." *10/7/23.*
"An occasional table, inlaid with 180 different woods, each in its natural colour and depicting a galleon in full sail, is the most interesting exhibit at the Fifth Annual London Fair and Market at the Agricultural Hall, Islington, which opened yesterday."

Tunbridge Wells Manufacturing Co., Ltd.
SOLE PROPRIETORS AND MANUFACTURERS.

Registered Office and Factory—
128 30, CAMDEN ROAD, TUNBRIDGE WELLS.

London Office -

36, RUSHOLME ROAD, PUTNEY HILL, S.W. 15.
Phone—PUTNEY 1830.

56a. Front page of a trade price list of the Tunbridge Wells Manufacturing Co. c1925.

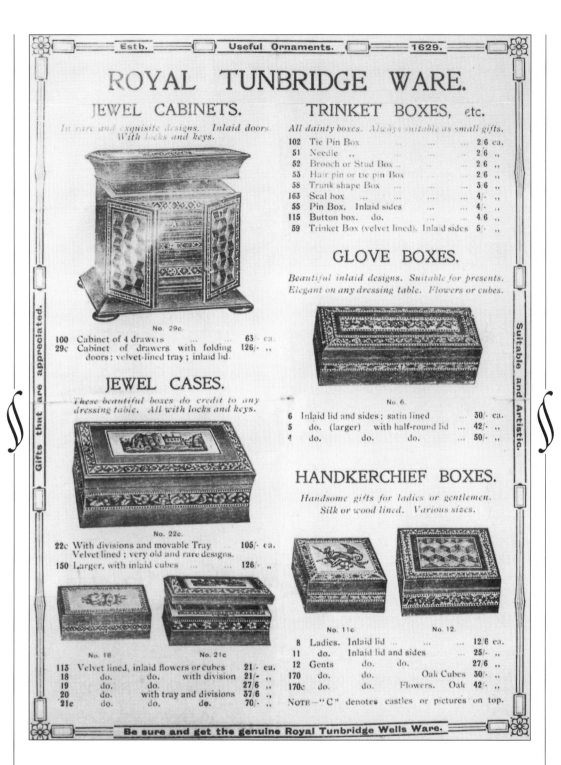

ROYAL TUNBRIDGE WARE.

JEWEL CABINETS.

*In rare and exquisite designs. Inlaid doors.
With locks and keys.*

No. 29c.

100	Cabinet of 4 drawers	63/- ea.
29c	Cabinet of drawers with folding doors ; velvet-lined tray ; inlaid lid.	126/- ,,

JEWEL CASES.

*These beautiful boxes do credit to any
dressing table. All with locks and keys.*

No. 22c.

22c	With divisions and movable Tray Velvet lined ; very old and rare designs.	105/- ea.
150	Larger, with inlaid cubes	126/- ,,

No. 18   No. 21c

113	Velvet lined, inlaid flowers or cubes		21/- ea.
18	do.	do. with division	21/- ,,
19	do.	do.	27/6 ,,
20	do.	with tray and divisions	37/6 ,,
21c	do.	do. do.	70/- ,,

TRINKET BOXES, etc.

All dainty boxes. Always suitable as small gifts.

102	Tie Pin Box	...	2/6 ea.
51	Needle ,,	...	2/6 ,,
52	Brooch or Stud Box	...	2/6 ,,
53	Hair pin or tie pin Box	...	2/6 ,,
58	Trunk shape Box	...	3/6 ,,
163	Seal box	...	4/- ,,
55	Pin Box. Inlaid sides	...	4/- ,,
115	Button box. do.	...	4/6 ,,
59	Trinket Box (velvet lined). Inlaid sides		5/- ,,

GLOVE BOXES.

*Beautiful inlaid designs. Suitable for presents.
Elegant on any dressing table. Flowers or cubes.*

No. 6.

6	Inlaid lid and sides ; satin lined	...	30/- ea.
5	do. (larger) with half-round lid	...	42/- ,,
4	do. do. do.	...	50/- ,,

HANDKERCHIEF BOXES.

*Handsome gifts for ladies or gentlemen.
Silk or wood lined. Various sizes.*

No. 11c   No. 12

8	Ladies.	Inlaid lid	...	12/6 ea.
11	do.	Inlaid lid and sides	...	25/- ,,
12	Gents	do. do.		27/6 ,,
170	do.	do.	Oak Cubes	30/- ,,
170c	do.	do.	Flowers. Oak	42/- ,,

NOTE—"C" denotes castles or pictures on top.

Suitable and Artistic.

Gifts that are appreciated.

56b. *Second page of the c1925 catalogue, featuring small boxes and
cabinets.*

TEA CADDIES.

It takes a long time to make one of these beautiful tea caddies. Hence they are rare. Both useful and ornamental. All with inlaid lids, locks and keys.

27c Double ; very rare, grey ash ... ... 84/- ea.

28c Double ; rosewood ; a beautiful caddy ... 126/- ea.

No. 24c.   No. 26c.

23	Inlaid lid ; plain sides (cubes)	...	21/- ea.
23c	do.	do. (flowers)	25/- „
24c	do.	Mosaic band on sides	30/- „
25c	Round inlaid top ; plain sides	...	35/- „
26c	do.	with mosaic sides	42/- „

STAMP BOXES.

Dainty and useful.

49	Single. Inlaid sides	...	...	2/6 ea.
50	With divisions for 3 kinds	...	...	3/6 „

PHOTO FRAMES.

Three popular sizes, made in beautiful inlaid frames. Any size can be made to special order.

No. 78.   No. 80.

76	Snapshot	...	...	...	...	2/- ea.
78	Postcard	...	...	...	...	3/6 „
80	Cabinet	...	...	...	...	10/6 „

INKSTANDS.

An ornament which is useful. A gift that is always welcome. Crystal inkwells.

No. 92.   No. 93.

117	Glass Inkwell	...	...	...	5/- ea.
114	do.	...	...	...	10/6 „
92	Crystal glass ; N.P. fittings	...	...	15/- „
93	do.	with 2 stamp boxes	...	25/- „

PLAYING CARD BOXES.

All in beautiful designs. Flowers and Cubes.

No. 35.   No. 156.

34	Tom Thumb Card Box. (Two packs.)		5/- ea.
35	One Pack. Satin lined, velvet bottom...		7/6 „
36	Two Packs		12/6 „
37	Bridge Box (2 Packs & Score Sheets)		17/6 „
156	do.	do.	50/- „

Encourage English Crafts.

Mosaics of Inlaid Woods.

56c. *Third page of the c1925 catalogue, featuring tea caddies, stamp boxes, photo frames, inkstands and playing card boxes.*

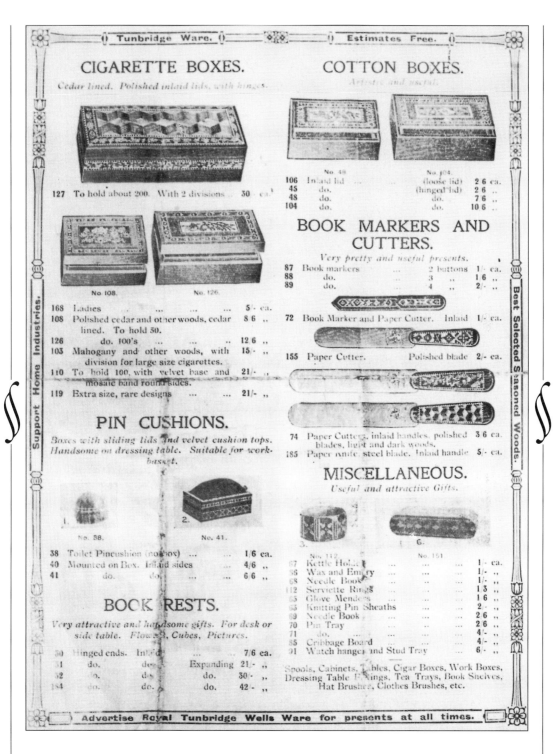

CIGARETTE BOXES.

Cedar lined. Polished inlaid lids, with hinges.

127 To hold about 200. With 2 divisions ... 30/- ea.

No. 108.   No. 126.

168 Ladies ... ... 5/- ea.
108 Polished cedar and other woods, cedar 8/6 ,,
        lined. To hold 50.
126   do. 100's ... . 12/6 ,,
103 Mahogany and other woods, with 15/- ,,
        division for large size cigarettes.
110 To hold 100, with velvet base and 21/- ,,
        mosaic band round sides.
119 Extra size, rare designs ... ... 21/- ,,

PIN CUSHIONS.

Boxes with sliding lids and velvet cushion tops.
Handsome on dressing table. Suitable for work-
basket.

No. 38.   No. 41.

38 Toilet Pincushion (no box) ... ... 1/6 ea.
40 Mounted on Box. Inlaid sides ... 4/6 ,,
41   do.   do. ... ... 6/6 ,,

BOOK RESTS.

Very attractive and handsome gifts. For desk or
side table. Flowers, Cubes, Pictures.

50 Hinged ends. Inlaid ... ... 7/6 ea.
51   do.   do. Expanding 21/- ,,
52   do.   do.   do. 30/- ,,
54   do.   do.   do. 42/- ,,

COTTON BOXES.

Artistic and useful.

No. 48   No. 104

106 Inlaid lid ...   (loose lid) 2/6 ea.
45   do.   (hinged lid) 2/6 ,,
48   do.   do. 7/6 ,,
104   do.   do. 10/6 ,,

BOOK MARKERS AND CUTTERS.

Very pretty and useful presents.

87 Book markers ... 2 buttons 1/- ea.
88   do.   ... 3 ,, 1/6 ,,
89   do.   ... 4 ,, 2/- ,,

72 Book Marker and Paper Cutter. Inlaid 1/- ea.

155 Paper Cutter.   Polished blade 2/- ea.

74 Paper Cutters, inlaid handles, polished 3/6 ea.
        blades, light and dark woods.
185 Paper Knife, steel blade, inlaid handle 5/- ea.

MISCELLANEOUS.

Useful and attractive Gifts.

No. 112   No. 151

87 Kettle Holder ... ... 1/- ea.
66 Wax and Emery ... ... 1/- ,,
68 Needle Book ... ... 1/- ,,
112 Serviette Rings ... ... 1/3 ,,
65 Glove Menders ... ... 1/6 ,,
66 Knitting Pin Sheaths ... ... 2/- ,,
69 Needle Book ... ... 2/6 ,,
70 Pin Tray ... ... 2/6 ,,
71   do. ... ... 4/- ,,
85 Cribbage Board ... ... 4/- ,,
91 Watch hanger and Stud Tray ... 6/- ,,

Spools, Cabinets, Tables, Cigar Boxes, Work Boxes,
Dressing Table Fittings, Tea Trays, Book Shelves,
Hat Brushes, Clothes Brushes, etc.

56d. *Fourth page of the c1925 catalogue, featuring boxes, pin cushions,*
book rests and miscellaneous items.

127

57. *Rosewood stamp box decorated with simple geometrical mosaic bandings and the 2½d stamp of the Festival of Britain commemorative set made by Albert Botton, a former employee of the Tunbridge Wells Manufacturing Co. 1951. w:9cm d:5cm h:2.5cm. (Tunbridge Wells Museum).*

bandings and veneers from the collapsed company was Richard Kemp, the son of one of the partners of Boyce, Brown & Kemp. He probably produced no great quantity of material at Tunbridge Wells, though he was important in ensuring a temporary stay of execution for the industry.[10]

Kemp was to form a partnership with Thomas Littleton Green which although it was not to endure, did help Green establish a manufactory that was to function until the outbreak of the Second World War. Green had been born in Maidstone in 1892 and attended Tonbridge School before qualifying as an engineer. After service in India, Egypt and France in the First World War he entered the family business, a paper mill near Maidstone, in 1918. This was not, however, to prove a successful venture, and when the mill closed Green was obliged to seek an alternative outlet for his talents. It was then by chance that he met Richard Kemp at Winchelsea Beach, East Sussex. By October 1931, a partnership had been established and business premises found in Market Road, Rye. Kemp brought with him not only the skills that he had acquired in the family business but also quantities of mosaic veneers. In April 1932, the partners exhibited their wares at the Ideal Home Exhibition in London. The association was not to prove successful, however, and in 1934 it was dissolved, Green now assuming sole management. He proved

16. Writing accessories. Top: *rosewood ink pot and pen stand w:12.5 cm d:7cm.* Middle: *three stamp boxes,* Left: *top: decorated with tessellated mosaic and having a 1d red stamp of the 1841 issue in the centre.* Centre: *Queen Victoria's head in mosaic on a black ground,* Left: *mosaic spelling out the word "STAMPS".* Front: *paper knife with ebony blade, and book-marker.*

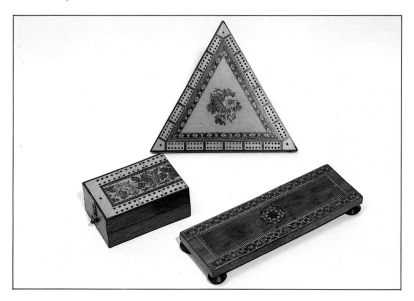

17. Cribbage boards. Top: *rosewood triangular, a shape also found in print-decorated with whitewood boards, central floral mosaic panel. c1850. sides 21cm.* Left front: *rosewood card box which opens to form a cribbage board, mosaic rose bandings in the centre. c1900. closed w:12cm d:8cm h:5cm.* Right front: *yew wood decorated with miniature parquetry, on turned feet. c1835. w:24.5cm d:8cm.*

18. *Stationery box veneered in ebony with floral mosaic panel and bandings. The base bears the label of "T. BARTON, Late NYE, Manufacturer, MOUNT EPHRAIM AND PARADE, TUNBRIDGE WELLS" (as fig. 61b p. 136). c1870. w:32.5cm d:26cm h:7.5cm.*

19. *Rosewood stationery boxes with mosaic floral central panels of a similar nature. The right-hand box has a border of trailing foliage and the base is covered with tartan paper, both characteristic of items bearing Alfred Talbot labels (see figs. 76, 77). c1850. Left: w:23.5cm d:18cm h:5.5cm, Right: w:25.5cm d:19cm h:6.5cm.*

himself an enterprising maker, utilising electricity to operate his saw, lathe and sander, and with a workforce of never more than three to help him, he developed a flourishing trade. The business not only sold to visitors to Rye but supplied retailers on a much wider basis. However, at the outbreak of the Second World War in 1939 Green joined the Royal Engineers and his business was obliged to close. During the war, a bomb fell close to his workshop damaging the roof, and allowing rain to affect the stock. The business did not re-open after the war.

Green's enterprise could not compare in size with the large commercial businesses at Tunbridge Wells in the nineteenth century, and therefore he rightly concentrated on the smaller decorative items. He produced a wide range of boxes for playing cards, cigarettes, matches and stamps (fig. 55a). Although he did not mark the wares with his name, a few boxes were stamped 'RYE', and others can be recognised by a very characteristic vertical tongue joint at the corners not found on other Tunbridge ware makers' products. Apart from boxes, he manufactured mirror and picture frames, pin trays, penholders, inkstands, needle-cases, ring-stands, thread-waxers, yo-yos, brooches, cribbage boards, kettle-holders, silk-winders and book-markers. He used a number of traditional Tunbridge ware designs, including perspective cube work and the Hollamby technique of spelling out words in mosaic, as a number of boxes have their lids decorated with the word 'RYE'. He did, however, develop a range of new designs. In late 1931, work was in progress to produce veneers illustrating Rye parish church and the Landgate. It was intended to offer these to the public in 1932 but to date no Tunbridge ware items so decorated have been discovered and this project may not have been carried through to the production stage. A Green design does survive, however, for the clock and jacks on Rye church tower. Other designs that exist include two for a windmill, a parrot (dated July 1938), a butterfly, and a pattern endorsed 'Paisley Jan. 10 '36'. For the anticipated coronation of Edward VIII a block with a crown flanked by the letters E.R. and the date numbers 1 9 3 7 in the corners was designed. This was subsequently modified and put into production for the coronation of King George VI. Not all objects were small; one box made in June 1939 measured 15¾in (40cm) by 9¾in (24.8cm) by 4in (10.2cm) and incorporated 18,956 pieces of mosaic. It thus seems that there was an attempt to diversify away from the traditional Tunbridge ware designs by the late 1930s. Although a considerable quantity of topographical blocks, floral panels and bandings of Hollamby design and a limited quantity from Barton's manufactory came to the business through the Kemp connection, there is little evidence that these were used on any scale. Large amounts remained when the business closed in 1939.[11]

Chapter 11

MODERN CRAFT WORKERS IN TUNBRIDGE WARE

With the closure of Thomas Green's business in 1939, commerical production of Tunbridge ware ceased. The immediate post-war period brought no attempts at revival, but in the 1960s periodicals aimed at the practical craftsman began to feature articles discussing the techniques. This craft interest, coupled with the need for restoration services, led to the regeneration of commercial production.

The only craftsman working in one of the old centres of production is Peter Benjamin of Tonbridge who manufactures in partnership with his wife Daphne. Time is divided between restoration and the production of new mosaic. Seasoned oak and mahogany are used for body construction, and other timbers in their natural colours for mosaic. The range of goods produced includes mosaic ear-rings, two types of paper-knife – one with an extra serrated edge – and mosaic picture frames for pyrographic pictures. For the wedding of H.R.H. the Prince of Wales to Lady Diana Spencer, a box with concave sides veneered in figured satinwood was produced, the top inlaid in ivory with the Prince of Wales's feathers and with floral Tunbridge bandings decorating the sides. This box was presented to the Prince and Princess as a wedding gift. Another commemorative item produced was a plaque of Tonbridge School Chapel in silhouette framed in tessellated mosaic. The Benjamins produce furniture including a cigar table based on a late nineteenth-century example by Thomas Barton (fig. 58). A more ambitious project for a games table, also in the Barton tradition, is now in production. The tables are marketed through Derek Roberts of Tonbridge, an antique dealer who specialises in Tunbridge ware.[1]

At Dibden Purlieu near Southampton, Albert Fickling started producing Tunbridge ware in 1977. His first range consisted of framed pictures or plaques in mosaic which were featured on BBC television. The simplest is an abstract pattern containing 350 tesserae which could be framed as a 13½in (34.3cm) by 14in (35.6cm) picture or an 8in (20.3cm) by 7in (17.8cm) plaque. The other design is a Tudor town house in a street setting, based on features of

58. *Cigar table, rosewood with geometrical and floral mosaic bandings and parquetry work in various woods by Peter Benjamin of Tonbridge, based on a late nineteenth-century design. h:67cm w:31cm. (Peter Benjamin).*

timber-framed buildings seen at Stratford-upon-Avon. This contained 2,500 tesserae and was available as a 21in (53.4cm) by 17¾in (45.1cm) picture or as a plaque. A three-dimensional effect was given to the house by laying the mosaic on blocks which increase in thickness for each storey corresponding to the jettying of the building. Parts of the design could be obtained, such as just the Tudor house (fig. 59) or the front entrance. A chess table involving 15,000 tesserae was also in the process of manufacture.

A third producer was Robert Vorley who initially manufactured at Laindon in Essex but then worked from Canvey Island in the same county. He took up a career as an architectural model maker, and his interest in Tunbridge ware was first aroused by articles in the *Woodworker* and visits to Tunbridge Wells Museum. Production started about 1978 and by 1981 about half his working time was spent on Tunbridge ware production. Robert Vorley specialised in boxes for cards, cigarettes, jewellery or stamps and production was in the region of 200 to 300 a year. Ninety different woods were used. Modern electrically powered machinery enabled him to cut very accurately. He made up blocks from 4in (10.2cm) to 6in (15.2cm) sticks and had over 75 different blocks available, ranging from perspective cube work through a number of floral and abstract designs to a range of fine butterfly, moth and dragon-fly veneers (fig. 60). Sometimes conventional marquetry borders of the Greek key pattern were used. One of the largest projects was a box 7in (17.8cm) square and 3¾in (9.5cm) deep veneered in wenge, as a souvenir of the 1981 Royal Wedding. The top depicts the west front of St Paul's Cathedral and contains 45,000 tesserae. Over 80 of these boxes were produced and sold for £120 each. Other boxes ranged in price from around £17 for a stamp box with a simple mosaic pattern on the lid to about £200 for the larger octagonal boxes. Initially production was marketed through a number of retail outlets but later was concentrated through the Casson Gallery in Marylebone High Street, London. At the time of writing, production has been suspended.

In the Brighton area production is being carried on by Len Garrett of Saltdean. He was educated at Chatham Technical School and undertook a five-year apprenticeship at the Dockyard, entering the Admiralty Drawing Office. In 1982 he took early retirement as Chief Draughtsman at the Department of the Environment in Reading. He was first introduced to marquetry in 1950 when in hospital. After retirement his first product was a range of wooden cottages, 2½in×1in×1½in (6cm×3cm×4cm), inspired by the ceramic houses produced by several manufacturers. He found, however, that the application of individual pieces of veneer to the core was laborious. A visit to Tunbridge Wells Museum indicated a solution: the construction of blocks from which ready-made veneers could be sliced. These cottages are still excellent sellers and are produced in batches of 50 at a time. Once the blockmaking techniques had been mastered he prepared blocks depicting a butterfly, perspective cube work, a floral panel and various geometrical and floral bandings for borders to be used for box decoration. He does not make his own boxes. Other items decorated with tessellated mosaic include

59. Plaque depicting a Tudor town house in mosaic and containing 1,500 tesserae by A.J. Fickling, Dibden Purlieu, Hants. 23cm sq. (A.J. Fickling).

bookends, matchbox covers, blotters, napkin rings, pipe racks, paper-knives and thimbles. Card and cribbage boxes, and boxes with chess boards, are included in the extensive range. Initially Len Garrett sold through craft fairs held at the Brighton Centre but now finds the Tunbridge Wells craft fairs a better market. His wares are on sale at the attraction 'A Day at the Wells' on the restored Lower Walks of the Pantiles. His work is easily identified as his mosaic bandings incorporate a discrete LG monogram. By selling direct to the public, prices are kept at modest levels ranging from a simple paper-knife at around £2.80 to the most elaborate boxes which rarely exceed £100. A recent introduction is a mosaic block of Leeds Castle which he hopes to put into production for sale at the castle.[4]

Bill Adams works from Harborne, Birmingham. For about 20 years he ran a building company but in the late 1970s set up an antique business. He concentrated on restoration work in a workshop at the rear of his shop. His interest in Tunbridge ware was aroused when he purchased a tea caddy with a Tonbridge Castle view. This inspired him to seek out publications and experiment with manufacture. He spent time at Tunbridge Wells Museum photographing items and making notes. He mastered the

60. *Range of boxes by Robert Vorley of Canvey Island, Essex and marketed through the Casson Gallery, London. Perspective cube and vandyke parquetry combined with mosaic work, including veneers representing butterflies. (Robert Vorley).*

process and has manufactured a number of blocks which include a view of Warwick Castle, a dog and a number of leaf, floral and geometrical bandings. Perspective cube and vandyke work are also employed. His aim is to copy accurately past designs. Current production is about two boxes a week and these are marketed through high-class retailers. Hampson Silks of Kingswinford, West Midlands acted as marketing agents.[5]

Chapter 12

TUNBRIDGE WARE MAKERS

A number of makers, and families of makers, in the Tunbridge ware industry stand out because of their innovative talents, the length of their span of production, or the extent of their productive capacity. Inevitably, those firms whose activities were commented upon by their contemporaries and whose products were identified by the use of trade labels feature large, whereas others whose names are known only from directories and rent and rate books are omitted. This is not to imply that the latter are of no significance, and it is possible that new information may come to light that will enable a better assessment to be made of their significance. Makers working in the Tunbridge Wells and Tonbridge area are listed first in alphabetical order, followed by those from Brighton and other south coast towns.

A. Tunbridge Wells

Thomas Barton (1819–1903)
Figs. 40, 53, 61–66, 73   Colour pls. 18, 24, 25

Thomas Barton was born in Clerkenwell and spent his early life in London. Clerkenwell was an area where many cabinet-makers, turners and even London Tunbridge ware makers had their workshops, and it is possible that he obtained some experience here before, still in his youth, he obtained employment with George Wise. he could not have stayed there long, however, for around 1836 he entered the service of Edmund Nye. He was to stay with this employer until Nye's death in 1863, when he took over the business. Nye was quick to appreciate Barton's talents, especially his adeptness at producing new designs, and he was rapidly promoted to the position of foreman. He appears to have played a major part in the design and production of the exhibits displayed by Nye at the Great Exhibition of 1851.[1] Nye, in his will dated 21 October 1862, stipulated that on his death Thomas Barton should have the option of purchasing the lease of the house, shop and premises on Mount Ephraim and the shop and house on the Parade

61a. *Rectangular workbox in coromandel wood, the top decorated with perspective cube work and parquetry and mosaic borders, the sides decorated with wide mosaic rose bandings. Label on base 'T. BARTON, Late NYE, Manufacturer, MOUNT EPHRAIM AND PARADE, TUNBRIDGE WELLS'. c1870. w:26.5cm d:20.5cm h:11cm.*

61b. *Label on the base of the rectangular workbox.*

62. *Ebony-veneered boxes decorated with marquetry by Thomas Barton.*
Left: *labelled 'T BARTON late NYE Manufacturer 93 MOUNT*
EPHRAIM TUNBRIDGE WELLS'. c1895. w:12cm d:8.5cm h:5.5cm.
Right: *labelled 'T BARTON late NYE Manufacturer MOUNT*
EPHRAIM AND PARADE TUNBRIDGE WELLS'. c1890. w:23cm
d:11.5cm h:6cm. (Tunbridge Wells Museum).

63. *Work-table top by either Edmund Nye or Thomas Barton, veneered*
in ebony and decorated with tessellated mosaic geometrical and floral
bandings. The centre features a butterfly and foliage carried out in
cross-grain marquetry. c1860–70. (Maidstone Museum).

64. *View of Battle Abbey gatehouse constructed so that individual pieces of wood, some shaped, represent each piece of masonry. This view was displayed by Thomas Barton at the Industrial Exhibition at Tunbridge Wells in 1864 and favourably commented upon. The panel was presented to Tunbridge Wells Museum by Miss Barton, his niece, and shows an early version of this view. Versions used to decorate boxes, blotter cases, etc. omit the tree at the right. 17.5cm by 24cm. (Tunbridge Wells Museum).*

with the goodwill of the business for £400. The stocks and tools were to be valued and charged in addition. Barton exercised this option indicating his financial standing even at this stage of his career.[2]

Barton retained the Chalet on Mount Ephraim as his manufactory and place of abode, and also the shop on the Pantiles. He established a reputation for the quality of his wares, and in September 1864 at the Industrial Exhibition held in Tunbridge Wells received first prize in the class for skilled workmanship for a display of Tunbridge ware. Visitors to the works on Mount Ephraim during Barton's service with Nye and the period of his own enterprise included Queen Victoria, the Prince Consort, the Prince of Wales (later King Edward VII), Benjamin Disraeli, the Marquess of Abergavenny and the Marchioness of Lorne. Thomas Barton did not wholesale goods but still managed to maintain a substantial manufactory. In 1871, he was employing 14 men and the goods manufactured ranged from small decorative inlaid mosaic games and occasional tables through smaller cabinet wares, such as work and writing-boxes, and tea caddies. He used, in the main, blocks showing floral designs, perspective cube work and, to a lesser extent, birds. He particularly fond of dark veneer woods such as ebony and coromandel wood (colour pls. 18, 24). Decorative bandings of floral or geometrical designs were used on the tops and sides of his wares. Small boxes and turned wares were produced for those patrons with more modest requirements. He also undertook many individual commissions and a number of items are known with his labels which are quite unlike the conventional Tunbridge wares produced at this period (use of mother-of-pearl, boxes decorated with water colours, fern-decorated pieces and even painted whitewood wares). Like other makers, he provided accommodation for visitors. He even acted as agent for two insurance companies.[3]

By 1891, however, the business was starting to contract and in March of that year he gave up the lease of the premises at 48, the Pantiles and concentrated his activity at the Mount Ephraim address. Despite his advanced age, Barton continued to promote

65. *Ebony desk stand with ink pot flanked with two lidded compartments decorated with mosaic and geometrical marquetry. Paper label on base 'T BARTON late NYE Manufacturer MOUNT EPHRAIM AND PARADE TUNBRIDGE WELLS'. c1870. w:27cm. (Sotheby's).*

66. *Coromandel tilt-top table on a turned tripod stand. The centre of the top is decorated with a star pattern in cross-grain marquetry, the edge with a lily banding. Attributable to Thomas Barton. c1880. h:94cm w:46cm. (Sotheby's).*

the trade and helped to organise an exhibition held at the Town Hall in October 1899, designed to revitalise the industry. However, his health was beginning to fail by that date, and in 1901 a paralytic seizure left him a virtual invalid, looked after by his two nieces.[4]

Apart from his enterprise as one of the leading producers of fine Tunbridge ware, Thomas Barton played a very active part in the local government of the town. He was elected a councillor in 1870 and later chaired the Water and Health Committees. He was made an alderman and borough magistrate in 1889 when the town received its charter of incorporation as a borough. Barton served as chairman of the Tradesmen's Association until 1885, and for many years was District Treasurer and Provincial Grand Master of the Manchester Unity of Oddfellows. He was obliged to relinquish this activity in his later years as his health failed.

With his death in July 1903, the business did not immediately cease. Some activity continued in the making-up and selling-off of stocks under the supervision of his nieces. A locally published guide of 1906 states that specimens of the ware could be viewed 'at the establishment of Mr Thomas Barton on Mount Ephraim, where it is sold by a descendant of the original maker'. Barton's name continued to be inserted in local trade directories until 1911, though from 1905 the word 'depot' was used in the description.[5]

Boyce, Brown & Kemp
Fig. 52

This partnership of Thomas Amos Boyce, James Brown, Jnr. and John Kemp was stated by Alfred Brown, son of James Brown, to have been founded in 1873. It was certainly trading by March 1878 when James Hollamby was indentured as an apprentice for five years, receiving wages ranging from 3s (15p) a week in the first year to 12s (60p) in the fifth year. Strangely, trade directories ignore the firm until 1882. James Brown Snr., father of one of the partners, was already an independent manufacturer. He was born in Tunbridge Wells in 1843 but at the age of three moved to Tonbridge. In 1856 he moved back to Tunbridge Wells and two years later started work at the manufactory of Henry Hollamby. His son James worked for him for a time before setting up with his partners the independent business of Boyce, Brown & Kemp. James Brown Snr.'s business was located at Violet Place, Camden Road in 1862 and it then moved to Goods Station Road (1865), Tunnel Tip (1871) and 9, Mercer Street (1878). It was a small factory employing only four men and a girl in 1871. The business subsequently merged with that of Boyce, Brown & Kemp. James Brown Jnr. had been apprenticed to Henry Hollamby at his works in Frant Road, Tunbridge Wells, but of the background of the other partners little is known except that Amos Boyce was an uncle of James Brown Jnr.[6]

The connection of James Brown Jnr. with Henry Hollamby was important in influencing both the nature of the business and the design of the products. As the business premises were situated away from the fashionable shopping and residential streets of Tunbridge Wells, the firm was largely of a wholesale nature. A showroom was maintained at the Camden Road premises, but probably more for trade than retail customers. The wholesale nature of the trade accounts for the fact that very few items from the factory were labelled. With the closure of Henry Hollamby's business which had a similar bias towards the wholesale trade, in 1891, Boyce, Brown & Kemp became the sole supplier to retail outlets, and after Thomas Barton had ceased production, the sole manufacturer. Boyce, Brown & Kemp took over many of Hollamby's designs and blocks, and even prior to 1891 it was probably buying veneers from Hollamby. A visitor to the Camden Road works in February 1890 was shown the mosaic pictures of Eridge Castle, Battle Abbey, Hever Castle, Tonbridge Castle, Penshurst Place and the Pantiles which Hollamby had been featuring for several decades. Original work introduced by Boyce, Brown & Kemp seems to have been largely novelties calculated to appeal to a market less concerned with quality than with superficial attraction. These included penholders fitted with miniature lenses through which six local views could be glimpsed and pin cushions shaped like a teapot. Although good work was produced to Hollamby designs some boxes were decorated with floral blocks of a coarse, inferior quality, and border bandings were often poorly matched at the mitred corners. To keep prices at levels at which the goods would sell was more important than quality.[7]

Despite the fact that they were the sole suppliers of Tunbridge ware, the firm was never large. In 1910 only 11 persons were employed and this number was to fall with the onset of war. Amos Boyce died in 1917, leaving James Brown the sole surviving partner, but already by 1916 John Ellis, the proprietor of Porter's, a fancy goods dealer on the Pantiles, had, in effect, taken over the enterprise.[8]

The Burrows family
Figs. 42, 46

In an advertisement inserted in the 1844 edition of *Colbran's New Guide for Tunbridge Wells,* Humphrey Burrows Jnr. claimed that his business was the original manufactory and had been established in 1685. There appears to be no evidence to substantiate such a claim, but the premises that he was trading from was called Jordan House and it appears that he might have been claiming to be the successor to a Mr Jordan who first set up his manufactory in 1685. There certainly was a Mr Jordan, a prominent Baptist, who bought a cottage and garden on Mount Sion, Tunbridge Wells on the site of which he erected a chapel which was opened in August 1720. It was this man who gave his name to Jordan's Lane (now Church Road), Tunbridge Wells and also Jordan House situated at the corner of Jordan's Lane and London Road. Jordan House appears to be early eighteenth century in date and is marked on John Bowra's map of 1738. The occupation of this Mr. Jordan is, however, unknown for certain, though he may have been a Tunbridge ware maker. It has been suggested that it was *c*1740 that a member of the Burrows family acquired Jordan House, but again concrete evidence is missing.[9]

Members of the Burrows family may well have been active in the industry by this date, for there was a tradesman called Burroughs on the Walks in 1739. The trade is not stated but it is likely that the tenant in question was Frances Burrows who was paying a yearly rental of £8 in 1741. A new ten-year lease at £10.10s (£10.50) was entered into on 24 August 1752 by William Burrows who took over from Frances. There can be no certainty that these people were concerned with the manufacture or sale of Tunbridge ware as no trades are indicated, but by the 1770s we enter upon more certain ground. Between 1772 and 1782 Mary Burrows was renting at the same sum of £10 10s a shop on the Walks and this is clearly named as a toyshop, which in the Tunbridge Wells context, certainly meant a seller of Tunbridge ware. In 1782 the lease was transferred to Thomas Burrows described as a turner, who remained in occupation until 1808. He may well be the person recorded in the Speldhurst registers as being buried on 20 July 1810. These premises on the Walks might have been supplied from a manufactory elsewhere in the town, possibly Jordan House. The picture is, however, complicated by the discovery of a trade card which can be dated to 1802 which names a 'BURROWS' with a manufactory at Lower Green near Tunbridge Wells and showrooms on the Parade next to Strange's Library. He offered 'Tunbridge Ware' either 'Inlaid, Painted with elegant Devices or with fashionable Prints'.[10]

In the early nineteenth century the picture becomes clearer, and the involvement of the Burrows family reaches its zenith. Three distinct enterprises emerge, and although the exact relationship of the principals to one another is not entirely clear, a close family connection can be surmised.

At Jordan House, Humphrey Burrows Snr. presided. T.T. Barrow's plan of Tunbridge Wells (1808) marks Jordan House occupied by a Mr Burrows and this is certainly Humphrey Burrows who in 1803 paid 10s (50p) to avoid militia duty. A lithograph c1834 published by Burrows shows the Princess Victoria out for her morning ride passing Jordan House. The Church Road face of the building displays a board inscribed 'Original Manufactory of Tunbridge Ware'. A later tessellated mosaic block of a girl on a donkey may have been inspired by this print and be the work of Humphrey Burrows. Humphrey Burrows Snr. in common with a number of other Tunbridge ware makers, offered rooms as lodgings. In about 1833, however, Humphrey Burrows Snr. appears to have leased the property and business to his son Humphrey Jnr. (b. 1811). The father continued to live at Jordan House and remained active in the business. By 1840 the business was trading as 'The Royal Tunbridge Ware Repository' and was operating a retail showroom on the Parade. The son carried out alterations, building a new shop and workshops, and, in 1844, announced that he had added a circulating library to his other enterprises. Amongst items manufactured were small pieces of furniture, and a parquetry work table bearing Humphrey Burrows' label is known dating from the mid-1830s. For a reason which is not entirely clear, but may possibly have been concerned with the death of his father in April 1845, Humphrey Jnr. shortly after gave up the business, despite the fact that he was only in his mid-thirties. The premises at Jordan House was taken over by G. & J. Cottington, another Tunbridge ware maker. Humphrey Burrows continued to live in Tunbridge Wells, and in 1847 and 1850 was one of the town improvement commissioners. He was living at Alpha Cottage, Grosvenor Road and was offering lodgings there as late as 1851, but died in February 1854.[11]

A contemporary of Humphrey Burrows Snr. was William Burrows, who from 13 April 1820 took over the lease of a shop on the Parade previously rented to Christopher Roberts Jnr., also a Tunbridge ware maker. He was also leasing Gibraltar Cottage on Tunbridge Wells Common in 1825. By 1827 he had a partner, James Burrows, and on 27 June of that year a 21-year lease was taken out on premises in the Parade. It is James Burrows who is credited with the major developments, (inlaid turnery, miniature parquetry and possibly tessellated mosaic) which took place in the nature of Tunbridge ware in the late 1820s and early 1830s.[12] The partnership with William was relatively short-lived and from 1828 he appears to have been in partnership with George Burrows, son of Humphrey Burrows Snr. Additional addresses for the new partnership were given as Culverden Cottage, Mount Ephraim and Hanover Lodge, Hanover Road, the latter being their manufactory.[13] The partnership does not appear to have labelled its wares but a thermometer, the frame decorated with miniature parquetry, is known with the inscription 'G. & J. BURROWS/LEWES' stamped on the reverse of the ivory scale. There is no evidence that the partners traded directly in the Sussex county town but they may have sold items through a retailer, possibly a clockmaker, optician or jeweller. After 1845, the business was conducted solely by George Burrows using

67. *Work-table, rosewood with vandyke and perspective cube parquetry, bearing the label of J.T. Ubsdell. c1830. h:75cm w:39.5cm d:34cm.*

20. *Glove box, stained ash, with broad mosaic leaf veneer on top and cross-grain perspective marquetry bandings on the sides. The base bears the label of "EDMUND NYE, Manufacturer, MOUNT EPHRAIM AND PARADE, TUNBRIDGE WELLS" (similar to Barton label fig. 61b p. 136). c1860. w:24cm d:9cm h:7.5cm.*

21. Left: *rosewood box, the top decorated with an abstract mosaic panel and geometrical borders. Base with the label of "EDMUND NYE, Manufacturer, MOUNT EPHRAIM AND PARADE, TUNBRIDGE WELLS" (fig. 72b p. 152). c1860. w:11.5cm. d:7cm h:3.5cm.* Right: *rosewood box with central floral panel. Attributable to Edmund Nye. c1860 w:18cm d:12.5cm h:5.5cm. Both boxes incorporate a chain banding known only on Nye items.*

22. *Rosewood writing desk decorated on the slope with a mosaic view of Battle Abbey gatehouse. Additional oak leaf and floral decoration. Attributable to Henry Hollamby. c1870. w:30.5cm d:24.5cm h (at back): 8.5cm.*

23. *Box, ash, decorated on the lid with a mosaic view of the ruins of the church of St. Mary in Castro and the Pharos, Dover Castle, surrounded with a geometrical border. Mosaic rose bandings on the sides. Attributable to Henry Hollamby. c1860. w:23cm d:15cm h:7cm.*

the premises on the Parade and the manufactory at Hanover Lodge. By 1855, at the age of 65, he had retired from manufacturing and merely operated a lodging house at the Hanover Road premises.[14] The picture is complicated further by another William Burrows, almost certainly the son of the previous William Burrows, trading from addresses in london Road and High Street from 1845 to 1851, in which year he was aged 32.[15] The last member of this family to trade as a proprietor was Thomas Burrows who had premises at 59, High Street, Tonbridge from *c*1877 to 1883, following the retirement of the last of the Wise family.[16]

William Fenner
Figs. 67, 68

William Fenner, in common with other Tunbridge ware makers, sought to impress potential customers with the longevity of his enterprise by announcing on his trade card 'established 1720'. There is no evidence to support such a claim, and the earliest member of the Fenner family known to have been associated with the industry was John Fenner who leased a shop on the Walks from 1782 to 1787, the year of his death. He carried on the trade of a turner and toy seller. The relationship between John Fenner and William Fenner is unknown, but the business of the latter opened very shortly after the closure of the former. William Fenner subscribed five guineas (£5.25) in 1792 towards the repaving of the Walks, which might suggest that he was already in business here by this date. A trade

68. Print of Fenner's Tunbridge Ware Manufactory, Mount Ephraim, Tunbridge Wells mounted in a parquetry frame, confirming the strong involvement of this firm in this type of Tunbridge ware. c1835. 27cm by 19.5cm. A version of the print showing John Ubsdell's name on the building is known. (Tunbridge Wells Museum).

card, probably dating from 1796, also survives, indicating the sale of a considerable range of print-decorated wares 'in the TURNER or CABINET line' at his shop on the Walks.[17] By the next year, however, he was associated with the business in the same line that had been carried on by James Nye certainly since 1772 and probably from 1757. It is possible that Nye was elderly and realised the advantages of taking the young and active Fenner as a partner. The partnership did not last long for by 1809 the rental payments on the business premises were being recorded in the name of 'Fenner Mr Wm late Nye & Fenner'. It is possible that at this point the young Edmund Nye took his father's place, for by 1810 Fenner & Nye are once more recorded as paying the poor rate. It is also significant that this partnership is described as 'late Foley' having absorbed the Tunbridge ware manufactory of William Foley. William Fenner appears to have retained a shop under his own name, possibly the one shown on Barrow's map of 1808 near Mount Sion Grove and described as 'Fenner's Turnery'. The partnership of Fenner & Nye ended in 1817. William Fenner immediately surrendered his Mount Sion premises and centred production at Mount Ephraim in the 'Repository' later known as 'the Chalet'. The workshops here had been used by Fenner & Nye as early as 1808 and were probably extended in 1813 when a Baptist chapel on Mount Ephraim was acquired by William Fenner.[18]

Fenner's work was admired for its quality. In 1826, the inhabitants of Tunbridge Wells raised 25 guineas (£26.25) by subscription to pay for a fine work- and writing-table as a gift for Princess Victoria. William Fenner was selected by lot to undertake the commission. By 1829 Fenner had disposed of his business to John Talbot Ubsdell (1797–1879) who traded from the same premises advertising his business as 'Late Fenner & Co.' He published a print of the manufactory identical to that shown in fig. 68, but with his name displayed on the outside of the building. His products included work-tables decorated with perspective cube and vandyke parquetry (fig. 67), and he used trade labels to identify his products. Ubsdell was baptised at Newport, Isle of Wight, on 22 October 1797 and was living in Tunbridge Wells in March 1828, the date of his marriage to a widow, Jane Butler, at St George's, Hanover Square, London. He is last recorded as a Tunbridge ware manufacturer in 1834, after which the business reverted to Fenner. Ubsdell moved to Lymington and later to Portsmouth where he died in 1879, aged 81. In the 1840s and 50s he was employed as a bank manager. After regaining his business Fenner traded as Fenner & Co., and under this title he tried direct marketing of his goods in London (see p. 27). In 1840, he advertised a wide range of fashionable wares 'at very reduced prices, owing to the introduction of new machinery', and in the same year he was operating an additional sales outlet at Bath Square on the Parade. He was supplying Edwin Marks, who had taken over the Calverley Library, Calverley Promenade, in Decimus Burton's new development on Mount Pleasant. Marks stocked a wide range of Fenner's wares from book markers and waxers at 6d (2½p) each to tables from £2.12s.6d (£2.62½) to £15 and teapoys from £6 to

12 guineas (£12.60). In view of all this activity, it is surprising to find that this year was the last one of trading. The Speldhurst tithe award map of 1841 shows the Chalet and workshops unoccupied. He appears to have enjoyed a long retirement from the trade, and in both 1847 and 1850 was one of the town improvement commissioners. As late as 1855 he was offering lodgings on Mount Pleasant.[19]

Wares decorated in perspective cube and miniature parquetry work bearing Fenner labels are known. The labels describe the business of Fenner & Co. as 'Inlaid & Mosaic Wood Manufacturers to HER MAJESTY & THE ROYAL FAMILY' and must therefore date from the late 1830s. This strongly suggests that he never produced tessellated mosaic pieces. The advertisement regarding the new machinery and the selling off of stocks in 1840 may represent an intention of moving into this field, which for reasons which are unclear, was never realised.

69. Mosaic panel of Shakespeare's Birthplace, Stratford-upon-Avon, by Henry Hollamby in a geometrical mosaic frame typical of the bandings used on much of Hollamby's work. c1875. 24cm by 21.5cm. (Sotheby's).

James Friend (1782–1878)

James Friend was born in Tunbridge Wells in 1782 and was certainly in business on the Parade by 1810. His work must have been highly regarded for in 1826 he was one of the four manufacturers selected by the citizens of Tunbridge Wells to ballot for the honour of making the work- and writing-table for Princess Victoria. Subsequently, he was to advertise that he was 'Tunbridge Ware Manufacturer to their Royal Highnesses the Duchess of Kent & the Princess Victoria', but like many such claims to royal patronage in this period, it may have had only slight foundation. The few surviving labelled pieces by Friend must come from this early period and consist of painted whitewood wares or pieces of high-quality small cabinet work in conventional Regency style, some veneered in cubic parquetry. James Friend was not solely a Tunbridge ware maker, however. As early as the 1830s, he was offering a range of needlework and fancy wares aimed mainly at a female clientele, and this side of the business was to increase in importance. By 1865, the business was listed as a 'Berlin wool repository' in a directory, and although it continued to sell Tunbridge ware it is possible that production had ceased by this date. James was assisted in his business by his elder brother John (1779–1867) who was living with James at the address on the Parade in 1851 and also declaring his trade to be 'Tunbridge Ware Manufacturer'. James Friend's daughter, Ann (b. 1809), had married a Mr Allen, but in 1851 was living with her father and uncle, and also declared the same trade as them. After 1865, the business traded as Friend & Allen until 1878, the years of James Friend's death.[20]

Henry Hollamby (1819–95)
Figs. 34–35, 37–38, 44–45, 47, 49, 69, 80, 94 Colour pls. 14, 15, 22, 23, 28a

The Hollamby family was extensively involved in the Tunbridge ware industry by the early nineteenth century both in west Kent and to a lesser extent in Brighton. Most were, however, employees and only one rose to distinction as a proprietor. This was Henry Hollamby who was apprenticed by his father, Henry Hollamby Snr. of Frant, at the age of 12 in 1831 for seven years to George and James Burrows. Henry Hollamby Jnr. must have been an adept pupil and a person of some ambition, for only seven years after the termination of his apprenticeship he was operating his own business at 6, Edgar Terrace, High Street. The enterprise was successful and ten years later, he was trading from premises in Chapel Place and on the Parade and had a manufactory in Frant Road. The manufactory was possibly the one maintained by George Wise until he withdrew from Tunbridge Wells. Hollamby's enterprise is also to be seen in the way that he publicised his products by showing them at international exhibitions.[21]

The reason for Hollamby's concern to display his wares widely can be seen in the nature of the business that he conducted. Although he maintained retail outlets to sell his goods directly to

70a. Ebony box with a centre block of Eridge Castle using a mixture of tessellated mosaic and cross-grain marquetry. The top is additionally decorated with geometrical and abstract mosaic bandings. c1840–45. (Pinto Collection, Birmingham City Museum).

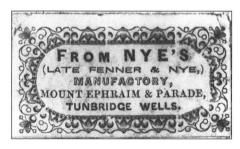

70b. Label on base of ebony box 'FROM NYE'S (LATE FENNER & NYE,) MOUNT EPHRAIM PARADE, TUNBRIDGE WELLS'.

visitors to Tunbridge Wells, and would permit the public to inspect his workshops, a large part of his trade was wholesale. He was not only the leading supplier of local shopkeepers, but sought to dispose of his goods as widely as possible. It was for this reason that he was anxious to develop mosaic blocks depicting topographical subjects. Many were designed for local sale but the production of blocks of Shakespeare's Birthplace Stratford-upon-Avon and Muckross Abbey and Ross Castle Killarney suggest that he was marketing to shopkeepers at some considerable distance. His blocks, which also included floral subjects, hawks and deer, are

149

71a. Stationery boxes. Left: *Satinwood with a mosaic spray of roses on the lid and floral bandings on the sides. c1845. w:10cm d:14cm h:8cm.* Centre: *rosewood with mosaic panel of rose and convolvulus blossoms, and floral and geometrical bandings. c1855. w:18cm d:12cm h:9.5cm.* Right: *bird's eye maple veneer, the domed top decorated with a mosaic spray of flowers, geometrical and broad floral mosaic bandings. c1860–65. w:18cm d:11cm h:11.5cm.*

71b. Label on the base of the rhomboidal box (below left) *'EDMUND NYE, MANUFACTURER, Mount Ephraim and Parade, TUNBRIDGE WELLS'.*

71c. Label on the base of the box (below right) *of the retailer 'W H TOOKE Goldsmith & Jeweller, 24 CHURCH ST LIVERPOOL OLD POST OFFICE BUILDINGS'.*

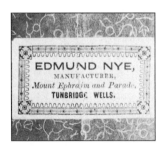

combined with naturalistic or geometrical mosaic bandings, usually of good quality. Apart from mosaic Tunbridge ware he also advertised 'Grey and White Wood Articles for Painting and Fern Printing'. It is unlikely that such wares will ever be identified, however, as Hollamby seldom labelled his work. He maintained a substantial manufactory which in the 1880s employed about 20 staff. The business appears to have closed down in 1891, Boyce, Brown & Kemp taking over many of the blocks and designs. His workshops were subsequently burnt down.[22]

Edmund Nye (1797–1863)
Figs. 1, 36, 63, 70–74, 80   Colour pls. 20–21

Edmund Nye was the son of James Nye, a Tunbridge ware manufacturer who appears to have been in business as early as 1757. On his father's death in 1809, he went into partnership with William Fenner, and worked as the junior partner in this enterprise until it was dissolved in 1817. From 1810, a Sarah Nye, probably a relative, was paying rates for a shop on the Parade, which she operated as a retail outlet for Tunbridge ware, and it was this shop and a manufactory in nearby Market Place that were to be the centre of Edmund Nye's operations from *c*1818 to the mid-1840s.[23] He built up a reputation for his products and in 1826 was a one of the makers selected to ballot for the honour of producing a work- and writing-table to be presented to Princess Victoria. Although he lost this commission to his erstwhile partner William Fenner, he did receive patronage from the Duchess of Kent in 1836, and was later to advertise himself as 'Manufacturer … to, the Queen and Royal Family'. Some of his early wares were decorated with topographical prints. A view of Tunbridge Wells is known bearing his imprint and dated 1827 (fig. 1). A painted and print-decorated whitewood box of *c*1825, bearing a print of the Parade, is known. The shop depicted in the foreground bears a prominent inscription on the fascia board 'MANUFACTURER E. NYE TUNBRIDGE WELLS'. In publishing prints, he was following a tradition established by Fenner & Nye who, as early as 1808, were producing Brighton views. Edmund Nye also maintained a retail outlet at 10, Castle Street, Hastings from 1826 to 1835 and a Hastings print published in April 1827 has an imprint of Nye at this address. It was while Nye was at the address on the Parade that Thomas Barton joined the firm as an employee.[24]

Edmund Nye took full advantage of the retirement of William Fenner from the trade in 1840. Although he did not take over Fenner's business and could not assert that he was his successor, he did emphasise in his advertising the words 'late Fenner & Nye', and by 1845 he had taken over the Chalet, Mount Ephraim, which had formerly been the main centre of production of Fenner & Nye, and subsequently William Fenner. He centred his business on the Mount Ephraim address, at which he lived, and gave up the manufactory in Market Place. In connection with the Great Exhibition of 1851, Edmund Nye prepared a number of fine pieces which were to constitute the largest and most elegant display of such wares. Nye's manufactory was renowned for the quality of the mosaic work produced which was frequently decorated with varied floral blocks and rose and leaf bandings, of considerable width in some cases. A number of mosaic topographical views were used, but the superb tropical butterflies which decorated the bookstand at the 1851 Exhibition, and a number of other high-quality pieces, some decorated with birds, were of conventional marquetry. Many of

72a. *Pin cushions. Back left: combined with four perfume bottles veneered in satinwood with wide mosaic leaf bandings. Attributable to Edmund Nye.* c1850. *w:24.5cm d:12cm h:10.5cm.* **Right:** *rosewood by Edmund Nye, top mosaic banding identical with previous item.* c1860. *w:17cm d:12cm h:8.5cm.* **Front left:** *circular, inlaid turnery.* c1870. *dia:3cm.* **Centre:** *bird's eye maple by William Upton, with mosaic garlands on sides and rose heads at ends.* c1855. *w:23cm d:7.5cm h:5.5cm.* **Right:** *rosewood.* c1870. *w:9.5cm d:6cm h:3 cm.*

72b. *Far left: Label from base of rosewood pin cushion (rear, right) reading 'EDMUND NYE Manufacturer, MOUNT EPHRAIM AND PARADE TUNBRIDGE WELLS.*

72c. *Left: Label on the base of bird's eye maple pin cushion (front centre) reading 'Wm UPTON, TUNBRIDGE WARE MANUFACTURERS, No 5, KINGS ROAD, BRIGHTON'.*

72d. *Left: Label on base of rosewood pin cushion (front right) reading, 'W CHILD JR, 51 KINGS ROAD, BRIGHTON, DESK & DRESSING CASE MAKERS'.*

73a. Rear: *rosewood box with mosaic floral centre surrounded by a mosaic chain border. Circular label on base, 'EDMUND NYE Manufacturer MOUNT EPHRAIM, AND PARADE Tunbridge Wells'. c1855. w:17.5cm d:11cm h:5cm.* Left: *square maple box with floral mosaic centre on a dark ground, geometrical bandings to top and sides. Label on base 'T BARTON, late NYE, Manufacturer, MOUNT EPHRAIM and PARADE, Tunbridge Wells'. c1875. 8.5cm sq h:4cm.* Right: *rosewood, lid decorated with a geometrical pattern of mosaic and parquetry. Label inside lid identical to square box to the left. c1880. 7cm sq h:1.5cm.* Front: *rosewood with perspective cube parquetry top. Stamped on base 'THOMAS BARTON Tunbridge Ware Manufacturer MT EPHRAIM TUNBRIDGE WELLS'. c1895. w:7.5cm d:5cm h:3cm.*

73b. *Label on base of both items, centre row, of plate 73a.*

153

74. *Ebony veneered octagonal games box with central tessellated rose block and geometrical and floral bandings. Edmund Nye label on base. c1860. l:26.5cm (Bracketts).*

Nye's products of the 1840s and 50s were veneered in light-coloured woods such as satinwood, holly and box, though rosewood was more commonly used. Some later pieces favoured darker woods such as ebony and coromandel and used distinctive geometrical bandings, and for these Thomas Barton was undoubtedly responsible. Barton took over Nye's business on his death in June 1863.[25]

Although Nye did not label or stamp all of his production, labels are found with some frequency and in varied forms, which makes it possible to suggest date spans for the main types which are:

  i. Rectangular 30.5 x 17mm inscribed 'NYE/
    Late Fenner & Nye/manufacturer/Tunbridge Wells',
     bordered and with concave corners.   *c*1835–40
  ii. As illustrated fig. 70b   *c*1840–45
  iii. As illustrated fig. 71b   *c*1845–55
  iv. As illustrated fig. 72b   *c*1855–63
  v. Circular, though sometimes cut square, as fig. 73b
    but with top inscription reading 'EDMUND NYE/
    Manufacturer' with convex circular line below
    before the address section in the lower half *c*1855–63
  vi. Circular label 70mm in diameter, often used
    on large circular pincushions   *c*1855–63
  vii. Oval stamp 20 x 10mm inscribed 'EDMUND NYE/
    MANUFACTURER/TUNBRIDGE WELLS

Tape measures and tapes in needle cases are also known with Nye's name printed on them.

Robert Russell (1812–73)
Fig. 75

Robert Russell was a maker of high-quality wares of a very distinctive character. He was born in Tunbridge Wells and is recorded as living there at the time of the 1841 census, but the date at which he commenced manufacturing is unknown. He is not recorded in any trade directories before 1851 but was obviously manufacturing before this date. As early as 1849, he was supplying the Duchess of Kent who in August and November of that year made small payments to him. The nature of the purchases is not entirely clear, but a sum of £2 15s (£2.75) paid on 20 August was recorded as 'for Tunbridge Ware Table'. Russell also exhibited at the Great Exhibition of 1851 a 'Tunbridge ware marquetrie inlay lady's work-box fitted with a till'. The box was said to be 'in Gothic style and showing native woods'. His initial address was Vale Place, London Road. At first he probably produced wares of a fairly conventional Tunbridge ware character and a fine octagonal walnut-veneered box exists with perspective cube work in the centre of the lid and Berlin woolwork-style bandings of roses and leaves. This box bears a label with the Vale Place address.[26]

75. *Examples of Robert Russell's 'Tunbridge Wells Marquetrie'. Rear: workbox, bird's eye maple, with top and front decorated with Russell marquetry. c1860. w:27.5cm d:21cm h:11.5cm. Front left: rosewood handkerchief box, the top decorated with Russell marquetry. c1860. 17.5cm sq h:6cm. Right: domed rosewood box with Russell marquetry on the lid surrounded by a chevron banding and tessellated mosaic. Mosaic rose bandings on sides. c1850. w:20.5cm d:11.5cm h:12cm.*

Russell was, however, to develop a very distinctive style of marquetry which he advertised as 'Tunbridge Wells Marquetry … analogous to the Tunbridge ware, but of a superior character'. This consisted of segments of finely figured veneers cut with a lobed outline which were either fitted together to form a central block, or symmetrical lobed shapes joined together to form 'chains' for border decoration. These were sometimes combined with perspective cube work, a marquetry panoramic view of Tunbridge Wells from Mount Ephraim, or even conventional Tunbridge ware mosaic bandings. Boxes produced ranged from the fine and elegant to those decorated on the top with a distinctive Russell marquetry panel but otherwise plainly veneered. He used templates made from bone to produce the marquetry segments required.

In 1862, Russell moved his manufactory to Chapel Place though he continued to live at Vale Place. He had already received important patronage; in 1863 he included amongst his clients, apart from the Duchess of Kent, Baroness de Spith, Lady Ann Marie Dawson, Lady Mary Rose, Lady Franklin, Lady Cornwallis and Lady Harding. In 1871, his workforce consisted of his daughter Harriet and – rather unusually – four women. Russell appears to have continued production until 1873, the year of his death.[27]

John, James and Ann Sharp
Fig. 76   Colour pl. 6

It is remarkable that for an enterprise which traded in Tunbridge Wells for half a century, and was regarded by contemporaries as one of the leading manufacturers, so little is known. The date of the founding of the enterprise is uncertain but it was operating by 1807. As with other Tunbridge ware manufacturers of this date, prints were published for sale to the public as well as for the decoration of woodwares. Two prints of Tunbridge Wells exist both with the imprint 'published by I. & J. Sharp', one dated 1807 and the other 1809, while a satirical print entitled 'Matrimonial voyages' was published in 1810. The Barrow map of 1808 marks Sharp's manufactory on the western side of Culverden Down. The business was, however, to expand and much larger premises at Oldenburgh House on the opposite side of the road were used in addition. These became the main centre of activity, though the other premises were retained, and on the tithe map of 1838 are described as a 'turnery manufactory'. Ann had joined the business as early as 1823. This was, no doubt, the period of their greatest prestige. In 1826, they were one of the four leading manufacturers who balloted for the honour of making the work- and writing-table for Princess Victoria, and in an 1830 guide were listed amongst the principal makers of Tunbridge ware. By this year they were claiming that they had received the patronage of the Queen, though such claims generally are apt to prove insubstantial if investigated. John was one of the town improvement commissioners in 1847. There is some evidence to suggest that John or James either exhibited or intended to exhibit at the 1851 Exhibition, but no description is available of the nature of the exhibit. Ann was the last survivor of the triumvirate and is mentioned in directories as late as 1858, but probably little production was continued this late, and the main source of her income may have been the provision of lodgings, an activity conducted for many years in addition to the manufactory.[28]

76. *Octagonal card box veneered in yew with parquetry banding to the top, and decorated with a coloured drawing of a display of cards. The duty card incorporates the maker's name 'I.J. & A. SHARP TUNB WELLS'. c1815. w:26cm d:21cm h:8cm. (Tunbridge Wells Museum).*

Surprisingly little is known about the products of the business. A few card boxes of rectangular or hexagonal shape veneered in fine woods such as yew or kingwood, exist. These feature on the top of the lid a display of playing cards, the prominent duty card (the ace of spades) being inscribed at the base 'I.J. & A. SHARP TUNB WELLS'. The playing cards are hand drawn, suggesting either a small production run or the fear of prosecution for printing the ace

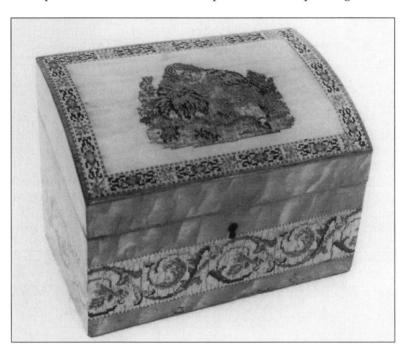

77a. Satinwood stationery box with a curved top, decorated with a mosaic panel of a boy and a dog. The sides are decorated with a curvilinear foliage banding in mosaic often found on Talbot's productions. c1855. (Tunbridge Wells Museum).

77b. Base covered with tartan paper and bearing the label 'FROM TALBOT'S TUNBRIDGE WARE MANUFACTORY, CHAPEL PLACE, TUNBRIDGE WELLS'.

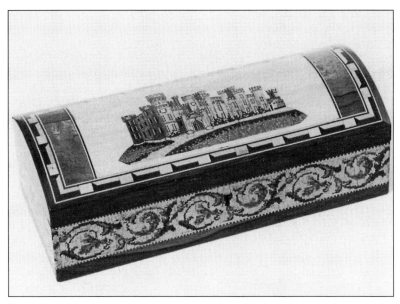

78. *Glove box, rosewood, with a domed top displaying a mosaic view of Eridge Castle. Attributable to Alfred Talbot on the basis of the characteristic curvilinear foliage mosaic bandings on the sides and the tartan paper on the base. c1850. (Pinto Collection, Birmingham City Museum.)*

of spades on which government duty was imposed. At a slightly later date the manufactory used an oval trade label printed on blue paper. It is known on a fine table cabinet decorated all over with large-scale, finely grained perspective cube work.

Alfred Davies Talbot (b. 1813)
Figs. 77–78   Colour pl. 19

Talbot is one of the lesser-known makers, but from the evidence of his surviving wares, he was a maker of quality mosaic items. He was born in Speldhurst parish in 1813, but about 1835 moved to the adjoining parish of Frant, where his daughter Sarah was born. By the time of the birth of his third daughter, Harriet, in 1843, he was living in Tunbridge Wells and had probably already set up his own business. He advertised in the 1844 edition of *Colbran's Guide* seeking repair work, as well as the sale of new wares. His manufactory was in Chapel Place near the Parade and he lived close by at 6, Bedford Terrace, an address that he also used in advertisements. The business continued to operate until 1858.[29]

Pieces bearing labels of this manufacturer or stamped on the base 'A D TALBOT' are uncommon, but a stationery box and a thermometer exist in the Tunbridge Wells Museum collection, and a comparison of the mosaic bandings used on these enable other items probably by this maker to be identified. One very characteristic banding, consisting of interconnected scrolled foliage, appears to be a particularly good indicator, and is found on a box in the Pinto collection, which uses a fine but unusual block of Eridge Castle, while a tea caddy in the Tunbridge Wells Museum uses this banding in conjunction with the block of Tunbridge Wells viewed from Mount Ephraim, also known to have been used by Robert Russell. Talbot also used floral and geometrical bandings and blocks featuring clusters of roses. The bases of a number of Talbot boxes are found covered with a distinctive 'tartan' pattern paper printed in black which is not known to have been used by other makers; the interiors are seldom finished with lining paper. These again are useful indicators of a Talbot origin.

79. *Rosewood stationery box, the curved top showing an identical flower head to the book rack in fig. 80a, the sides decorated with wide floral bandings and with additional geometrical bandings similar in style to those used by Henry Hollamby. Attributable to Thomas Waterman. c1860. w:16cm d:11.5cm. (Sotheby's).*

24. (Above left) *Domed glove box, veneered in ebony, with broad rose and geometrical mosaic bandings. Label on the base of 'T. BARTON''* (*fig. 61b p. 136*). *c1880. w:24cm d:10cm h:8cm.*

25. (Above right) *Octagonal tray with handle, ebony veneer on rosewood, floral mosaic veneer in the centre and geometrical and floral bandings. Attributable to Thomas Barton. c1870. w:22.5cm.*

26. *Late productions of the Tunbridge ware industry.* Top: *cigarette box, plane wood, the top decorated with perspective cube work and geometrical mosaic bandings. The interior of the lid bearing the trademark of the Tunbridge Wells Manufacturing Co. Listed in their catalogue as a No. 127 cigarette box with a trade price of 30s (£1.50). c1925. w:27cm d:10cm h:8cm.* Front left: *rosewood handkerchief box, the top decorated with a floral mosaic veneer and geometrical bandings. The base bears the price label of ''PORTERS TOYLAND TUNBRIDGE WARE'' and a manuscript price of 7s 6d ($37\frac{1}{2}$p). c1910. 15cm sq. h:5.5cm.* Front right: *cedar wood box, the top decorated with mosaic floral veneer and geometrical bandings. The base inscribed in manuscript ''From Mrs Mould/Xmas 1919''. At this date John Ellis was the sole manufacturer. w:9.5cm d:6.5cm h:3.5cm.*

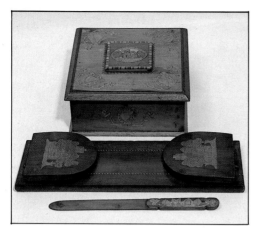

27. (Above left) *Killarney arbutus wares.* Top: *box decorated with an inlaid view of Muckross Abbey and harps and shamrock. Inscribed on top "Killarney Lakes". c1900. 22.5cm sq. h:9cm.* Centre: *book stand, the ends inlaid with views of Muckross Abbey. c1900. w:37cm d:12cm.* Front: *paper knife inlaid with a view of Muckross Abbey and shamrock. Blade inscribed "Killarney 1886". 1:27cm.*

28a. (Above right) *Killarney arbutus box of typical shape, the top decorated with a tessellated Tunbridge ware panel of Muckross Abbey probably supplied by Henry Hollamby (view reversed). c1880. 21cm sq. h:8cm*

28b. (Above left) *Interior of box (plate 28a) showing pyrographic view of Ross Castle, Killarney.*

29. (Above right) *Portable writing desk, arbutus and other woods, the top displaying a pyrographic view of Muckross Abbey, Killarney. Trails of shamrock and an Irish harp decorate the top and sides. c1900. 1:33cm d:25.5cm. (National Museum of Ireland).*

80a. *Book racks.* Left: *rosewood, cubic work and floral spray on the ends. Bears the label of 'T WATERMAN & SON, GRAFTON HOUSE, Parade, Tunbridge Wells'. The style of the floral spray and the construction of the rack may help in the identification of other unlabelled items by this maker.* c1855. *w:33cm d:15cm.* Centre: *rosewood, an abstract design on one end and view of Eridge Castle on the other. Attributable to Edmund Nye (see fig. 69).* c1845. *w:26.5cm d:12.5cm.* Right: *rosewood, the ends decorated with views of Eridge Castle and Netley Abbey in mosaic. Attributable to Henry Hollamby.* c1870. *w:33cm d:16cm.*

80b. *Waterman's label as it appears on book rack above.*

Thomas Waterman (b. 1809)
Figs. 79–80

Thomas Waterman's label has been found on a number of pieces of Tunbridge Ware but little is known concerning his business. He was born in Brighton and is possibly related to another Thomas Waterman, a Tunbridge ware maker though not a proprietor, who between 1828 and 1843 lived in Chesterfield Place and Ivory Place, Brighton. The young Thomas Waterman must have moved to Tunbridge Wells at an early age, certainly before 1833. He is not recorded as a manufacturer in directories until 1859. His main business premises were at Grafton House on the Parade, but in 1859 his address had changed to High Street. It is likely that he occupied Grafton House for longer than a year, however, for all his labels bear this address and give the title of the business as Thomas Waterman & Son. The son referred to is uncertain for he had four sons, two at least of whom followed the same trade as their father. The eldest was 18 at the time of the 1851 census. The last directory entry for Thomas Waterman is 1865. He was still living in Tunbridge Wells in 1871 and declaring his trade as Tunbridge ware maker.[30] Glove boxes, tea caddies and book racks have all been noted with Waterman labels. The quality of the pieces in general is good though rather conventional, with Berlin-type rose-and-leaf bandings, rose and other floral blocks (sometimes rather coarse) and perspective cube work.

B. Tonbridge

George Wise (1703–79) and his successors
Figs. 9–10, 14, 16, 25, 30, 33, 81–84

The business conducted by four successive generations of the Wise family in Tonbridge High Street is, without doubt, the enterprise with the longest history in the Tunbridge ware industry. It was also the only enterprise in the town of Tonbridge to achieve real success and distinction. The small country market town of Tonbridge could provide little local patronage, had few facilities to attract tourists to

81. Circular engravings prepared for the decoration of whitewood Tunbridge wares (see fig. 14). Left: River frontage of George Wise's manufactory showing the bridge and castle in the background. Right: Wise's manufactory viewed from the bridge showing the face to Tonbridge High Street. c1810. (John & Jill Ford). Similar rectangle engravings also exist.

82. Rosewood writing desk, the top veneered with mosaic bandings of roses, oak leaves and geometrical patterns. The panel depicts the State Apartments, Windsor Castle. A panel with this identical veneer in the Tunbridge Wells Museum is inscribed in pencil on the reverse, 'This specimen of Gauge work was made at Mr. George Wise's manufactory, Frant-rd by William Harris Jr.'. c1840. w:30.5cm h:(front) 5.6cm (back) 8.2cm d:24.2cm. (Guildhall Museum, Rochester).

lodge there, and was a full five miles from the centre of spa life at Tunbridge Wells. Although George Wise Snr. opened Tunbridge Wells showrooms in the early 1830s and traded in the spa town for around a quarter of a century, the firm had to rely heavily on the wholesaling of its products, which it did with singular success.

The founder of the enterprise, George Wise, was born in 1703 but was not baptised at Tonbridge. The family was, however, domiciled in the area and Simon Wise who in April 1737 leased a workshop, probably in Tunbridge Wells, may possibly have been a Tunbridge ware maker.[31] In 1746, George Wise started to lease premises in Tonbridge and set up the business that was to bring renown to the family. At this period, the town was set for expansion following the opening of the Upper Medway navigation as far as this point in 1741. Although the production of Tunbridge ware may have commenced in 1746, for George was by trade a turner, direct

163

evidence of this is lacking and it would have been insufficient in itself to support him. By 1784, his son, Thomas, was involved in the business and the firm was described as 'Turners, Chair-makers, Dealers in Medicines, Tunbridge Ware, Haberdasheries, Cutlery, Silver and divers other wares'. On his death his widow, Elizabeth, carried on the business in association with Thomas, until her death in 1793.[32]

Thomas Wise (1750–1807) certainly carried on the production of Tunbridge ware and possibly looked for some of his custom to the travellers on the Hastings road who might find Tonbridge a convenient half-way stage at which to take refreshment. Instructions survive for a 'POST PUZZLE made by Tho. Wise, Tonbridge' which involved counters and an 'urn' to contain them, and which was sold as an amusement to travellers. Thomas also published prints of Tunbridge Wells and Brighton intended for sale and probably box decoration. These are known dated between 1800 and 1806. He also acted as agent for other print publishers, and in July 1800 was taking orders for a print of an arch erected during the previous year in Maidstone in honour of a visit by George III. Thomas also acted as an auctioneer and a considerable number of his auction bills and catalogues survive in the Sprange collection in Tunbridge Wells Museum. Most of the properties, household and trade goods sales were in the Tonbridge area. Included in one sale of the effects of William Woodhams at Nonsuch Green in April 1797 was 'a Complete Chest of Tunbridge-ware Turners' Tools belonging to the late John Brooks'. In 1804, Thomas Wise bought the premises, previously leased, at the north end of the bridge over the main channel of the River Medway in Tonbridge High Street, which was the centre of the firm's activity.[33] In 1838, this property was described as 'Five Houses, Workshops, Yards and Garden' totalling in all 3 rods and 19 perches. It had a convenient river frontage for the reception of timber and large sheds for its storage, while the other buildings provided adequate space for the workshops, showrooms and dwelling-house required by the family. It was probably in the time of Thomas Wise that the business started to concentrate its attention on Tunbridge ware production and the associated trade of print publishing. The rise of Brighton and Margate followed by the similar development of other Sussex and east Kent coast resorts provided new opportunities for the sale of souvenir wares, while these continued to be popular at the more established inland spas. However, his nephew, the second George Wise (1779–1869), appears to have built the reputation of the firm on the basis of the move already made towards specialisation.[34]

The earliest print recorded with a George Wise imprint carries the date 1 March 1806, and the latest with a Thomas Wise imprint 24 March 1806. It thus seems likely that George Wise took over the business from his uncle about March 1806. For the next 25 years he specialised in producing workboxes, tea caddies, games and other good-quality boxes, the majority being decorated with prints. Articles incorporating views of Tunbridge Wells, Tonbridge, Brighton, Hastings, Worthing, Margate, Broadstairs and Cheltenham with Wise labels show evidence of his wide

83. *Games table, rosewood, the tip top displaying a draught-board veneered alternately with ebony and fruitwood squares. The top, stand and base additionally decorated with floral and geometrical mosaic bandings. The table bears an indistinct handwritten inscription 'Geo Wise town 1854'. Top 42.5cm square. (Christie's, South Kensington).*

84a. *Four-drawer walnut cabinet, the top decorated with a mosaic view of Warwick Castle, the back with an oval rose panel and the doors, drawer fronts, etc. with additional rose panels and bandings. Edge of plinth worked in vandykes. Label in the back of each drawer 'FROM G. WISE, JUN, Manufacturer, TUNBRIDGE'. c1865–70. w:27.5cm h:24cm d:195.cm (Tunbridge Wells Museum).*

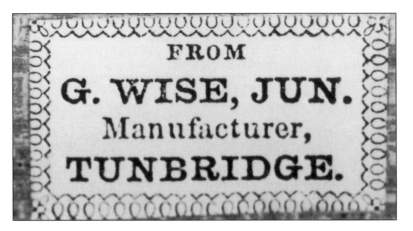

84b. *Label from four-drawer walnut cabinet.*

distribution. He also made commemorative items. A sewing box with a view of Margate church, and painted decoration including a crown, bears the date '19th July 1821' – the Coronation of George IV. George Wise was active in persuading libraries to stock his goods. Non-topographical prints were also used, including those published by Rudolph Ackermann of the Strand, London, who sold Wise's Tunbridge ware in his Repository. Penwork and gilt borders were used on boxes, and it is likely that Wise produced items entirely decorated with penwork.

The growing popularity of veneered Tunbridge ware also attracted Wise, who was in a good position to exploit the new developments in miniature parquetry and mosaic work pioneered by James Burrows at Tunbridge Wells about 1830. With his wide trade in topographical, print-decorated wares, it was to be expected that Wise would be early in the field of designing in the new mosaics and especially developing views of buildings. Tunbridge ware decorated with blocks of Windsor Castle was supplied to Princess Victoria, indicating a pre-1837 genesis. This is confirmed by post-1837 advertisements stating that Wise was a maker 'to their Royal Highnesses the Duchess of Kent and Princess Victoria'.[35] The wholesale trade developed with print-decorated goods was continued with these mosaic items. In the early 1850s one of his stockists, William Tiffen, a Folkestone bookseller, advertised ranges of inlaid and mosaic turnery and cabinet goods produced at Tonbridge.[36]

It was in the second George Wise's period that the plan for opening a branch at Tunbridge Wells was put into effect. This was designed to facilitate direct retail sales to fashionable residents and visitors as an addition to the existing wholesale trade. The repository was opened at 11, Calverley Promenade (now Calverley Park Crescent), a new development built between 1830 and 1835 to provide fashionable facilities to the new town recently established at the top of Mount Pleasant. The Promenade had 17 shops on a raised walk, with a circulating library in the centre and a vapour bath and shampooing establishment at one end. In front of the shops were to be gardens, a fountain and a bandstand. Wise's business was established here by 1832. The development was designed to compete with the Parade and attract fashionable society away from the traditional focus of the town, but in this is failed and within a few years of opening the whole was converted into lodging houses. By 1845, George Wise had moved his Tunbridge Wells repository to the Parade, where the retail outlets of the other Tunbridge ware makers were clustered. It traded at this address until 1857. Wise also maintained a manufactory in Frant Road at this period, possibly the one later occupied by Henry Hollamby (fig. 82).[37]

Although George Wise did not exhibit at the 1851 London Exhibition he was spurred on, no doubt because of the publicity afforded to his rivals, to participate in the next major international exhibition, which was held in New York in 1853. It would seem likely that he also wanted to develop sales in the United States. He displayed a 'table, boxes, desks and fancy articles' in inlaid and mosaic Tunbridge ware' and was awarded a bronze medal for his exhibit. A fine mosaic games table in a late Regency style with a written inscription 'Geo Wise town 1854' provides an indication of the prestigious items that the firm was capable of manufacturing at this period (fig. 83).[38]

George Wise's son, given the same Christian name as his father, was born in 1816 and followed him into the family business. On his father's death in March 1869 'all manufactured stock, tools, plant and utensils' were bequeathed to his son.[39] He had, however, already traded independently as early as 1862 from an address at 59, High Street and the businesses of George Wise and George Wise Jnr. are separately shown in directories. In 1864, when the sixteenth-century school house of Tonbridge School was demolished to permit new buildings to be erected as the school expanded its numbers, George Wise Jnr. obtained oak timber from the structure which he used to manufacture souvenirs. A small paper-knife with an oak blade is known, displaying a paper label indicating that the wood came from this source, and naming George Wise Jnr. as the maker. The father had only infrequently labelled his mosaic work, but the son appears to have done so on a more systematic basis and it is therefore possible to assess the nature of the wares produced in this last phase of the business. The range of goods and their decoration was fairly conventional, though of good quality. Pictorial topographical blocks were used, including those of Tonbridge and Warwick Castles, and Cobham Hall[40], and also Berlin rose and other floral subjects and bandings. The use of borders of small vandykes, sometimes with an edging consisting of small dashes, appears to have been a characteristic of Wise's work at this period. By the time George Wise Jnr. entered the trade as an independent producer, fashionable demand was in decline. In 1851 his father had employed nine men, but ten years later this had been reduced to three men and a boy. George Wise Jnr. appears to have bought in veneers from Henry Hollamby and may even have bought completed items from this source and placed his own labels on them. About 1876 he closed his business, though T. Burrows attempted to take over the custom and possibly the stock of materials. This business, too, closed in 1883. Most of the manufactory occupied for so long by the Wise family was pulled down in 1886 to widen the road and provide better access to the bridge over the River Medway. The last George Wise was to enjoy a long retirement for he did not die until February 1899. In his will he left the fairly considerable estate of £3,960.[41]

C. Brighton

The Morris family
Figs. 7–8, 85

The surname Morris is not known in either the Tunbridge Wells or London Tunbridge trades, though an early advertisement states 'from London' (fig. 8). The success of the Kentish makers such as Thomas and George Wise and Fenner & Nye in supplying the rapidly growing Brighton market was inspired by the Morris family. The business is usually referred to as Morris's Royal Fancy Tunbridge Ware Repository, but when the principal is named in directories and rate books, John or Serjeant John and Sergeant Witten appear as Christian names. The enterprise claimed to have been founded in 1808 and as early as July 1814 was at Trafalgar Place. A trade card from this early phase is illustrated with engravings showing that both turnery and small cabinet wares were produced (fig. 8). Whitewood items were painted, decorated with prints or finished in penwork. By 1822 the business had moved to a prominent position at the north end of the fashionable Steine – 26 and 27, Richmond Place. The main manufactory was here but the Trafalgar Place premises were retained for a time as a sawmill. The three-storey building occupied by the firm in the Steine is featured in a number of Brighton prints for it faced the much-admired, new Gothic parish church of St Peter which was begun in 1824 and consecrated in 1828. Few of this firm's products have been recognised as it seldom marked its wares, but a labelled whitewood box with a view of the 'North Parade & Donaldson's Library on the Steine', 'Published by S.W. Morris Manufacturers', one with a view of the Chain Pier in a roundel with a gilt edge to the top of the frame incorporating a cartouche inscribed 'From Morris's Repository Brighton', and a small box with a view of the 'Royal Mews' are known (fig. 7). Apart from the print, the decoration consists of a few simple penwork lines. These items come from this early phase of the firm's existence. It is likely, too, that more decorative and

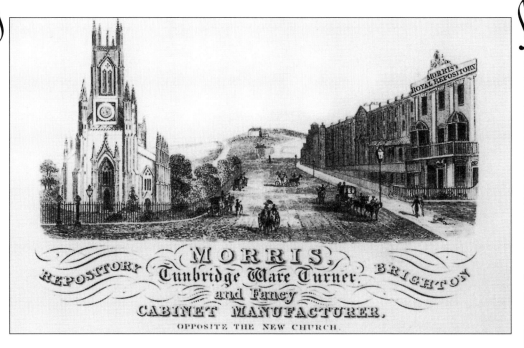

85. *Trade card of Morris, Brighton, showing St Peter's Church by Charles Barry (1824–28) on the left and Morris's Royal Repository, Richmond Place opposite. c1830. (Henry Smith Collection).*

prestigious wares were produced as Morris's Royal Fancy Repository was mentioned in various guides as one of the fashionable bazaars. It stocked a wide range of jewellery, stationery, perfumery, French fancy wares, children's games and amusements, including Wallis's dissected maps, apart from the items that were produced in its own workshops.[43]

In 1835, S.J. Morris died and the business passed to Abraham Morris (b. 1817), the son of John Morris, who was fully in charge by 1837. It was in this period that the firm started to produce inlaid turnery and mosaic wares, following the Tunbridge Wells pattern, though the existence of a tessellated mosaic box with a Tonbridge Castle view suggests that completed items were being bought in for sale. Throughout their period of trading the firm produced a wide range of desks, dressing-cases, workboxes and caddies, both decorative and utilitarian, carried out repairs and renovations to items of furniture and Tunbridge ware, and stocked jewellery,

86a. Whitewood workbox, decorated with a coloured engraving of the Marine Parade and Chain Pier, Brighton. The box is additionally finished with penwork borders and simulated rosewood. c1825. w:28cm d:23cm h:14cm. (Tunbridge Wells Museum).

stationery and perfumery. A branch repository was operating in 1839–40 on the seafront at 79, Kings Road. The firm even received small commissions of a utilitarian nature from the Lord Chamberlain's department, justifying the royal coat of arms which surmounted the advertising board fronting their premises. The business, however, ceased trading in 1848. Edward Morris, who traded from Richmond Gardens from 1839 into the late 1840s, and also maintained a branch at 47, George Street, Hastings from 1839, was probably related.[44]

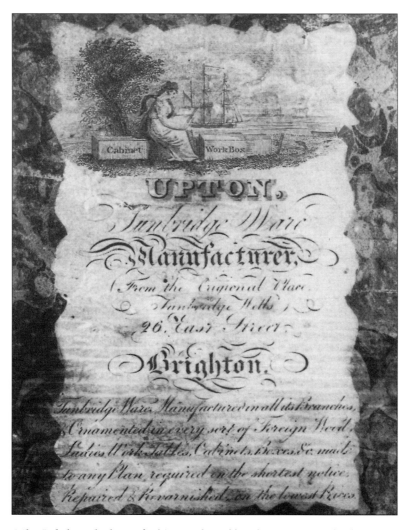

86b. *Label on the base of whitewood workbox 'UPTON, Tunbridge Ware Manufacturer, From the Original Place, Tunbridge Wells 26 East Street, Brighton'.*

William Upton
Figs. 7, 27, 72, 86

A trade label on a fine, print-decorated workbox by Upton in the Tunbridge Wells Museum (fig. 86) lists his occupation as 'Tunbridge Ware Manufacturer From the Original Place, Tunbridge Wells', and the Tunbridge Wells association is confirmed by his declaration in the 1851 census returns that he was born in Speldhurst parish. It is likely that he was related to Sarah Upton who maintained a toy shop on the Parade, Tunbridge Wells from 1772 to 1787. The date of his move to Brighton is unknown but he was certainly there by February 1815 when his daughter Sarah was baptised. He declared his trade as a turner and at the time was living in Trafalgar Place, the address of Morris's workshop, and may have been an employee. By 1818, he had moved to New Road and four years later was trading as a Tunbridge ware manufacturer from this address. A rectangular, rosewood-veneered tea caddy, with chamfered corners, and with large-scale perspective cube work on the top, in a private collection, has an Upton billhead pasted to the base giving his address as 'Near the Theatre, New Road'. The following year, he moved to 26, East Street, using 6, Boyces Street as a workshop. He remained in East Street until 1828 when he briefly traded from 5, Somerset Place before settling at 4, later 5, Pool Lane and moving back to 26, East Street by 1835. Whilst using these addresses he was near to the heart of Brighton and probably selling retail to the fashionable company that visited the resort. He was selling prints, too, for one exists with his imprint that would have been much larger than could have been used normally for box decoration.[45]

The workshops moved in 1834 to 1 and 2, Kensington Street and in 1838 are listed as 94, Gloucester Lane, which was to remain the centre of his production until the business closed *c*1859. This property was owned by John Upton, possibly a relative, who may also have had some connection with the business. These addresses were, however, at a distance from the fashionable part of the town, and showrooms were maintained at 34, Old Steine by 1845, 1, later 2, Marine Drive (1845–48), and later still 5, Kings Road or 40a, Old Steine (1859). Pieces sold from the Kings Road address are frequently labelled, and often incorporate tessellated mosaic veneers. It has been stated that these mosaic pieces were the work of his son, William Upton Jnr. He was born in 1821 and his marriage is recorded in November 1846. As his trade was listed at this time as a Tunbridge ware maker, it is not unlikely that he assisted his father. Three years later, however, William Upton Snr. was still active in the trade and living at 94, Gloucester Lane and it is probable that he retained control up to the termination of the manufactory. Trading continued from 40a, Old Steine and later 68b, East Street under the proprietorship of a Miss Upton until 1864.[46]

D. Worthing and Weymouth

James Medhurst (d. 1877)
Fig. 29

James Medhurst is the only nineteenth-century manufacturer of mosaic Tunbridge ware known to have worked outside the counties of Kent and Sussex. His baptism is recorded in the parish of Maresfield, Sussex, a village 15 miles from Tunbridge Wells, on 29 March 1796. Thomas Medhurst, his father, was a Tunbridge ware maker who later moved to Frant, a part of which parish was included in the town of Tunbridge Wells. James Medhurst married Sarah of Buxted, Sussex and was living in Frant in September 1813 when their daughter, Sarah, was born. He moved to Brighton prior to 1819 and the marriage of his daughter Mary was recorded there in July 1838. The father's trade was stated to be 'Tunbridge Ware Manufacturer' and the address 11, Cumberland Place. This would seem to imply that at this date he was manufacturing in the town and later he was to claim that he had 'the honour of attending on H.R.H. Princess Augusta several times while at Worthing and Brighton'. He does not, however, appear in any of the Brighton directories. It is possible that in the 1830s he may have been devoting more of his time to activities other than those of his main trade. James Medhurst was greatly interested in archaeology and in 1828 whilst excavating a Roman site at Lancing, discovered a tessellated mosaic pavement 4.8 metres (16 feet) square. He saw its potential for attracting visitors from Brighton and Worthing and by 1832 it was on view to the public and mentioned in local guide books as an attraction. James Medhurst also showed on the site 'some small altars, lavatories &c, and a really valuable collection of coins'. He had erected 'a neat species of hut to receive visitors, and enclosed the ground in a neat style' and advertised the site by means of a red and white flag inscribed 'Roman Pavement'. He was assisted by his son, and both were stated to 'evidence a gratifying intelligence'. He was later to claim that 'one Thousand persons have inscribed their names in a book which was kept at the Roman Pavement'. These visitors were also customers for painted whitewood Tunbridge ware objects that he sold on the site, these bearing a printed label inscribed 'A TRIFLE from the ROMAN PAVEMENT'. So important did the project become that he set up house at Sompting near by. For reasons which are not clear the landowner, on whose property the Roman pavement had been discovered, decided to terminate Medhurst's enterprise by destroying the site (*c*1833). After this setback, Medhurst initially showed his collection of antiquities, 'consisting of a number of Roman and Ancient British Coins together with Broaches, Rings, Combs, Bracelets, Lockets, Spear-heads etc.', at his house. However, as the 300 exhibits had been 'obtained by his own researches on the South Downs, within five miles of Worthing' the latter was seen to be the obvious place to display them to the public. In 1839 he moved from Sompting to 11, West Buildings, Worthing where he concentrated on his trade of Tunbridge ware maker offering print-decorated whitewood items with an emphasis on turnery. In March

1851, his wife Sarah and his sons Robert and Edmund were living at West Buildings and all declared their trade as 'Tunbridge ware turner'. James Medhurst was to trade from this address until 1859.[47]

He not only formed the Worthing business but at the same time established a similar business at 11, Maiden Street in Weymouth. In 1846 this was described as a 'Tunbridge Warehouse'. He excavated a number of Roman and Romano-British sites in the area in the early 1840s and by 1851 had moved his Weymouth address to 9, Chesterfield Place, Esplanade and there set up a 'Museum of Antiquities illustrating the Celtic, Roman and Saxon eras in Britain'. A reflection of this interest in history and collecting can be seen in the material that he incorporated into his Tunbridge wares. Boxes of his manufacture bear labels indicating that they were made from wood of the wreck of either the *Earl of Abergavenny,* an East Indiaman lost off Portland on 5 February 1805, or the *Columbine* wrecked on Portland Beach on 28 November 1838. Both labels have descriptions of the wrecks printed on labels attached to them, and as both bear the Chesterfield Place address they must date from the 1850s (fig. 29). Medhurst also advertised goods made from the wreck of the *Royal George* which sank at Spithead in 1782, but was dispersed by explosives between 1839 and 1843, hence the availability of timber. Material from this vessel was exploited by a number of makers of souvenirs, including George Wise of Tonbridge. The labelled boxes are of good quality but of fairly conventional Tunbridge ware character with floral blocks decorating the lids and geometrical or floral bandings on the sides.[48]

The businesses at both Worthing and Weymouth appear to have ceased trading by about 1860 though in the following year a Phoebe Medhurst was still operating from 9, Chesterfield Place as a fancy ware shopkeeper and Sarah Medhurst, his wife, continued to live at West Buildings, Worthing until 1862. James Medhurst appears to have retired to Bristol, and items from his archaelogical collections passed to the City's Museum. He died at Great Malvern on 4 November 1877. Of his five sons, four took up the trade of their father, George, Robert and James at Worthing and Edmund at Sidmouth, Devon.[49]

RELATED DECORATIVE WOODWARES

Chapter 13

KILLARNEY INLAID WOODWARES

An interesting parallel with the Tunbridge ware industry is to be found in the manufactures that commenced in the Killarney area of south-west Ireland in the first half of the nineteenth century. The height of prosperity of this industry from *c*1845 to 1880 roughly coincides with the zenith of the Tunbridge mosaic marquetry wares and, like that of the Kentish resort, the industry continued at a declining level of production well into the next century. Its wares were produced to satisfy the demands of visitors to a resort centre and the range of marquetry and inlaid goods produced have many parallels both in form and decoration with those produced at Tunbridge Wells. There is even a direct involvement by a Tunbridge Wells manufacturer in the Killarney trade, for blocks were produced and goods sold showing mosaic views of Muckross Abbey (more correctly referred to as Muckross Friary), Ross Castle, and Glena Cottage, sites near Killarney which were recommended for tourist visits. Killarney furniture has also been illustrated and mistakenly described as Tunbridge ware in English publications.

Killarney, in common with Cumbria and the Scottish Highlands, has the combination of mountain and lake best calculated to appeal to the lover of the picturesque. From the late eighteenth century, the taste for the picturesque was being stimulated by such writers as the Rev. William Gilpin, whose works taught the visitor to appreciate natural scenery through such critical faculties as would be applied to major works of fine art. Killarney did, however, suffer a major disadvantage. Compared with English, Welsh and even Scottish areas of picturesque beauty it was remote to the British visitor, and furthermore Ireland with its smaller population and lower levels of wealth was unable to generate sufficient native tourists. Visitors did come in small numbers and the first guide book to the lake and mountain scenery was published in 1776, the year in which Arthur Young visited Killarney. Young declared that the scenery he had witnessed 'can scarcely be said to have a rival' and compared with other parts of Ireland 'to be in reality superior to all comparisons'. However, he was fiercely critical of the facilities provided, especially the lack of suitable accommodation, the

87. *Davenport, arbutus wood decorated with marquetry, detail in pyrography, depicting ferns, mountain eagles, deer, arbutus sprays, ivy, shamrock, thistle and rose. Stamped 'J O'CONNOR Arbutus & Bog Oak Manufacturer Killarney'. c1860.*

distance from the town to the lake and the extravagant prices demanded for certain services, complaints endorsed by early nineteenth-century travellers. He recommended that an enterprising promoter provide 'a well built inn … on the immediate shore of the lake' and 'a large rendezvous-room for billiards, cards, dancing, music &c to which the company might resort'.[1] Yet no promoter appeared, and what prosperity the town enjoyed relied more upon the local industries of agriculture, corn-milling, textiles, tanning, copper mining and smelting. In 1810, it was stated that the 'improving state' of the town was 'not so much owing to the great concourse of visitants whom the beauties of the Lake attract, as to the judicious attention of the respectable proprietor, Lord Kenmare … to the extension of the Linen Manufacture'. As late as 1834, the town could be described as being 'good without being at all picturesque' and apart from its two good streets was said to contain also 'many bad alleys, and close filthy lanes and yards'. Rural distress in the south-west of Ireland, caused by pressure of population, was already by this date encouraging the poor of the district to invade the town in the hope of being able to serve or excite the pity of visitors, a feature unfavourably commented upon by some who visited the resort. The population by 1831 had risen to 11,333, appreciably above the present census figure.

Some improvements had, however, been made to the town by the 1820s and 30s. There were two 'spacious inns', several lodging houses providing accommodation, and two subscription reading rooms, one of which had a billiard room. The race meeting was revived, a regatta held on the lakes and deer-hunting was advertised as an attraction for sporting gentlemen. The greatest drawback to attracting visitors was still, however, the remoteness of the town. Although only 54 miles from Cork and served both by jaunting cars and a mail-coach to Tralee, English tourists taking this route had to endure an 18- to 24-hour sea crossing from Bristol. The distance from Dublin was 191 miles but with no direct mail-coach service. This deficiency was not redressed until late in the 1840s, when the completion of the Dublin to Cork railway enabled visitors to take advantage of a connecting coach at Mallow, reducing the road element of the journey to a mere 42 miles. A railway branch from Mallow reached the town in July 1853.[2]

The manufacture of souvenir woodwares commenced in Killarney in the mid-1820s, when bog oak and bog yew started to be carved for sale. Both of these woods were dug up from turf bogs near the town. Bog oak, dense black in colour and close grained, proved an excellent medium for carving, and took a fine polish. Bog yew was said to resemble rosewood. The carving of these woods was not confined to Killarney and a substantial sale of such items developed in Dublin. By tradition, the production of such souvenirs was popularised by the presentation of an elaborately carved walking stick of bog oak to George IV when he visited Ireland in 1821. The work was executed by a man called M'Guirk who obtained additional orders because of admiration for the royal walking stick. He is recorded in Dublin directories in the mid-1830s at 1, George's Hill as a bog oak manufacturer and continued to make such wares there until 1846. This success was exploited by a man called Denis Connell, who initially lived at Killarney and sold his carvings to visitors. He prospered and subsequently established a business at 10, Nassau Street, Dublin in 1845. Connell displayed a number of examples of his carving from 'bog oak found in the Lakes of Killarney' at the Great Exhibition in 1851. Already by 1849, he appears to have had a business relationship with his son-in-law, Cornelius Goggin, who is recorded at the same address and in the same trade. On Connell's retirement, the business passed to Goggin who, in 1851, had premises at 13, Nassau Street, Dublin and the 'Royal Irish Bog Oak Warehouse' at 26, Nassau Street. He claimed the patronage of Queen Victoria and was offering his wares for sale at the Pantheon Bazaar, Oxford Street, London. Goggin maintained his Killarney connection as well, however, and in 1858 was in partnership with Jeremiah Crimmin in Main Street. An advertisement of that year claimed that the business was established in 1825 and this may well be the date when Connell initiated the production of souvenir woodwares at Killarney. Pigot's directories of 1824 and 1826 fail to mention the presence of such a trade and the only woodworkers listed in the Killarney area are carpenters. Guide books, several of which were issued in the 1830s, do not mention such an industry and the conclusion must be that it was on a small scale at this date.[3]

By the late 1830s a new timber had started to be exploited. This was arbutus *(Arbutus unedo)*, a tree-shrub of Mediterranean origin, which grew profusely in the mild and damp conditions of the south-west of Ireland. The earliest reference to its use in producing souvenir wares was in 1837 when it was stated that 'a variety of useful and ornamental articles' were made from the wood for sale to tourists. In 1858, Jeremiah O'Connor was claiming to be 'the original arbutus and Irish bog oak factor' and if we assume that this claim refers to the arbutus side of the business it may well be that this commenced in the mid-1830s. Certainly, by the end of the next decade, the industry was well established and beginning to develop a reputation extending beyond the Killarney area for the quality of its work. Denis Connell, in addition to his bog oak display at the Great Exhibition of 1851, also showed 'bookstands, chess boards, card cases &c from arbutus wood, grown at the lakes of Killarney'. It is not known whether he made these particular items or merely retailed them.[4]

The most prestigious of the wares produced in Killarney were a range of cabinets, chiffoniers, Davenports, and games and loo tables, elaborately decorated with marquetry, assisted by pyrographic detail, and reflecting a full understanding of the fashionable styles current in the cabinet-making trades of the British Isles (figs. 87–90, 92, colour pls. 30–31). A feature of this furniture was the incorporation of pictures of local tourist attractions such as Muckross Abbey, Ross Castle, Glena Cottage, Innisfallen, Dunloe Castle, Killarney House and Aghadoe, each contained in an oval or circular frame. The design of these was based upon engravings contained in guide books and topographical works on the area. On some pieces, as many as 12 of these pictorial panels were used. In addition, representations of local wildlife such as the mountain eagle and deer were used, as well as the Irish harp. Borders of shamrock, ferns (abundant in the area), arbutus sprays, oak leaves, acorns, roses, holly leaves and thistle flowers provided additional decoration. Arbutus was one of the main timbers used in the construction of such furniture, and different effects could be obtained by using veneers from the root, trunk and branches.[5] Other local timbers were used such as holly, sycamore, laburnum, maple and yew. Similar items of furniture were also produced without the marquetry and a centre table, veneered in yew in triangular segments, is known stamped on the base 'Killarney'. It is interesting to speculate on where the skilled craftsmen necessary to carry out the cabinet work, turning and marquetry came from. Cork was the nearest cabinet- and furniture-making centre and of the 26 furniture exhibitors at the National Exhibition held at Cork in 1852, eleven were from the city and only seven from Dublin.[6] It has been suggested that at least some of the furniture and marquetry work was produced in Dublin by Arthur Jones, Son & Co. of 135, Stephen's Green West.[7] This firm was established by William Jones at Ormond Quay in the late eighteenth century and continued in business until 1881 when they gave up the cabinet and upholstery side to concentrate upon their estate agency and auctioneering activities. As cabinet-makers and upholsterers, they enjoyed a considerable reputation in the mid-nineteenth century, especially on the basis of an extensive suite of bog yew furniture carved with figures and devices reflecting the history and culture of Ireland. This was shown both at the Great Exhibition of 1851 and the Dublin Exhibition of 1853. Jones was a regular exhibitor of his wares, and showed a wide range of furniture in the fashionable styles of the day, but he never appears to have displayed or advertised Killarney-style marquetry pieces at such exhibitions, though Killarney manufacturers certainly did.[8]

Apart from the tables and large items of cabinet furniture, Killarney makers produced a wide range of smaller items for the souvenir trade including boxes and containers, smaller examples of the cabinet-maker's art, and turnery wares. The range of items closely parallels that produced in the Tunbridge ware trade at the same period (figs. 91, 93). In 1858, Jeremiah O'Connor, one of the leading Killarney manufacturers, was offering for sale 'Sugar and Tea Stores, Chess-boards, Work Boxes, Writing Desks, Envelope Boxes, Card Cases &c, &c'. To this list can be added bookstands, dressing-cases, backgammon boards, needle-cases, silk-winders, paper-knives, trays, and toys such as a cup and ball. These wares never appear to have been marked with the name of their maker, but they sometimes incorporate inscriptions such as 'Killarney Lakes', 'Killarney' and a date, or 'Made in the Gap of Dunloe' which provide some guidance to their age or maker. Apart from the wares in bog oak and bog yew, virtually all woodwares sold at Killarney were advertised as being manufactured from arbutus. There were, however, attempts to pass off other woods on the ignorant visitor as arbutus. One visitor in 1844 cynically remarked, 'All arbutus, save when growing, is stained birch', while a guide book of 1846 stated:

'dark olive green, and variegated reds are the prevailing colours of the arbutus; though in the shops they will assure you that every article they have is made from that tree alone.'[9]

The fame of the Killarney woodware industry as a producer of prestigious and fashionable furniture was relatively brief. It was not until the late 1840s that the town was able to produce such items, and by the 1870s the industry was already starting to decline. The maker whose products set the standard of excellence was James Egan, whose premises were 8, Main Street, at which address he is listed in the 1846 edition of *Slater's Directory*, though it has been stated that the business was established two years earlier in New Street. Egan publicised his wares not only locally, but by taking every opportunity of displaying his inlaid furniture at national and international exhibitions which included London (1851), Cork (1852), Dublin (1853), London (1862) and Dublin (1865). This publicity helped to attract an influential clientele to his business. Unfortunately, he never marked his furniture, and although all fine furniture of this type is commonly attributed to his factory, this cannot be justified. Egan was unique amongst the mid-Victorian producers in that he appears to have advertised entirely arbutus woodwares, though there is evidence of him also making and selling bog oak and bog yew items in the 1850s and early 60s. In 1870, James Egan was also proprietor of the Innisfallen Hotel.[10] His main rival was Jeremiah O'Connor whose business, originating in the bog oak souvenir trade, antedates that of Egan. His manufactory was also in Main Street and was supplemented in 1858 by a retail shop in the same street. O'Connor also produced fine arbutus furniture and a table and a Davenport exist stamped 'J. O'Connor, Arbutus & Bog Oak Manufacturer Killarney' (fig. 87). It is not known, however, whether all his furniture was so marked. He adopted the same policy of exhibiting as Egan, and his wares were on show in London (1851), Cork (1852), and Dublin (1853). As late as 1882, he displayed inlaid arbutus and carved bog oak at the Exhibition of Irish Arts and Manufactures in Dublin.[11] Another firm was established early in the history of the industry by a person called Neate, and was being operated by his widow in 1841 with the help of her daughters. She gave up the business before 1850 and moved to Dublin. It was carried on by her son-in-law, Jeremiah Crimmin, who appears to have had a close business relationship with Cornelius Goggin of Nassau Street, Dublin, a bog oak manufacturer who had formerly worked at Killarney. In 1858, the firm was advertising as Goggin & Crimmin with a factory in Main Street. They claimed prize medals at Dublin (1853), New York (1853) and Paris (1855) but these refer to exhibits entered by Goggin alone, and it is probable that the impressive list of patrons that they claimed in 1858 were equally customers of Goggin's business. Goggin appears to have maintained some trading association with Killarney earlier in the 1850s, for the bronze medal that he was awarded at the New York Exhibition was for his entry of 'Irish Bog Oak, Killarney Wood, Marble and Horse-Hair Ornaments'. The 'partnership' does not appear to have lasted for long, for at the 1862

London Exhibition Jeremiah Crimmin exhibited 'Fancy cabinet articles in bog oak &c' under his sole name, while Goggin's business continued to flourish in Dublin. As late as 1914, however, E.M. Goggin, successor to Cornelius at Nassau Street, Dublin exhibited 'arbutus wood carving' amongst other wares at the St Louis World Fair, suggesting a continuing association with the marketing of Killarney-made wares.[12] The fourth major manufacturer was James Coakley of 4, Main Street, Killarney, whose factory appears to have been established in the mid-1850s. He made and sold both arbutus and bog oak articles and displayed inlaid arbutus at both the Dublin Exhibition of 1882 and the Cork Exhibition in the following year. By the 1890s, however, he was concentrating on bog oak manufactures. The business lasted well into the twentieth century, but there is no evidence to suggest that he was a producer of furniture. Others are mentioned in nineteenth-century directories but they appear to have been stockists rather than manufacturers.[13]

The main Killarney makers were anxious that the visitors to the town should be aware of their work, and like a number of the Tunbridge ware makers of Tunbridge Wells, invited the public to inspect craftsmen at work in their factories in anticipation of the patronage that might be received in the adjacent showrooms. Tourist guides featured the factories as one of the attractions to be sampled by visitors. The word 'factory' used by most of the woodware makers must not mislead us into thinking of large-scale enterprises. Like the workshops of the main Tunbridge ware makers and many provincial cabinet-makers, the number of employees was never large. James Egan was employing a work force of 15 to 16 persons in the early 1850s. This no doubt included members of his own family, for in 1861, one of his workmen was a Thomas Egan. As James Egan was regarded as the largest and most famed of the factories, it is not unreasonable to assume that the work forces of the rival establishments were smaller, in some cases substantially so. Jeremiah O'Connor added further attractions at his factory which included an upper room where caged mountain eagles could be seen, the head of a wild deer inspected, and other curios observed. James Egan also exploited the interest in the local wild deer by identifying his workshop with the sign of the wild deer's head.[14]

The arbutus works of Killarney rapidly established a firm reputation not only in Ireland but also in other parts of the British Isles for the quality and general attractiveness of their wares, which brought the patronage of the wealthy and influential. Royal patronage was even to be bestowed on the industry. The Prince of Wales was the first important member of the Royal family to visit the town. He arrived on Saturday, 17 April 1858, and that evening viewed a special exhibition of ware organised by James Egan and Jeremiah O'Connor. The Prince showed an interest in the items and purchased from Egan's display 'a beautiful chessboard and some other small but elegantly-finished articles'. In order to dispel the idea that he was favouring only one manufacturer, he promised that on the Monday he would visit the factories generally. This he did, attending those of Jeremiah O'Connor and Jeremiah Crimmin 'in both of which his Royal Highness made some large and select purchases'. The nature of these purchases is not described but one item purchased from O'Connor must have been a fine table, as a facsimile of it was made and displayed in his workshops to attract visitors.[15] An even greater event was the visit of Queen Victoria in August 1861. The Queen was accompanied by the Prince Consort and the Prince of Wales and stayed at Killarney House as the guests of Lord and Lady Castleross. They were presumably responsible for ordering from James Egan two pieces of furniture for presentation to the Queen. One of these was a cabinet and desk of arbutus wood richly inlaid, which was fully described in the local and national press:

> *'The inlaying represents designs of some of the principal points of interest about the lakes, all exquisitely finished, each design being surrounded by wreaths of shamrocks, roses and thistles. On the lid, a representation of Glena Cottage encircled with a wreath, and around the edges a border of shamrocks. On one side of the desk is represented Ross Castle, and on the other Killarney House. On the inside of the lid is a harp encircled with a wreath of shamrock, rose and thistle. The cap is beautifully inlaid with the Royal Arms with the initials V.R. on either side. In the cabinet are five drawers on the front of which is an inlaid design. Those designs are Muckross Abbey, Ross Castle, Innisfallen, Aghadoe and Dunloe Castle each being encircled with oval panels composed of herringbone inlaying. At each angle is a representation of the rare and peculiar fern leaf which is found only on the mountains of Killarney.'*

The other item presented was a bog oak casket carved with similar views on the lid, back, front and sides, surrounded with wreaths of shamrock, rose and thistle. The lid was also adorned with the Royal arms. The work was carried out by James Egan himself and three of his workmen, Michael Fleming, Thomas Egan and James Lynch. Jeremiah O'Connor also seems to have produced a fine cabinet and table for presentation to Queen Victoria for in 1870 he was advertising that facsimiles of these could be seen at his factory. Although these pieces are no longer in the Royal collection, a desk with a cupboard base in the collection of the National Museum of Ireland corresponds to the description of that made by Egan for Queen Victoria (colour pl. 31), while the Ulster Museum has a similar item with the Royal coat of arms in marquetry on the doors. The history of this piece of furniture is unknown (fig. 88). In 1858, Goggin & Crimmin were claiming to be 'Furnishers to Her Majesty, His Royal Highness the Prince of Wales and the Irish Court'. They also claimed the Empress of the French amongst their patrons. Although, as has already been indicated, the Prince of Wales when he visited Killarney in 1858 made purchases from Jeremiah Crimmin, the other patronage must refer to the bog oak manufactures of Cornelius Goggin's Dublin establishment. As early as 1851, he was advertising himself as 'Bog Oak Carver to Her Gracious Majesty the Queen'.[16]

The larger pieces of elaborately inlaid furniture produced could

88. Arbutus cabinet decorated with marquetry, detail in pyrography, of local fauna and flora of the Killarney area and views of tourist features. The coat of arms of the United Kingdom of Great Britain and Ireland displayed on the doors. c1860. (Ulster Museum).

only find a market amongst the wealthy. They provided a useful attraction and advertisement when displayed in the factories, but it would be unlikely that the majority of visitors would wish to purchase these relatively expensive items. It was necessary, if a regular sale was to develop, that the resident aristocracy, gentry and wealthy middle-class Irish should provide much of the patronage. In finding commissions, the manufacturers of arbutus furniture were aided by a growing feeling of Irish nationalism which began to voice itself in opposition to British trade domination in manufactured goods. John Francis Maguire, Member of Parliament and Mayor of Cork, expressed this feeling when, in connection with the furniture exhibits of the 1852 Cork Exhibition, he stated:

'In no department of the whole Exhibition is the skill and taste of the Irish workman more conspicuous than in this; and yet, singularly enough, we hear of repeated instances of our gentry, and even our mercantile classes, purchasing their furniture in London and Paris.'[17]

The Killarney furniture, with its use of local floral, fauna and antiquities, and symbols of Irish nationalism, was calculated to appeal to those who desired to reverse this trend and support the products of Ireland. The proprietors of the arbutus factories were only too willing to take advantage of the rising national consciousness, and realised that the attraction of orders for such furniture would provide valuable employment in the winter months once the tourist season had ended. They therefore gave full publicity to prestigious aristocratic patronage. James Egan maintained a book in his showrooms listing the orders received and the sales of his finer wares. This was witnessed by S. Reynolds Hole, Dean of Rochester, in the late 1850s when he visited the factory:

'Here you may learn from a ledger, opening, as ledgers will, at a brilliant galaxy of noble names, which make a commoner's eyes wink, how the Right Honourable the Earl of Cash bought an elaborate table for my Lady's boudoir, and how Rear-Admiral Sir Bowline Bluff made purchase of a Backgammon board, marvellously inlaid over which I venture to surmise, has ere discoursed in stormy language, when the gout and dice have been against him. Let us tread softly and at a distance in these illustrious footsteps, and buy our meek memorials of Killarney.'[18]

By 1858, Egan was able to boast the patronage of the Earl of Clarendon, the Earl of Lanesborough, the Earl of Eglington, the Earl of Kenmare, Viscount Hill and Lady Headly, amongst others. One commission by Egan for the Earl of Eglington, probably carried out in the early 1850s, was displayed under the Earl's name at the Dublin Exhibition of 1853. This consisted of 'a loo table made in Arbutus wood from Killarney, Ladies' work table, with work box, writing stand and book stand, formed from the pillar of the table, the whole elaborately inlaid with 157,000 pieces'. Egan was not the only Irish craftsman the Earl patronised, for there was also on show a carved oak chair by Curran and Son of Lisburn. Goggin & Crimmin listed some of their patrons in an advertisement in 1858; these included the Duke of Cambridge, the Duke of Devonshire and local Killarney gentry such as the Earl of Kenmare, the Dowager Countess of Kenmare and Viscount Castleross. Some of this patronage may, however, have been in connection with Goggin's bog oak warerooms. When the Tralee to Killarney Railway was inaugurated on 19 September 1855, the Earl of Carlisle, the Lord Lieutenant, used an inlaid Killarney wheelbarrow in connection with the cutting of the first sod. With such aristocratic favours bestowed, those of lesser social stature were tempted to follow suit, such as 'a small tourist' that S. Reynolds Hole saw departing from his hotel in the morning for Connemara with a caged wild eagle, 'a large Arbutus table, ditto case of Killarney ferns and a hillock of general luggage'. The relative frequency with which Killarney furniture appears at auction sales or in collections in Britain would seem to indicate that the 'small tourist' was far from unique amongst British tourists in purchasing such items.[19]

Smaller wares, apart from being sold at the factories, were also hawked round the town by young girls and women. They haunted places where tourists were likely to assemble and were very forward in touting the wares carried in their baskets, both arbutus and bog oak souvenirs. Hole recounts an onslaught of such peddlers on passengers waiting for the departure of the Glengariff jaunting car, which was not without success, for when it did eventually start it was 'bristling with paper knives'. When the car stopped a few miles on at the Muckross Hotel to pick up passengers, another wave of sellers descended. Tourists were warned in guide books not only of the persuasive powers of these sirens but also that they would 'be expected to pay for these pretty things in proportion to the assumed length of their purse'. Even the hotels were not sacrosanct to these vendors of trinkets. The author of one guide of 1853 referred to them as:

> 'those shrewd, smiling, demure foragers, who hover, hawk-like, within the precincts of the hotels, biding their time for the "ennui-ish half hour" before dinner, or better still, that same enjoyable period after it, when satisfied appetite, and nothing-to-do-ishness, combine to open the heart and purse-strings'.

Apart from the sale in Killarney, smaller wares also enjoyed some success away from their place of manufacture. Cornelius Goggin was certainly offering Killarney arbutus ware for sale in Dublin in 1851 as part of his stock. Jeremiah Goggin, who maintained showrooms at 74, Grafton Street, Dublin between 1855 and 1901 as a bog oak ornament manufacturer, also stocked Killarney arbutus wood wares and advertised a New York address at 723, Broadway. The use of views and motifs closely identifying them with Killarney would have made some of these wares less suitable for sale outside their place of manufacture, however.[20]

From the 1870s, the Killarney arbutus ware industry entered on a path of decline. It was no sudden collapse, but a long-drawn-out twilight which extended to the final extinguishing of the industry in the mid-1950s. The reasons for this decline are similar to those that affected the Tunbridge ware industry. By the 1870s, the wealthy were less inclined to holiday in the British Isles. The railway had opened up the delights of Switzerland to the British tourist seeking mountains and lakes, with a journey little more lengthy or inconvenient than that to the south-west of Ireland. This removed much of the patronage at the top end of the market, while the souvenir trade at the other extreme faced fierce competition from cheap foreign wares. Egan's factory closed in the 1870s and although O'Connor's business managed to survive for a further decade, it appears in the final years to have been little more than a 'bog oak warehouse'. James Coakley, whose factory had been established in the mid-1850s was still producing arbutus furniture in the early 1880s but by the next decade was being described as a 'bog oak manufacturer'. He was still trading in 1905. To some extent, new businesses filled the gaps, but they were not on the same scale or even of the same nature as those of the mid-nineteenth century. Daniel O'Connell who established his business in New Street in the mid-1880s was a carver both in bog oak and arbutus but there is no evidence that he ever produced cabinet wares. One interesting enterprise did, however, follow the old tradition, though in a new location. James French established his workshops in the middle of the Gap of Dunloe, a tourist beauty spot about eight miles from Killarney town. The business was probably already well established by 1883 when it was awarded a medal at the Cork International Exhibition for an inlaid cabinet and card table. The tradition of furniture-making persisted and a visitor in 1901 noted that 'the good woman of the shop deals principally in ginger beer and arbutus wood articles, some of the latter large and elaborate. A big escritoire that she shows us is destined for New Zealand.' By this date, furniture forms were simpler in outline to conform with the revival of interest in the styles of the late Georgian period. Games tables adopted straight square section legs, and nests of tables were produced similar in style to the quartetto tables of the Sheraton period. French or his successors may have attempted to imitate the mosaic techniques used in Tunbridge ware. An arbutus wood box exists, the top decorated with a rather crude attempt to depict Muckross Abbey in mosaic with, on the back, an inscription 'MADE IN THE GAP OF DUNLOE KILLARNEY'. French also produced articles in bog oak and as the manufacturers in Killarney town gradually ceased trading he no doubt became the main source of supply for the souvenir shops of that place.[21] The practice of using young women to hawk goods round the main hotels and tourist spots appears to have died out by the 1880s.[22] French's business may well have continued until the late 1920s, for a Ward Lock guide of about this date mentioned 'French's (or Arbutus) cottage' as the limit in the Gap of Dunloe to which cars could proceed.[23]

A determined attempt to reverse the decline of local woodworking crafts was made in the mid-1890s. A Killarney inlaid arbutus wood cabinet shown at the Arts and Crafts Society of Ireland's Exhibition in Dublin in 1895 was described as 'a specimen of an old industry which shows gratifying signs of a modern revival at the same place'. This no doubt referred to the Killarney School of Arts and Crafts opened in that year. It originated some years earlier when the Countess of Kenmare formed a class for drawing and wood carving, but in 1895 the Earl of Kenmare gave a house, which was fitted up as a permanent school and 'a master engaged from London'. A German carver, Anton Lang, from Oberammergau was invited over by Lady Kenmare and stayed for ten months. Amongst his pupils was a Daniel O'Connor. The equipment donated to the Killarney School of Arts and Crafts included a turning lathe and a circular saw. By 1897, 12 men and boys were regularly employed at the school and evening classes attracted an enrollment of 20.[24] Goods produced were exhibited and marketed under the name 'The Killarney Furniture Industries', and substantial commissions were already being received by 1897. A carved crucifix was displayed in the arts and crafts section of the Irish International Exhibition,

89. *Work-table on octagonal stem with curvilinear base supported on claws. Marquetry with pyrographic detail, the top featuring an Irish harp with trails of shamrock, thistle and rose. c1870. (Sotheby's).*

90. *Arbutus centre table decorated with parquetry, detail in pyrography. The centre views on the top are of Muckross Abbey, Glena Cottage and other local views are depicted around the edge of the table and on the base. Sprays of shamrock, thistle and rose and oak leaves and ferns are used on the top and base. c1860. (Sotheby's).*

Dublin in 1907 and at the St Louis World Fair of 1914 a carved oak bedstead, two chairs, a settee, gilt candlesticks and sconces and a fire screen and mirror. Its life, however, appears to have been short, as the school closed soon after. It appears to have concerned itself mainly with the craft of carving and does not appear to have involved itself with inlaid woodwares. A green letter-box and casket, the latter the property of the Earl of Mayo, were, however, illustrated in 1901 and do seem to indicate some interest in small cabinet wares.[25]

The business of James French was taken over by John Kiernan who maintained a similar type of business at Arbutus Cottage in the Gap of Dunloe until the industry's final expiration. Large pieces of furniture were produced and the inlay pictures of Muckross Abbey, Ross Castle and Glena Cottage continued to feature together with shamrock trails and other leaf borders. The views are, however, often less detailed and appear almost as silhouettes, the dark arbutus wood and the white holly providing a striking contrast which makes such work recognisable from that of the nineteenth century. The trails of shamrock, thistle and rose which feature on mid-nineteenth-century items symbolising the union of Ireland with England and Scotland, were less used by the end of the nineteenth century and disappeared entirely soon after. Trails of

91. *Souvenir gift wares of the type sold at Killarney. The small writing desk, box and ends and base of the book rack feature views of Muckross Abbey, Ross Castle and Glena Cottage in marquetry, the detail in pyrography. Late nineteenth to early twentieth century.*
Desk w:34cm d:26.5cm h:10cm, book rack w:37cm, book h:17.5cm w:12.5cm, box 16cm sq h:6cm. (Muckross House, Killarney).

92. *Games table with swivel top, when open displaying provision for backgammon, chess and cribbage. Decorated with marquetry and pyrography view of Muckross Abbey on top and bandings of fern and ivy foliage. Made in 1929 by John Donoghue at a cost of £60 for Fr Walsh, curate of Tuogh. w:83cm d:45cm h:77cm. (Muckross House, Killarney).*

oak, ivy, shamrock and ferns continued in popularity. An inlaid games table of this period, now at Muckross House, was made in 1929 at a cost of £60 for Father Walsh, a curate in Tuogh. This table, which has provision for backgammon, chess and cribbage, was made by John Donoghue, a craftsman employed by the Kiernan family (fig. 92). The work force there in 1946 consisted of John Kiernan, his son John Peter, his daughter Eleanor and John

30a. *Games table, arbutus and other woods. The top with a central marquetry and pyrographic panel of Muckross Abbey. Additional views of Glena Cottage and other places of interest in the Killarney area. Marquetry trails of shamrock, ferns etc. Centre front the Union motif of a rose, thistle and shamrock on a single stem. c1860. h:72.5cm 1:59.9cm w:39.2cm. (Portsmouth Museum & Art Gallery).*

30b. *Table with top open displaying facilities for the games of chess, backgammon, cribbage etc. 1:78.7cm.*

31a. *Desk and cabinet veneered in arbutus and other woods made by James Egan and presented to Queen Victoria on her visit to Killarney in 1861 (see p. 182). The Cabinet bears a small ivory tablet inscribed "Arbutus Wood Cabinet especially manufactured for the Queen's Boudoir. On the occasion of Her Majesty's visit to Killarney and afterwards Presented by Viscount Castlerosse to the Poor of that District. Much of the Lake Scenery is Depicted throughout the inlaying." h:115cm w:84cm d:59.5cm. (National Museum of Ireland).*

31b. *Cabinet open displaying the nest of drawers behind the doors. These are decorated with views of Muckross Abbey, Aghadoe, Ross Castle, Innisfallen and Dunloe Castle. The desk top raised to reveal the fitted interior.*

Donoghue, who by this year was said to have had 60 years experience in the industry. It was in 1946 that the last major piece of furniture was produced, a folding card table. Thereafter the trade was solely in smaller pieces such as boxes, trays and portable writing desks, inlaid in a similar manner to the furniture. Disaster struck in 1952. The workshop was gutted by fire and its contents destroyed, and soon after John Donoghue, whose long experience was a vital asset to the firm, died. Eleanor Kiernan married and emigrated to England and John Peter also died. The business could hardly be expected to survive such blows and probably expired completely in 1955 or soon after, and Arbutus Cottage and the gutted workshops now stand derelict. As with the Tunbridge ware industry, families continued from one generation to the next in the trade. The Kiernan family could count four generations in the wood-carving and inlaying trades.[26]

The Killarney industry provides some interesting parallels with

93. *Three-drawer cabinet of arbutus and other woods, the hinged top, sides and doors decorated with marquetry and pyrography panels depicting Glena Cottage, Muckross Abbey, an Irish wolfhound and tower and trails of shamrock and oak leaves. Early twentieth century. w:29cm. (Sotheby's).*

that of Tunbridge Wells, both in the span of operation and in its products. Both were set up in response to an influx of visitors to a holiday resort, and produced their finest wares around the middle of the nineteenth century. Both were in decline by the 1870s. The Tunbridge ware industry had been established for a century and a half before that of Killarney, and it would therefore seem fruitful to examine whether the English industry influenced that of south-west Ireland. In one sense the wares are fundamentally different. Killarney seldom used mosaic and was content to adopt conventional cross-grain marquetry, with much of the detail scorched into the wood. In design, however, it is not unreasonable to suggest that Tunbridge ware, with its use of marquetry views and borders of leaves and flowers, may well have influenced the Killarney patterns. In Tunbridge ware, these elements were being developed in the late 1830s and early 1840s whereas there is no evidence of pictorial arbutus wares existing this early.

94. *Tunbridge ware bookstand with tessellated mosaic views of Muckross Abbey (left) and Ross Castle (right) set in a rosewood ground. Floral and geometrical mosaic borders. Attributable to Henry Hollamby, Tunbridge Wells. w:36cm h:28cm. c1870. (Muckross House, Killarney).*

Contemporary commentators were fully aware of the resemblance of the Killarney products to those of the Tunbridge Wells area and the compiler of the entry for Killarney in *Slater's Directory* of 1856 commented that 'an important branch of business has originated here, in the manufacture of fancy articles similar to the Tunbridge-ware goods'. It has been well known for some time that a pictorial Tunbridge ware mosaic block of Muckross Abbey existed, for it is commonly found on workboxes, tea caddies, etc. as frequently as some of the local Kentish views. Although most of the objects decorated with this view must have been sold in England on the basis of its attractiveness as a representation of a ruined abbey, it is highly likely that it was initially produced to meet the needs of a Killarney retailer. This has been confirmed by the location in Ireland of two Tunbridge ware reading stands, both of which incorporate this common Muckross Abbey view alongside a much rarer mosaic representation of Ross Castle (fig. 94). The history of these two items suggests that they were bought in Ireland.[27] Neither piece carries a maker's label but these are subjects recorded as being produced by Henry Hollamby in 1882 though their first use was considerably earlier. A workbox decorated with the Muckross block is known bearing a label indicating that it was given as a present on 6 June 1862. A writing desk and glove box exist decorated with a Tunbridge ware view of Glena Cottage near Killarney which in style appear to be the work of Henry Hollamby who was probably the maker of a small rosewood box inscribed in Tunbridge mosaic 'Lakes of Killarney'.[28] Boxes with English views also appear to have been sold in Killarney and one with the Cloisters, Battle Abbey bears the inscription 'From a Grant to Mrs Miller, Killarney Lakes 1861' placed there by the seller. Hollamby not only supplied complete items of Tunbridge ware for sale in Killarney but was also prepared to offer veneers for use by Killarney makers. Boxes of obvious Killarney manufacture and decoration have been noted incorporating the Tunbridge block of Muckross Abbey (colour pl. 28) and also mosaic lettering 'Killarney Lakes'. A Tunbridge ware needle case is also known, with a photographic view of Muckross Abbey on one face. The use of a vandyke border has been noted on a Killarney workbox, the top decorated with a rather crude and non-typical marquetry depiction of Ross Castle. This may be an early production and point again to the Tunbridge ware industry influencing that of Killarney.

It might seem unlikely that Killarney ware should be mistaken for the products of the Tunbridge Wells industry in view of the fundamentally different techniques used in their decoration, and the use of Irish motifs and symbols in the former, yet this has, however, happened and has been recorded in print. An article which appeared in *Country Life* in 1948 identified a Killarney games table of late nineteenth- or early twentieth-century date showing views of Ross Castle and Glena Cottage as well as shamrock and fern borders, as a Tunbridge ware table made about 1845 by Fenner & Co. for the Prince Consort.[29] Unfortunately, both photograph and text were repeated by the Pintos in their book on Tunbridge ware,[30] and this has misled at least one subsequent writer.

Chapter 14

SPA WOODWARES

Thomas Benge Burr, the first historian of Tunbridge Wells, wrote in 1766 about the commercial life of the town that:

> 'The trade … is very similar to that of the Spa in Germany, and chiefly consists in a variety of toys in wood, such as tea-chests, dressing-boxes, snuff-boxes, punch-ladles and numerous other little articles of the same kind.'

Taking their cue from this source, a considerable number of other Tunbridge Wells guide books and accounts as late as 1840 repeated this comparison.[1] Those who are familiar solely with Tunbridge wares of the Victorian period and later, which are veneered and often decorated with tessellated mosaic, will find no warrant for such a comparison, and it is probably for this reason that writers and collectors of these items have largely ignored the Spa industry, whose wares are little appreciated in Britain. Now that the earlier Tunbridge wares are being recognised and studied, however, the truth of Burr's assertion is being increasingly recognised. Very little is known about mid-eighteenth-century Tunbridge wares but those of the end of the century and the first 30 years or so of the nineteenth century are seen to have numerous parallels in form and decoration.

The town of Spa is situated in the wooded terrain of the Ardennes in southern Belgium, close to the borders of both Germany and Luxemburg. The chalybeate springs of the area were certainly attracting visitors as early as the sixteenth century and received publicity from the writings of a Dr Lymborth who in 1560 published simultaneously in Latin, French, Spanish and Italian a work entitled *The Acid Springs of the Ardennes Forest*. Spa's situation on the borders of Germany and France ensured at an early date an international clientele, and it was considered of sufficient importance as a centre of health and recreation that both sides in the Thirty Years War scrupulously respected its neutrality. Its development as a resort came at an opportune moment, for the iron smelting industry of the region, based on a plentiful supply of wood for conversion to charcoal and local ores, had entered a period of decline by the early seventeenth century. The international fame of Spa was such that, when after the Restoration of Charles II in 1660 similar towns were popularised in Britain, they adopted its name to describe and advertise their health-giving waters.[2]

The arrival of fashionable visitors at Spa provided opportunities for the sale of gifts and souvenirs, and local craftsmen were not slow to realise this. The heavily forested region provided a valuable resource from which such wares could be produced. The first product appears to have been walking sticks, a practical necessity because of the uneven paths and streets, the hilly terrain and the distance to walk to the spring sites. The makers of these long sticks with a large oval knob at the top were known as *bourdoniers*, a word closely resembling the Italian *bordoni*, the Venetian makers of staves for pilgrims embarking for the Holy Land. It became the custom for the magistrates of the town to present elaborately finished examples to distinguished visitors, and the art of decorating these in the fashionable styles of the day was the basis from which the production of a wide range of other objects, mainly of wood, was developed to tempt the visitor.[3]

Souvenir wares consisted in the main of either decorative boxes or turnery items including small bowls, brushes, and bellows to remove excess hair powder. Dr Edmund Nessel, who in 1699 published his work *Traité des Eaux de Spa*, has left a full account of the sophisticated wares that were on offer by the end of the seventeenth century. These were decorated with painted designs, including imitations of the fashionable oriental lacquer wares being brought to Europe in increasing quantities from China and Japan by the Dutch and other East India Companies, and at that time at the height of their popularity in Western Europe. Nessel describes wares *à la façon des Indes*, some having raised work, in a wide range of colours and embellished with gilding (fig. 94). By the end of the century, Spa was producing toilet boxes in lacquer, the interior filled with yet further boxes decorated in the same style, an arrangement continued through into the eighteenth century and very characteristic of the finer pieces produced in the town. Spa enjoyed an international reputation for the quality of its lacquer wares, not only because of the skill of the decorators, but also the finish imparted by the specially compounded Spa varnish. Of all the craftsmen, the most renowned was Gérard Dagly (1657–1726) to whom is attributed the discovery of this varnish. Most of Dagly's work was, however, carried out away from Spa, for in 1687 he was appointed Kammerkünstler (official court artist) to Fredrich Wilhelm, the Elector of Brandenburg, and for nearly a quarter of a century worked in Berlin for the Prussian court. He earned a reputation as the most talented japanner in Europe. Other members of the Dagly family probably continued at Spa, for Barton Pöllnitz writing in 1729 mentions Dagly at the White Pigeon as the maker of the best varnish.[4]

Another technique utilised by the souvenir industry of Spa in the late seventeenth century was inlay. Mother-of-pearl was frequently inlaid in painted boxes and other objects and was often cut and engraved in the form of flower heads. Parts of these might be tinted

95. *Box with domed top jappaned in green and inlaid with mother-of-pearl which has been engraved and coloured to form flower heads and cornucopia. Central medallion engraved with a rural scene. Spa. c1680. w:31.5cm d:23.5cm. (Musée de Spa).*

in various colours (fig. 95). The adoption of these floral subjects was probably an acknowledgement of the popularity of such decoration on Dutch and Dutch-inspired marquetry furniture. Other inlays, sometimes found in combination with mother-of-pearl, were ivory, tortoiseshell, pewter, copper and silver. Apart from floral designs, men, animals, insects, cornucopia and foliage subjects were imitated. The use of tortoiseshell and metal inlays was being popularised at this period in Western European furniture design by the work of Louis XIV's royal cabinet-maker André Charles Boulle, and imitated to some degree in England by Gerreit Jensen (fl. 1680–1715) who was employed by Charles II and his successors. The leading maker of these wares at Spa appears to have been Lambert Xhrouet, whose skill in engraving mother-of-pearl was mentioned by Nessel in 1699. Xhrouet's fame was sufficient for him to attract a visit to his workshops by King Gustavus III of Sweden. He was still working in mother-of-pearl in 1734, when his skill was commented upon by the anonymous author of the work

96. *Toilet box japanned in green displaying a rural scene peopled with figures of shepherds and shepherdesses. A cartouche on the top contains the inscription 'VINCENT ROUSSEAU FECIT A SPA'. Spa. c1720. (Victoria & Albert Museum).*

Amusements des Eaux de Spa. In December 1751 another member of the Xhrouet family was praised for his craftsmanship in using tortoiseshell and the painting of snuff boxes.[5]

In the eighteenth century Spa was at the height of its popularity as a health and pleasure resort for the fashionable of Europe. In this respect, it conformed to the pattern to be found in other European spas including Bath and Tunbridge Wells in England. Furthermore, it was not to suffer the same degree of competition from the vogue for sea bathing which increasingly siphoned off the younger and more lively society from the English spas in the second half of the century. One British visitor in 1771 could declare 'Spa has been much increased in building and company since the year 1763, and is of all others the most delightful spot for its natural beauties and its sound habits'. The international clientele of the spa was noted with rather a jaundiced anglophile eye:

> 'Spa collects together from nine hundred to a thousand of all descriptions and characters; a motley crew of crowned heads; bishops

both temporal; and spiritual, barons and boutiquiers, either for the purpose of health from the different springs or pleasure or profit.'

Visitors certainly included the 'crowned heads' of Europe, and it was the visit of Peter the Great of Russia early in the century that had greatly helped to popularise the resort. Apart from the royalty, aristocracy and nobility of Europe, the town attracted Europe's leading politicians, philosophers, writers and artists. A spate of new building occurred to provide hotels and lodgings, as well as places of public entertainment such as a theatre, assembly rooms and parades for this society. The fashions and habits of Paris society were adopted, and gambling played an important role. The faro table, one of the greatest attractions, was farmed by a company of bankers from the Bishop of Liège, while the introduction of horse-racing by the Duke of Lauzum in 1773 provided an additional outlet for gambling. As at other European resorts, a regular routine developed to occupy waking hours fully, which the company was expected to observe. One British visitor detailed the daily round:

'The amusements are fully sufficient for every hour of the day, what with making the tour of the springs in the morning, drinking, or seeing others drink, it is all the same, music and rouge et noir, or roulette, at noon, riding or driving until four, dining, going to the play, the rooms and the ball at night, you may pass the day tolerably.'

Part of the round was to visit the shops selling the fashionable souvenir specialities of the town. Here could be bought articles needed for the full enjoyment of the spa life, including the card and game boxes to satisfy a society eager for games of chance (fig. 97). The prizes for private lotteries could be acquired, and Baron Pöllnitz writing in 1729 recounts how 'toys' such as pin boxes, scissor and tweezer cases, necklaces, work-baskets and a complete set of toilette boxes were bought for this purpose. Presents for relatives and friends could be purchased and the range of attractive designs could be personalised for aristocratic clients by the addition of their coats of arms or cyphers.[6]

Two items made at Spa and associated with the use of the waters do not appear to have been produced in connection with the English spas. The first of those was the *bergamote* or *orangette*. This was a container for sweetmeats, herbs or spices such as aniseed, fennel, ginger or orange peel, which could be taken to counteract the unpleasant taste of the chalybeate waters. Initially these were produced from two half orange skins that were reversed, hardened, shaped in a mould, decorated and varnished. The other aid was a dial to record the number of glasses of water consumed. These were usually turned in ivory with a mother-of-pearl pointer and a scale reading up to 16 or 20 glasses. They were worn by ladies on their belts and by men in the button holes of their suits (colour pl. 33).[7]

In the late seventeenth century Spa had been noted for its boxes and other wares finished in imitation of oriental lacquer and inlaid with mother-of-pearl or metal. These wares remained popular for the first few decades of the eighteenth century also, but the technique of inlaying was on the wane by the 1730s. Oriental

97. *Whitewood card box decorated with polychrome chinoiserie scene on a yellow ground. The interior contains four smaller boxes similarly decorated and ivory counters and tokens. Spa. c1700. w:19cm d:14.5cm h:4.5cm. (Musée de Spa).*

subjects underwent some revival in the mid-eighteenth century as this style echoed the spirit of whimsy to be found in the prevalent rococo style. A much-increased range of objects was produced at Spa in the eighteenth century extending from small items such as a quadrille and toilette boxes, watch cases, desert trays and snuff boxes to pieces of furniture including fancy tables, hanging corner cupboards, clock cases and candlesticks. The main trade was in the smaller wares produced by family businesses and small workshops. Baron Pöllnitz noted that 'as these knick-knacks are the only things manufactured at Spa everybody works at this business that does not let lodgings, we went to a dozen of these shops'. Wares produced at Spa also sold at the less fashionable spa of Aix-la-Chapelle (Aachen).[8]

New styles of decoration developed in the eighteenth century to satisfy fashionable taste. The art of drawing with Indian ink on boxes became popular. In the early part of the eighteenth century subjects were taken from popular artists of the period such as François Boucher and depicted figures of men, women and children in romanticised landscapes. Frames of acanthus fronds were often reproduced in gilt work. A wide range of colours were used to paint the ground on such boxes. One artist who specialised in such pastoral scenes was Vincent Rousseau (fl. 1676–1720) who painted on his boxes a cartouche inscribed either 'Rousseau Pinxit Spa' or 'Vincent Rousseau Fecit à Spa' (fig. 96). Other boxes in this style had merely the lids decorated with ink drawings and polychrome decoration, the sides being left undecorated showing the natural plane or maple wood commonly used in the Spa industry for box construction. Several coats of varnish were applied to protect the decoration and enhance the appearance.[9]

Romanticised pastoral vistas became less popular in the second half of the eighteenth century and were replaced by views of the town of Spa and the surrounding countryside which were used to decorate wares. This style of work appears to have been inspired by the Spa artist Remacle Leloup (1711–49) who produced illustrations for the book *Les Délices du Pays de Liège*. This may have been the Leloup who in 1729 was recommended by Baron Pöllnitz for 'landskips and perspective'. More important was his son, Antoine, who was born at Spa in 1730. He was in his turn responsible for illustrating J-P. de Limbourg's work, *Noveaux Amusements de Spa* (1763) and contributed three engravings to the second edition of 1782. The Spa Museum has in its care no fewer than 120 small circular ink drawings featuring places in the town and the surrounding area executed on vellum by Antoine Leloup. These

98. *Oval whitewood tea caddy, decorated with ink drawings of the spring sites in the vicinity of Spa on a yellow ground. Gilt foliage borders on sides and top. w:15cm d:9.5cm h:10.5cm. Spa. c1775. (Victoria & Albert Museum).*

closely resemble in style and form the roundels used to decorate late eighteenth- and early nineteenth-century Spa boxes and other wares. In many cases the view is identified. The most popular views were the main spring sites such as La Géronstère and La Sauvenière, but Le Vaux Hall, Le Parc des Sept Heures and La Cascade de Coo were amongst others featured. Rectangular drawings in ink on paper or parchment, based in some cases on engravings sold in the town, were also used (figs. 98, 99). Boxes to which these views were attached were painted, the ground colour being often a pinkish-red or apple-green, though in some cases a marbled background was simulated. A number of examples are known where the earlier technique of drawing in Indian ink directly on to the wood was adopted, both the sides and the top being so decorated. Some turnery wares, such as skein-winders, were also decorated with such views. Colour was not used on the drawings themselves. Where a coloured view was required, the scene was painted directly on to the lids of boxes, the sides and borders being left undecorated, the natural wood being merely polished.[10]

Although much of the mother-of-pearl inlay work of the late seventeenth and early eighteenth centuries had utilised floral subjects, the popularity of this form of decorative motif was to wane from c1720. Flower painting took a minor role, merely being used for the decoration of the sides of boxes and orangettes. Such subjects did, however, return to popularity again at about 1770, paralleling their widespread adoption in European ceramics,

99. *Rectangular box painted in green and decorated with ink drawings of Spa locations (Le Tonnelet, La Géronstère, Le Vaux Hall) within pink rectangles. The top is decorated with a large medallion of figures in a rural setting. Spa. c1790. (Victoria & Albert Museum).*

enamels and japanned metal wares of the same period. Delicate polychromatic sprays of flowers of various species in their natural tints sometimes accompanied by brightly coloured butterflies, were much in vogue in the last years of the eighteenth century. About the same date, classical subjects gained a renewed impetus from the spirit of neo-classicism, and reflected the growing appreciation of Greek decorative art. Classical legend and literature had exercised some influence before this period and in 1729 Baron Pöllnitz described a table decorated with 'fourteen pictures out of Ovid's *Metamorphoses*'. Although legend still provided some of the subjects used in the late eighteenth century, many derived directly from classical antiquities and Greek vase painting. Penwork with backgrounds in dense Indian ink are most characteristic of the decoration of such wares. Boxes of this period, true to their neo-classical style, are mostly of simple rectangular shape, eschewing the elaborate curvature of some items produced in the mid-eighteenth century under rococo influence. The early nineteenth century saw the adoption, in common with other European nations, of shapes based on ancient sarcophagi, which were found to be very convenient for workboxes and tea caddies.[11]

Spa wares of the late eighteenth and early nineteenth centuries have a number of points of resemblance with Tunbridge wares of the same period. The use of topographical views, flower painting, the fondness for classical subjects, displays of cards on games boxes, and the use of penwork are all common to the two industries. Box shapes are also similar, and they were fitted for similar purposes, for cards, writing materials, sewing equipment or the storage of tea. Both industries produced small painted turnery wares. There are, of course, differences, such as the types of timber employed, plane, sycamore and maple being the most favoured woods at Spa, and there are numerous small variations in the style and technique of decoration. It would seem unlikely that the Tunbridge Wells industry was in close contact with Spa makers. There is no evidence of workers from Tunbridge Wells training at Spa or workers from the Belgian town settling in Kent. English visitors to Spa would, however, provide a line of communication through which ideas could filter back to Britain, though London makers may have been kept better-informed than those at Tunbridge Wells. The international reputation of Spa would have made its fashions and manufactures of interest to all spa frequenters and tradesmen.

Furthermore, Spa workers were prepared to disseminate their skills. The work of Gérard Dagly for the Prussian court has already been mentioned, but he was not alone in settling elsewhere to practise. The fame of Spa workers made them attractive to rulers seeking to establish royal manufactories or new industries. Renier Roidkin (fl. 1722–41) entered the service of Clemens August, Elector of Cologne and in 1763 the Margrave of Beyreuth was employing one of the Xhrouets at his residence. It was a Spa turner, Lambert Xhrouet, who taught Emperor Francis I the art, at a time when turning found favour amongst the royalty and gentry of Europe as a genteel hobby. Other examples could be cited of the way in which the Spa industry helped to fertilise the decorative arts of Western Europe in the eighteenth century.[12]

Of greater relevance perhaps to Britain was the part played by Spa workers in the establishment and popularisation of the souvenir woodware industry in Scotland. Lord Gardenstone, a Scottish law lord with estates in the Laurencekirk area, when travelling on the Continent in 1787, visited the lacquer workshops established at Chantilly by the Duc de Bourbon Condé. He was impressed by what he saw and started to formulate a plan to establish on his estates an industry producing and decorating snuff boxes and other wooden wares to provide local employment. At Spa he found similar wares being produced and set about finding an experienced craftsman willing to live in Scotland, and practise his skills there, and teach them to others. His choice fell on Vincent Brixhe who was born in Spa in 1756 and was 'bred to all branches of the art, particularly eminent for painting flower pieces, and imitations of marble chaffers'. He was said to have trained with 'Monsieur de Lou' (Antoine Leloup?) for twenty years. Brixhe was to receive £30 for the three years he was to stay in Scotland and five guineas (£5.25) for each apprentice he agreed to teach. All materials were to be supplied by Lord Gardenstone who was to be responsible for the sale of the items produced. After the three-year period Brixhe might trade on his own behalf if he wished to, and was to receive a house free of rent. In 1791, when the three-year period ended, Brixhe took advantage of this offer, and was assisted by another Spa worker, H. Henrard, who later elected to return home. The snuff boxes were to be produced by a local joiner, Charles Stiven. From this beginning, there developed a substantial industry with additional centres of production at Crumnock and Mauchline in Ayrshire. Early wares produced by the Scottish industry have a considerable resemblance in the style of decoration and the subjects chosen for illustration, to those of the Spa industry. Even in the materials used for snuff-box construction, plane and maple, similar woods were used to those employed at Spa. The main product of the Scottish industry in the first 30 years of its existence were snuff boxes and in this it did not compete significantly with the Tunbridge wares of southern England. The product range gradually widened however, and in the nineteenth century the development of the tartan-decorated (from c1840) and transfer-printed sycamore wares decorated with views (from c1850) helped greatly to increase the scale of the production.[13]

The last decade of the eighteenth century and the beginning of the nineteenth seriously affected the trade of Spa. The Revolution in France cut off many of the fashionable visitors from the resort, and this was followed within less than three years by a series of wars that were to plunge Europe into a state of uncertainty for over two decades. In the intervals between the periods of direct conflict trade continued, and to some extent the Napoleonic aristocracy replaced that of the Ancien Régime as visitors. Spa craftsmen adapted to the changed political situation, one entrepreneur even marketing a statuette of the Emperor Napoleon with a carved ivory dial on the plinth to record the consumption of chalybeate water. But it was not only the war that affected the trade of the town, for natural disaster struck also. In 1807 after a drought of three months duration, the forests around the town were devastated by fires. This was followed almost immediately by flood. The woodlands had, however, recovered sufficiently by the end of the war for society to be once more attracted, and in 1816 the town received 706 visitors consisting of Germans, Dutch, French, Poles, Russians and after a considerable absence, the British once again. Spa was never quite able to recover the glory of its fashionable zenith in the previous century, however, but for several decades was to enjoy a modest prosperity which continued to support the woodware industry.[14]

The fortunes of the industry at Spa after 1815 closely resemble that of Tunbridge Wells. Up to the 1870s, there was an air of continuing prosperity and in 1867, 130 craftsmen and artists of both sexes were still employed in the industry. As late as 1878, 15 firms were still selling wares. This suggests an industry over twice the size of that of the Tunbridge Wells area at the same period. Spa firms still produced wares for sale at Aix-la-Chapelle and surrounding towns but also sought to compensate for any local diminuition of trade by widening their markets. International exhibitions were used to publicise the wares of the industry and five Spa firms exhibited at the Great Exhibition in London in 1851, namely Henri-Joseph Jérin, Henri Bruno, Emile & Louis Mission, Jonas-Etienne Marin and Jean Massardo. A wide range of decorative tables, work, stationery and handkerchief boxes, baskets, desks and cigar cases were on display, decorated with painted floral designs, landscapes, including local Spa views, and other subjects. One of Mission's workboxes was painted with a representation of a bullfight while Massardo used the artist Créhay to decorate two large workboxes with subjects entitled 'The Indecision' and 'The Reconciliation'. Two other artists, Henrad and Rankin, were also responsible for decorating wares displayed by Massardo. Prices ranged from five guineas (£5.25) for large workboxes to as little as 2s (10p) for the smaller netting boxes. Marin was awarded a prize medal for one of his exhibits and E. & L. Mission an honourable mention. Commercially, their wares probably met with limited success in the English market, for no Spa makers exhibited at the 1862 Exhibition. As late as 1865, however, Rener made a bold attempt to export his wares with some success and others followed his lead. Yet, a rapid decline set in by the 1880s with the number of producers dwindling to eight in 1888, and of these about half had disappeared by the end of the century. Albin Body, the historian of the industry, writing in 1898, declared it little more than 'a sweet memory of the past'.[15]

The wares of the first half of the nineteenth century were in the main decorated with paintings which covered the full extent of the tops of boxes. Many of these were of local scenes, buildings and natural features painted in the romantic taste of the day. Also in the same vein were the hunting scenes, animals and children which displayed all the sentimentality that 'Victorian' patrons admired. Flower decoration was still practised but the delicate sprays of the late eighteenth century had now in most cases developed into profuse and robust displays of blossoms in vivid colours (fig. 100b). Some chinoiserie designs and subjects reappeared and Marin displayed some of these at the 1851 Exhibition. G.J. Créhay (1816–97), G.A. Créhay (1844–1937), Hubert Henrard (1816–98), Alfred Ledin (1846–1913), Victor Renson (fl. 1865), H. Hanse, Henri Deprez, D. Fassotte, Aristide Mission, H. Bronfert and P. Reigler are some of the artists whose signatures appear on work of this period. It is not uncommon to find nineteenth-century Spa wares signed by the decorating artist. Although most boxes were still of simple rectangular shape, there was a growing trend towards the reintroduction of some of the elaborately-shaped forms popular in the mid-eighteenth century. Although styles changed to some degree, the industry in the nineteenth century showed little of the innovative skill of the century before in the development of new wares, designs and techniques. One minor innovation was the discovery that wood immersed in chalybeate water will shade to a delicate grey colour, which formed a pleasing background to flower painting. This process was widely used in the industry by the 1850s and introduced into the Tunbridge ware industry from Spa in about 1860. By the middle of the nineteenth century, the industry was increasingly producing bourgeois art for a bourgeois market of a fickle and uncertain nature.[16]

100a. Whitewood sewing box, the top painted with a scene depicting a man and a dog, the interior painted with various flowers in bright polychrome. Spa. c1860. (Victoria & Albert Museum).

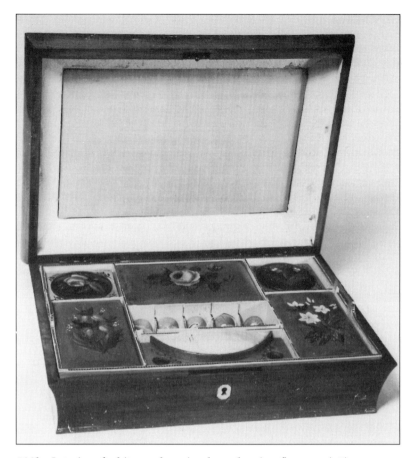

100b. *Interior of whitewood sewing box, showing flower painting on compartments.*

At the commencement of the twentieth century, the industry seemed set to expire within a few years, yet surprisingly it has managed to survive. It has even, at times, shown some modest expansion. By 1905, the number of firms selling Spa wares had risen to seven and in the early 1920s one maker, Van Sompel, tried unsuccessfully to produce on a factory scale. Despite all setbacks, the industry managed to struggle on and the wares are still produced in the town, even though the craftsmen working today consist of only two box-makers, one turner and two or three decorators. Modern pieces in the main follow traditional designs displaying floral subjects painted on natural wood (often stained grey). An attempt was made in 1970 by the Belgian artists, Jean Rets and Delahauf, to induce the Spa craftsmen to introduce contemporary abstract designs into their work, but their efforts found little favour and traditional styles still prevail.[17]

32. *Fine quality Sorrento marquetry writing desk on cabriole legs. The floral work and the peasant figures and scenes from rural life carried out in conventional cross-grain marquetry are characteristic of the work of the industry in the late nineteenth century. The writing surface bears the marquetry inscription "M. Grandville à Sorrento" and depicts the medals awarded at international exhibitions for this maker's work. c1870. (Sandro and Alma Fiorentino).*

33. (Above left) Top and bottom left: *Two sweetmeat boxes for sugared fruits or aniseed known as ''orangettes'' or ''bergamotes''. Orange peel reversed, shaped and decorated with paint.* Top: *cylindrical, yellow ground with representations in red, green and gold of two hearts, a bird and trophies, inscribed ''Je rend le mérite à l'amour''. dia:6.5cm h:2.5cm.* Left: *shaped like a soup tureen with floral decoration in red and green on a yellow ground. dia:5.5cm h:3.5cm.* Bottom right: *ivory engraved counter for recording the number of glasses of Spa water consumed, inscribed on the dial ''SES EAUX MINERALES SONT SANS EGALES''. dia:5cm. All second half of the eighteenth century (Musée de Spa).*

34. (Above right) *Games box for pêle-mêle and quadrille. The top decorated with a display of playing cards, music, landscapes etc. The interior contains three gaming boxes, a brush and a looking glass. Directoire period (1797–99). w:19.5cm d:14.5cm h:6.5cm. (Musée de Spa).*

35. *Mauchline ware turned spill vase constructed from two contrasting woods. This type of construction is unusual in Mauchline ware. Vases of this type have been wrongly identified as Tunbridge ware (Pinto plate 11). Tunbridge inlaid turnery uses a wider range of woods. The black transfer printed views of Edinburgh Castle and Holyrood Palace used on this piece are of typical Mauchline form. c1900. h:28cm.*

Chapter 15

SORRENTO WOODWARES

The art of working in mosaic is most familiar to the British through floors and wall decoration of Roman craftsmanship. It is therefore natural that when the same technique is used in wood an Italian origin should be sought. The nearest resemblance to the Tunbridge wares executed in Britain is in the mosaic woodwares produced in and around Sorrento in southern Italy. Inexperienced collectors could confuse the two, as similar techniques of construction have been used at times. The traditional date for the establishment of the industry at Sorrento is 1827, and the nearness of this date to the introduction of the tessellated mosaic techniques at Tunbridge Wells has led to the assertion that it was from Sorrento that the art of mosaic may have been learned. That the Tunbridge Wells industry owes its techniques to that of Sorrento or even directly to a Mediterranean source must, however, be strongly doubted. Not only is there absolutely no evidence of the existence of foreign proprietors or craftsmen in the Tunbridge Wells industry, but the use of tessellated mosaic wood techniques for souvenir woodwares in Italy is not known until at least 20 years after their introduction into Tunbridge Wells. In the case of the Sorrento industry the widespread use of tessellated mosaic appears to have developed later still.[1]

The town of Sorrento is situated on a promontory 16 miles south-east of Naples and close to the sites of Pompeii and Herculaneum, whose excavation had by the first half of the nineteenth century been publicised by an international literature of some magnitude. It was probably the increased flow of visitors, many foreign, to the area that prompted the development of the Sorrento woodware industry from the mid-1820s, though the art of marquetry was already flourishing in southern Italy well before this period. The expansion of the industry in decorative woodwares at Sorrento owes much in its early days to Antonio Damora (1811–1905) and Luigi Gargiulo (1806–83). Damora moved to Naples where he worked for the Bourbon monarchy in the royal workshops for a number of years before returning to Sorrento about 1845. Soon after this, another maker, Michel Grandville (1821–93), established his

209

business in the town. The fondness of the Neapolitan court for neo-classical furniture influenced by the French Empire style[2] coupled with the proximity to Pompeii and its visitors, dictated the style of the early wares, especially those of Luigi Gargiulo, which consisted of boxes and small pieces of furniture, such as circular tables constructed of orange or lemon wood inlaid with classical motifs and figures. Veneering does not appear to have been practised on these early items.[3]

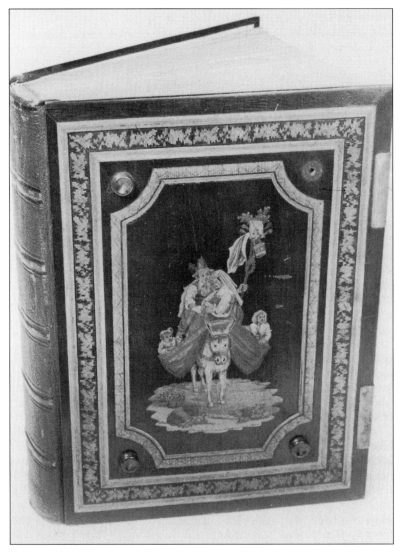

101a. *Photograph album, leather spine and wooden boards decorated with marquetry showing a peasant family riding a donkey. The edge border is carried out in tessellated mosaic marquetry. The inner cover displays the label of Michel Grandville. Sorrento. c1880. (Tunbridge Wells Museum).*

101b. *Michel Grandville's label inside the photograph album.*

By the middle of the century, the ease of rail travel had brought a much greater influx of visitors to the Naples region and many sought out the pleasant seaside resort of Sorrento as a base, yet further promoting the industry, which now started to develop the characteristic wares that were to be its stock-in-trade for the second half of the nineteenth and the first decades of the twentieth century. These woodwares were often veneered in walnut on a carcase wood such as olive. Conventional cross-grain marquetry was developed, depicting the peasantry of the district dancing barefooted or travelling on grossly overladen donkeys. The marquetry panels were usually oval in shape and initially the pictorial work utilised woods in natural colours. After *c*1880, however, woods stained red, green and more rarely blue, feature prominently in many cases. With the exception of a few early examples, the background to the marquetry panels is in dark or even ebonised woods. Floral marquetry was utilised for the fronts and sides of boxes and edge bandings of alternative contrasting woods employed (fig. 102). By the 1860s, the industry was sufficiently well established for the manufacturers to seek wider markets, and two Sorrento ware makers exhibited at the 1862 International Exhibition in London. One was Luigi Gargiulo, and the other Michel Grandville, and both displayed items decorated with marquetry. Gargiulo's pieces were merely described in the catalogue as 'small articles of furniture with native woods', a cigar case, a music desk and a box. The jurors were impressed with the items and awarded Grandville a prize medal while Gargiulo received an honourable mention.[4] Both Gargiulo and Grandville stamped names on items of their manufacture,

102. Box decorated with a marquetry scene depicting a peasant family riding a donkey, the detail in pyrography. Central reserve flanked by cross-grain decorative banding. Sides decorated with floral marquetry. Base of box stamped 'MICHEL GRANDVILLE IN SORRENTO'. c1880. w:25cm d:19cm h:9cm.

while Grandville also employed paper labels printed in French 'FABRIQUE D'OBJETS DE FANTASIE EN BOIS DE SORRENTO', also 'FIGURES DE POMPEI' and 'COSTUMES DE NAPLES' (fig. 100). His address is given as Rue du Tasso.

The earliest use of tessellated mosaic marquetry in Sorrento ware was claimed to be in 1871 when it was employed by Guiseppe Gargiulo (1830–1912) for a design showing two children enclosed by an oval frame.[5] However, there is some evidence to suggest that the technique was being used in Italy and southern Europe as much as 20 years earlier. One of the most admired of the foreign exhibits at the 1851 London Exhibition was a table made by a Spaniard called Peres which was said to contain three million pieces of wood in its decoration which was on 'the same principle' as 'a table by NYE of Tunbridge Wells'. A bronze medal was awarded in 1853 at the New York Exhibition to Claudio Guiseppe of Nice, then part of the kingdom of Sardinia, for a picture in 'wood mosaic'. Much more significant for Sorrento, however, was the display in London in 1862 of a 'toilet-table in mosaic' by Matteo Jannicelli of Salerno, a town less than 20 miles distant from Sorrento. Was it from this source that the art of mosaic was introduced into Sorrento? Although it is not always easy to define what technique is meant when the word 'mosaic' is used, the evidence is sufficiently strong to suggest that Sorrento was not the first place in Italy to manufacture wares similar to those of the Tunbridge ware industry. The decorative use of marquetry was flourishing in many localities in Italy by 1860 but most of the work was of a conventional cross-grain nature.[6]

The evidence concerning the development of wood mosaics at Sorrento appears to exclude the possibility that the Tunbridge ware industry learned the technique from this source. It is, however, possible that there was a reverse flow of information. By the 1860s, there would certainly have been English visitors to Sorrento who would have been aware of mosaic Tunbridge wares and in this connection it is perhaps significant that at the 1864 Industrial

103. Tilt-top table by Antonio Damora, the top decorated with a large tessellated mosaic panel of a dog with small reserves at the edges depicting birds. This mosaic work resembles in design similar subjects used in mosaic Tunbridge ware. c1875. (Alessandro Fiorentino).

213

104. *Wallet for the storage of letters and writing materials, leather spine and wooden boards. Marquetry central reserve featuring peasants dancing, with pierced fret surround. Edge border of tessellated mosaic marquetry. Back signed 'Sorrento'. c1900. w:26cm d:19cm.*

Exhibition in Tunbridge Wells, which included a prominent display of Thomas Barton's work, a Mrs Hooper displayed 'a number of articles, consisting of Indian wood from Sorrento'.[7] Further evidence suggesting a link comes from the designs utilised in the earliest mosaic wares produced at Sorrento. One table decorated with a fine tessellated mosaic panel of a dog shows a spaniel not unlike that used on some early mosaic Tunbridge ware and certainly not Italian in origin (fig. 103). The shape of some pieces of furniture produced in Sorrento in the late nineteenth or early twentieth centuries also shows strong English influence. Sets of quartetto tables, based on a design from Thomas Sheraton's *Cabinet Directory* (1803) are known decorated with conventional cross-grain marquetry panels of typical Sorrento form.[8]

Despite the appearance of the tessellated mosaic technique at Sorrento in the early 1870s, it appears initially to have been used rather sparingly by most makers. Conventional cross-grain marquetry featuring 'peasant' subjects formed the main part of the production of the industry as late as the 1920s, though such wares might have simple mosaic borders (figs. 101a, 104). The threat of such items to the then declining Tunbridge ware industry was, however, noted. In August 1910, James Brown of Boyce, Brown & Kemp referred to the way that the products of the Kentish industry had been 'imitated grotesquely abroad'. He emphasised that 'the imitation work' was 'stained, whereas in the genuine article every tint obtained is from the natural colouring of the wood'. Despite his opinion that these imitations were 'not a success', the lower costs in Italy enable the labour-intensive industry to survive and even flourish here, whereas in England it was to languish and expire.[9]

The Sorrento industry was still in a healthy state in the inter-war years. In 1921, there were six or seven workshops catering for the visitors to the town. Most of the production, about 70 per cent, was sold to Italians at this period, the remaining 30 per cent being bought by foreigners and going in the main to Latin America, Switzerland and Great Britain. By this period, tessellated mosaic wares were much more in evidence. Pictorial work in this technique was seldom attempted this late, but complex patterns of a pseudo-Renaissance character and floral designs were produced as veneers to decorate the tops and sides of boxes, needle-cases, napkin rings, photograph frames, clock cases and other items. Paper-knives in the form of a shoe, decorated with mosaic bandings, were sold in considerable quantities (fig. 105). Perspective cube work, again utilising stained woods, was also used as a veneer, though less frequently than tessellated mosaic. Carcase wood for the Sorrento ware of this period is usually olive and the marquetry woods not used in their natural colours were stained red or green. Locks, hinges and fastenings are markedly different from those found on Tunbridge ware and helpful in distinguishing them from Sorrento productions. Some pieces, usually of conventional marquetry, are boldly marked in ink, usually on the back, with the word 'Sorrento' (fig. 104). Wares obviously produced at Sorrento and in typical designs are known with the names of other Italian towns and cities and even places in southern France such as Nice. This seems to indicate a successful and widespread commercial marketing in this period.

The Sorrento industry survived the war years and is still in active production. As late as 1970, eight to ten makers were at work often displaying their wares in showrooms, and producing the goods in workshops open to the streets. Most were small family businesses producing similar ranges of goods. By this period, tessellated mosaic work was less in use and confined mainly to bandings on some items, and worked with woods stained in red and greenish blue. Decorative furniture veneered in conventional cross-grain marquetry, and utilising stained woods in many cases, was a major element in the trade. Marquetry patterns were often of stylised foliage forms. Some pictorial work was also attempted, such as figures of a woman and child, an outline representation of Apollo in his chariot, stylised figures of birds and foliage and others. Much of the marquetry was simple in outline, lacked detail and was designed to economise on labour costs. The marquetry work was used to decorate small pieces of furniture of which tilt-top and occasional tables were the most common. Tables of this type were exported in some quantity. Larger and more elaborate items, such as cabinets, were produced and these and larger tables often displayed curvilinear shaping and cabriole legs, based on French rococo Louis XV prototypes. Small items such as book racks and trays were also in the main veneered in cross-grain marquetry, some Pompeian

105. *Sorrento souvenir items decorated with mosaic and cross-grain marquetry, olive, inlaid with other woods in natural colours or stained. The shoe is intended to be used as a paper-knife. c1910–50. (Tunbridge Wells Museum).*

themes re-emerging. In some cases the motifs were displayed against a background wood stained green. The use of machinery is much more evident in the industry today. Thus, although the Sorrento industry is the only one of the four marquetry trades considered in this work to sustain volume production, it has only achieved this by a drastic alteration in the wares produced, to economise on labour.

A Note on Mauchline and Scottish Souvenir Woodwares

A wide range of decorative and souvenir woodwares was produced in Scotland from the late eighteenth century until the 1930s. From the mid-nineteenth century, the main centre of production was the small Ayrshire (now Strathclyde) town of Mauchline, and traditionally the wares produced in this period have been known by this name, regardless of the actual place of manufacture. With one exception, which will be described later, it is unlikely that they would be mistaken for Tunbridge ware as the types of wood used, the method of decoration and many of the forms are fundamentally different. There are already adequate published sources for the study of these wares.[1] For these two reasons, a detailed treatment is unnecessary here. Some mention may, however, be justified as Mauchline products were competitors with Tunbridge wares particularly in the cheaper range of souvenir objects, and they sold extensively in the south of England in the very markets which were crucial to the Tunbridge ware maker.

The Scottish industry was initially founded in the village of Laurencekirk, Kincardineshire (now Grampian) by a box-maker called Charles Stiven (1753–1820). By the 1780s, he was manufacturing snuff boxes in the village and as he used the coach office as his place of work, his wares were bought by travellers and enjoyed a more than local reputation. He exploited in the construction of his snuff boxes, a wooden knuckle joint the so-called 'invisible hinge' which had earlier been perfected by John Sandy of Alyth, Perthshire (now Tayside), a man who enjoyed considerable fame for his inventiveness and manual dexterity, despite being bedridden for most of his adult life. Stiven was fortunate in having the interest and patronage of the local landowner Lord Gardenstone, who was aware, through a personal visit in 1787, of the success of Spa woodwares. Gardenstone persuaded an artist from Spa to settle at Laurencekirk to decorate Stiven's boxes.[2] The wares produced set the pattern for these early Scottish products which are made of sycamore and decorated in penwork and paint, and then varnished. Stiven's business endured and boxes of early nineteenth-century date are known marked 'C Stiven Laurencekirk', 'Charles Stiven &

Sons' and 'Stiven & Son'. By the early nineteenth century, the success of the Laurencekirk enterprise attracted competitors, and W. Crab, W. & G. Milner and Robert Macdonald set up as snuff-box makers in the village; wares stamped with the name of the latter are known. Some diversification of wares occurred in the early nineteenth century, when tea caddies and chests also incorporating the 'invisible hinge' were produced to counteract the decline in the snuff-taking habit. Again, these were decorated with penwork and painted designs. It is thought that G. Meekison, who was working from an address in the High Street, Montrose in 1832 was a producer not only of snuff boxes, of which stamped examples exist, but also of tea caddies.[3] The eastern Scottish industry was not to endure, however. Despite royal patronage and attempts to use 'historic' timbers taken from specific trees or sites to attract custom, the Stiven enterprise and the industry itself expired in the region about 1868.[4]

It did, however, spawn a more successful offshoot in the south-west of Scotland, producing very similar wares. The initial maker in this region was William Crawford who started manufacturing snuff boxes at the village of Cumnock in Ayrshire (now Strathclyde) about 1810. The industry expanded rapidly in the area. By 1825, there were six makers and two painters in Cumnock alone, and the industry had expanded to other centres in the county, of which the most important were Auchinleck, Catrine, Mauchline and Ochiltree. In total, 57 Scottish makers have been identified as working between 1820 and 1830, mostly in the county of Ayr. This would suggest that, in the main, the workshops were small and the individual outputs limited. Collectively, however, the Ayrshire industry was of consequence. It capitalised on the enthusiastic nostalgia which the poet Robert Burns generated and which was characterised by the building of an elaborate mausoleum to the bard at Dumfries, in 1819. Scenes from Burns's works, portraits of Burns or Sir Walter Scott, coaching, hunting or drinking subjects, Scottish views, heraldry and royalty were the main subjects for snuff-box decoration. As the main product was snuff boxes, and all are characterised by the 'invisible hinge', none of these products are likely to be confused with Tunbridge wares, despite the fact that many of these at this period were of whitewood and decorated to some extent using similar techniques.[5]

Of all the Ayrshire businesses, the one that rose to greatest fame, and was to dominate the industry as a whole, was the firm of William & Andrew Smith of Mauchline. This business is said to have been founded by Andrew Smith in 1821 and the partnership existed by 1823. One of their earliest products was a hone for sharpening razors. Apart from the sharpening stone, it needed a strop or leather strap, a wooden handle and backing. An example is known dating from the reign of King William IV, the handle and backing printed in transfer with the Royal coat of arms and 'MANUFACTURERS TO HIS MAJESTY' and 'INIMITABLE STRAP'. It may have been the use of the technique of transferring prints on to the wooden parts of these utilitarian objects which gave the partners the idea of decorating whitewood souvenir wares more cheaply by using a similar process and avoiding the labour-intensive artistic work in pen and paint. Snuff boxes were made on an extensive scale, but with the decline in demand diversification occurred. Utilising the improving transport network, the Smiths looked to markets in England. The partnership may have been suspended between 1842 and 1849, for in this period both Andrew Smith and William Smith maintained separate warehouses in Birmingham, apart from the manufactories at Mauchline. William Smith had a London agent and Andrew Smith one in Paris. Both offered workboxes, cigar cases, tea caddies, inkstands, needle cases and a wide range of other decorative and souvenir wares. By the mid-century, manufacture was on a very extensive scale with a total labour force of some 400 people in the 1860s. The Smiths continued to flourish into the early years of the present century. In 1933, a fire badly damaged the works but already by this date the industry was in serious decline and this disaster appears to have been sufficient to mark the final run-down in trading. The extensive scale of the Smiths' production and marketing meant that the smaller Ayrshire producers with the high costs of production by traditional methods were unable to compete and were by degrees eliminated. Only one firm competed successfully with W. & A. Smith in producing the new wares and this was Caledonian Box Works of Lanark, founded about 1866 by Alexander Brown, a former employee. Brown sold his company to Mackenzie and Meakle about 1900.[6]

The wares produced from the late 1840s, largely by the Smiths, are the most commonly found and collected today. These are decorated with a number of finishes which will be considered next.

Tartan Wares

A strong revival of interest in the Scottish tartans occurred in the nineteenth century, promoted by an upsurge in national feeling amongst the Scottish people themselves and by the growth of tourism which was greatly encouraged by the Royal purchase of the Balmoral Estate.

The earliest record of the sale of tartan-decorated wares was in March 1841. By this date tartan cigar cases, razor strops and cases and finger plates for doors were being sold by the Smiths' London agency. The earliest woodwares so decorated had the designs applied directly to the wood with paint. Cheaper methods of applying the decoration were sought, and on 2 November 1853 W. & A. Smith took out a patent (No. 2639) for a machine using 16 pens (later to be replaced by wheels or rollers) which would rule tartan patterns on to paper which could in turn be applied to the wood before varnishing. This invention enabled souvenir wares decorated in this manner to be produced in quantity. Great care was taken when applying the paper to ensure that joins did not show. Tartan-decorated wares were manufactured by the Smiths right through to the final ending of production in the 1930s and a wide range of different useful or decorative items were so treated.

W. & A. Smith was the major producer of tartan wares but some were also made by Wilson and Amphlet of Mauchline and the Caledonian Box Works.[7]

Transfer-printed Wares

The most common forms of Mauchline ware are boxes and souvenir items in sycamore decorated with one or more engraved views of locations in the British Isles or overseas. As already indicated, W. & A. Smith were using the technique of transferring printed designs to whitewood – as early as the 1830s in the case of razor strops. For decorative souvenir wares, however, the process does not appear to have been used until *c*1850 and from then on was to be carried on as one of the main items of trade until the 1930s. The engraved views printed in black are usually enclosed in oval frames with the place named beneath. Scottish views and engravings associated with Burns or Scott form one of the major groups, but the extent of the marketing of the Mauchline products is clearly seen in the diversity of the views used as illustrations. That these wares competed for trade in the resorts where Tunbridge wares had traditionally sold well there can be no doubt. The south coast resorts such as the Isle of Wight, Worthing, Brighton, Eastbourne, Hastings, Folkestone, Ramsgate and Margate are well represented, and objects with Tunbridge Wells views such as High Rocks and the Toad Rock, Rusthall Common are known. Wares illustrated with Killarney views are also common, indicating competition with the locally made arbutus and imported Tunbridge wares at this Irish resort. Locations in France, Holland, Belgium, Spain, South Africa, Canada, Australia and the United States indicate a successful exploitation of the potential for export. Royal events and exhibitions also provided subjects for transfer-printed Mauchline wares.[8]

Photographic Wares

A range of wares exists, similar to those transfer-printed, but incorporating photographs. These were manufactured from the 1860s and some may well be the products of the Caledonian Box Works. Alexander Brown, the founder of this enterprise, had a great interest in photography. Production of such wares continued until the early years of the present century. As has been indicated,[9] some Tunbridge wares are also known decorated with photographs but these are most distinctive. The Tunbridge wares are veneered items, decorated with tessellated mosaic bandings, and the rectangular photographs occupy the major portion of the top of each object. In Mauchline wares, the photographs are usually smaller and in oval frames and decorate sycamore whitewood wares.[10] The Tunbridge Wells Manufacturing Company did, however, produce some plain whitewood boxes with photographic views and one of triangular shape which bears a photograph of the Queen Victoria Monument outside Buckingham Palace is known with their stamp.

Fern-decorated Wares

From c1870, some Mauchline ware was decorated with impressions of ferns in dark brown stipple in the popular late Victorian taste. W. & A. Smith and the Caledonian Box Works were both responsible for such articles. Coloured ferns and seaweeds were also depicted on whitewood wares. Not all items decorated with ferns are necessarily of Scottish manufacture, however. Craft and souvenir shops in general sold whitewood boxes for amateur decoration and even Henry Hollamby of Tunbridge Wells offered 'grey and white wood articles for painting, fern printing &c &c'.[11]

Lacquer Wares

Less commonly, Mauchline wares are painted black in imitation of lacquer and additionally decorated with views and coloured transfers.[12]

As has been indicated, none of these Scottish or Mauchline souvenir wares are likely to be mistaken for the products of the Tunbridge ware industry. Many of the objects made are common to both, especially in the smaller souvenir objects. The Cleopatra's needle (obelisk) type thermometer is found in Mauchline and Tunbridge ware for instance. After the mid-nineteenth century, the Scottish industry does not appear to have produced larger objects such as tea caddies, workboxes, games boxes, stationery cabinets, inkstands, writing desks or book racks in any quantity. Nor did it produce furniture. There is, however, one rarer form of Mauchline ware which has been mistaken for Tunbridge ware and recorded in a published work.[13] For a short while, the Scottish industry produced some turnery wares utilising bands of two contrasting woods, one white and the other brown. The most characteristic item produced in this form was a slim tall spill vase with a serrated top. Such vases are invariably decorated with transfer-printed views and are thus unlikely to deceive (colour pl. 35). A small jug was also produced, using light and dark contrasting woods. Tunbridge turnery is never as simple in decoration as these Mauchline wares, and used a wider range of woods. It also lacks the transfer-printing or seaweed or fern decoration that identifies the Scottish product.[14]

NOTES

The following abbreviations have been used:

BL – British Library (Reference Division); BM – British Museum; Bod. – Bodleian Library, Oxford; BRL – Brighton Reference Library; Cal. Tr – *Calendar of Treasury Papers*; ESRO – East Sussex Record Office; KCAO – Kent County Archives Office; MM – Maidstone Museum; PRO – Public Record Office; RBG – Royal Botanical Gardens, Kew; SH – Somerset House; TWM – Tunbridge Wells Museum; WBC – Worthing Borough Council; WM – Worthing Museum and Art Gallery; WRL – Westminster Reference Library.

Chapter 1

1. JAR Pimlott, *The Englishman's Holiday* (1957) pp. 24–27; Alan Savidge, *Royal Tunbridge Wells* (Tunbridge Wells 1975) p. 28.

2. Pimlott, pp. 27–29; Savidge, pp. 15–32.

3. Pimlott, p. 31; Savidge pp. 34–35, 43–45; CW Chalkin & MA Hammond, *Rural Change and Urban Growth 1500–1800* (1974) pp. 232–34.

4. Donald D Mackinnon, *History of Speldhurst* (Tunbridge Wells 1902) p. 53; (Speldhurst 2nd edn 1930) p. 66.

5. William Bray (ed), *The Diary of John Evelyn* Vol II (1879) pp. 41, 43, 134.

6. CW Chalklin, 'A Kentish Wealden Parish (Tonbridge) 1500–1750' Oxford B Litt 1960 p. 52; CW Chalklin, 'A Seventeenth Century Market Town – Tonbridge' *Archaeologia Cantiana* Vol LXXVI (1961) p. 152.

7. James Phippen, *Colbran's New Guide for Tunbridge Wells* (Tunbridge Wells 1840) advertisement p.14; Bod. John Johnson collection – trade card of Edmund Nye; MM Barton trade card; TWM Fenner trade card; *The Tunbridge Wells Advertiser* 12 Aug 1910.

8. Beauchamp Wadmore, *Some Details in the History of the Parish of Tonbridge* (Tonbridge 1906) p. 107; KCAO P371/12/4; William Stapley, *Stapley's Tunbridge Wells Visitor's Guide* (Tunbridge Wells 1847) p. 63.

9. C Morris (ed), *The Journeys of Celia Fiennes* (1947) p. 133. The Count de Grammont visited Tunbridge Wells in 1663 in the company of Charles II and Catherine of Braganza and recorded in his *Memoir* seeing one side of the Walks 'a long row of shops, plentifully stocked with all manner of toys, lace, gloves, stockings'. Although the word 'toys' used in the Tunbridge Wells context often means Tunbridge ware, this must not be taken to imply the sale of such wares as early as 1663. The *Memoir* was not written down until much later by Anthony Hamilton and was not published until 1714, and this description of the shops on the Walks clearly cannot refer to 1663.

10. KCAO TR8/1673; U38E1; PRO C11/2318/2.

11. KCAO U749/E15–19, E26–28, E35, E38; U749/T2; *The European Magazine* Sept 1820 p. 210; Savidge pp. 43–4, 62–3, 88–9, 103.

12. KCAO U749/T16; U55/T385; P371/1/12/4; P371/14/3–4.

13. 1801 census – Speldhurst parish 1,618 but this would have included the village of Speldhurst, 3 miles from Tunbridge Wells. Tunbridge parish, of which the market town of Tonbridge was the largest settlement, 4,371.

14. Chalklin & Hammond p. 234; Chalklin (thesis) p. 116; TWM Sprange 35, 74, 98, 124; List of subscribers to the paving of the Walks 1792; *The Post Office London Directory* (1812); *Johnstone's London Directory* (1818); *Baxter's Stranger in Brighton and New Brighton Directory* (Brighton 1822).

15. Arthur W Bracket, 'Tunbridge Wells and its Old Prints' *The Print Collector's Quarterly* Jan 1933 pp. 52, 55; *The Maidstone Journal* 22 July 1800; Phippen (2nd edn 1844) advertisement H. Burrows; *The Sussex Agricultural Express* 28 Oct 1837; WRL letter books of Hastings Nathaniel Middleton 26 Oct 1816.

16. Lady Llanover, *The Autobiography and Correspondence of Mary Granville* Vol I (1861) pp. 135–36; Ethel Younghusband, *Mansions, Men and Tunbridge Ware* (Slough 1949) p. 30; Samuel Derrick, *Letters Written from Leverpoole, … Vol II* (1767) p. 39; Fanny Burney, *Diary and Letters of Madame d'Arblay* Vol I (1842) pp. 263–66; Margaret Roake & John Whyman (ed) *Essays in Kentish History* (1973) p. 191.

Chapter 2

1. Chalklin & Hammond p. 248.

2. BM Banks 119.7; *Cal. Tr. Papers* 8 Dec 1686.

3. The print referred to is in a private collection, but one in the Guildhall Library, Department of Prints, on the same theme lists 'The Turners' Booth in New Thames Street with the Hand & Hand insured as long as the foundation stands'. This print shows a lathe in the booth.

4. Trade cards of London Tunbridge ware makers of this period occur in the Banks and Heal collections (Dept. of Prints, British Museum), the Department of Prints, Guildhall Library and the Victoria & Albert Museum. A list of known London makers is given at Appendix 4, pp. 255–59.

5. *A London Directory* (1794); *The Times* 4 Jan 1803, 6 Jan 1809; *John Bull* 7 Apr 1822; *Kent's Directory* (1825).

6. *Holden's Directory* (1799); *The Post Office London Directory* (1803), (1828), (1830), (1840), (1846); *The Times* 3 Jan 1806, 5 Feb 1806, 9 Jan 1807.

7. BM Heal 100.3; Banks 100.3, 100.4, 100.10; John Ford, *Ackermanns 1783* (nd). I am indebted to John and Jill Ford for the information regarding Ackermann's payments to George Wise which were extracted from the accounts books of Rudolph Ackermann & Co.

8. *The Post Office London Directory* (1826); BM Heal 100.31; *Holden's Triennial Directory* (1809); WRL Gardiner box 63 No 2A; Ford *op cit*.

9. TWM Sprange 149; map in print collection; unattributed newspaper cutting 28 May 1837; GA Cooke, *Walks Through London* (nd 1830) p. 357; J Britton, *The Original Picture of London* (28th edn nd *c*1832) p.318; Richard D Altick, *The Shows of London* (Cambridge, Mass. 1978) p. 211.

10. *Furniture History* XXX (1994) p. 27; Reading *Mercury and Oxford Gazette*

8 Oct 1770; BM Banks 93.8, 93.36, 93.37; *The Universal British Directory* Vol I (1793); EW Brayley, *Delineations, Historical and Topographical of the Isle of Thanet* (1817) p. 59. A Varley, *A History of Libraries in Cheltenham from 1780–1900* (1968) pp. 41–5.

11. *Pigot & Co's Metropolitan New Alphabetical Directory* (1826); *Robson's London Commercial Directory* (1830); *The London Post Office Directory* (1830) (1835) (1838).

Chapter 3

1. Pimlott pp. 50–32; Edmund W Gilbert, *Brighton – Old Ocean's Bauble* (1954) p. 12.

2. Pimlott pp. 52, 59–61; Gilbert pp. 10–11; Sue and John Farrant, 'Brighton 1580–1820: From Tudor Town to Regency Resort', *Sussex Archaeological Collections* 118 (Lewes 1981) pp. 333–34, 339–42, 347–8; RJ Goulden 'Edmund Baker and Jasper Sprange', *Factolum* No. 38, Feb 1994, pp. 17–19.

3. Thomas Benge Burr, *The History of Tunbridge Wells* (1766) p. 288; Savidge p. 87–89, RJ Goulden.

4. John & Jill Ford, *Images of Brighton* (Twickenham 1981), pp. 80, 294, 333–34, 345; Anon, *The New Brighthelmstone Directory* (1770) p. 41; Anon, *Description of Brighthelmstone and the Adjacent Country* (Brighton 1800) pp. 22–23; Clifford Musgrave, *Life in Brighton* (1970) p. 77.

5. For further details of this business see pp. 170–72.

6. PRO HO107/1645; ESRO PAR 255/1/2/1, PAR 255/1/2/14, PAR 255/1/3/11; PAR 259/1/3/18; KCAO DRb/RT2/371A/1/1; U749/E15; U749/E35, U749/E38, *Folthorp's General Directory for Brighton* (1864).

7. For further details of this business see pp. 168–70.

8. ESRO PAR 255/1/2/1; TH Boore, *Brighton Annual Directory and Fashionable Guide* (1822); *The Court Guide and General Directory for Brighton* (1848); *Post Office Directory of the Home Counties* (1855).

9. John & Jill Ford pp. 271–364.

10. Tea caddy, and a workbox in private collection, see fig. 26 and colour pl. 10.

11. C Wright, *The Brighton Ambulator* (1818) p. 98; *The Stranger's Guide in Brighton* (Brighton 1838) p. 28; TA Swaysland & J Gill, *Directory of Brighton* (Brighton 1832); *Baxter's Stranger in Brighton and New Brighton Directory* (Brighton 1822).

Chapter 4

1. Displayed by the Bath Preservation Trust at 1, Royal Crescent, Bath.

2. *The Universal British Directory* (1791); TWM Sprange 149.

3. BM Banks 17.6; *Pigot & Co's London & Provincial Directory* (1822), (1830).

4. TWM Sprange 82, 149; BM Banks 93.8; Margate Public Library YO60.940 Parker 602; Mary S Morris, *A Catalogue of English Painted Enamels 18th and 19th Century in the Wolverhampton and Bilston Collections* (Woverhampton 1973) p. 38; Brayley p. 59; Anon., *The Margate Guide* (1797) p. 46; Anon., *New Margate, Ramsgate and Broadstairs Guide* (8th edn nd *c*1825) p. 61; GW Bonnor, *The Picturesque Pocket Companion to Margate* (1831) pp. 68–70, 182; John Whyman, 'A Hanoverian Watering Place: Margate' in Alan Everitt (ed), *Perspectives in English Urban History* (1973) pp. 138–60.

5. *Pigot & Co's London & Provincial Directory* (1826); *Pigot & Co's National Commercial Directory* (1832), (1835); John Shearsmith, *A Topographical Description of Worthing* (Worthing 1824) pp. 16–17 (new edn 1832) pp. 33–34; TWM Sprange 61.

6. Morris p. 133; William Bonyton, *Bonython's Dover Guide* (1823) p. 16; Shearsmith (1832) pp. 33–34; Anon., *The New Brighthelmstone Directory* (1770) p. 41; Anon., *The Margate Guide* (1797) p. 54.

7. J Mackcoull, *A Sketch of Worthing* (1813) pp. 83–84.

8. John Ackerson Erredge, *History of Brighthelmstone* (Brighton 1862) pp. 201–05; R Sicklemore, *An Epitome of Brighton* (Brighton 1815) p. 60; Shearsmith (1824) p. 17; Wright (1818) p. 147; *Baxter's Stranger in Brighton and Guide* (Brighton 1826) p. 27; WJ Adams (publisher), *Adam's Illustrative Descriptive Guide to the Watering-places of England* (1848) p. 138.

9. V & A Dept of Prints Box GG 65A; *Wrightson's Directory of Birmingham* (1821); Peter CD Brears, 'The York Spinning Wheel Makers' *Furniture History* Vol XIV (1978) pp. 19–22; York Herald No 13 27 Mar 1790, No 267 14 Feb 1795; *York Courant* No 4082 2 Mar 1807, No 4447 28 Mar 1814, No 4550 18 Mar 1816; *Yorkshire Gazette* No 214 24 May 1823, No 216 7 June 1823; *Universal British Directory* (1798); *Holden's Triennial Directory* (1809); *Pigot & Co's Commercial Directory for 1818–19–20* (Manchester 1818), *The Times* No 5909 4 Jan 1803; TWM Sprange 35.

10. *Wilson's Dublin Directory* (1809); *Pettigrew & Oulton's Dublin Directory* (1834), (1836).

11. See pp. 175–93.

Chapter 5

1. For example see Wadmore pp. 107–08.

2. Connard trade card Messenger/Cavendish sale 21 July 1995, lot 899.

3. Morris p. 133; F Lewis Hinckley, *Directory of the Historic Cabinet Woods* (New York 1960) pp. 168–70; Burr p. 108; CW Chalklin, *Seventeenth Century Kent* (1965) pp. 90–92.

4. BM Heal 122.20; J Sprange, *The Tunbridge Wells Guide* (1780) pp. 11–12; R Campbell, *The London Tradesman* (1747) p. 243; Anon., *A General Description of All Trades* (1747) p. 211; John Evans, *An Excursion to Brighton, A Visit to Tunbridge Wells and a Trip to Southend* (1823) p. 139.

5. BM Heal 119.3; Llanover Vol I pp. 134–35.

6. TWM Sprange 35, 76; BM Banks 100.8; Simon Jervis, *Printed Furniture Designs Before 1650* (1974) p. 7; Ronald E Rowe, *English Dial Clocks* (Woodbridge 1978) pp. 71, 74, 76, 78.

7. BM Banks 100.11, 100.18; TWM Sprange 150; *The Times* 4 Jan 1806.

8. Ralph Edwards, *The Dictionary of English Furniture* Vol I (rev edn 1954) pp. 113–14; Saint-Sernin, *Healthful Sports for Young Ladies* (1822); E Berresford Chancellor, 'A Note on Tunbridge Ware' *Connoisseur* Vol XCV Jan 1935 p. 32; TWM Sprange 27, 117, 138, 149.

9. John & Jill Ford pp. 275, 296, 345; E Wallis (publisher), *Brighton as it is* (new edn 1830) p. 54.

10. Flavia Swann, *Introduction to Sotheby Belgravia Catalogue for Tunbridge Ware Exhibition and Sale* Nov-Dec 1980 p.4; Therle Hughes, *More Small Decorative Antiques* (1962) p. 63.

11. Edward H & Eva R Pinto, *Tunbridge and Scottish Souvenir Woodwares* (1970) p. 109.

12. BM Banks 93.36; *The Times* 9 Jan 1807; Clifford Musgrave, *Regency Furniture* (1961) pp. 134–36.

13. *Pelton's Illustrated Guide to Tunbridge Wells* (Tunbridge Wells 10th edn 1883) p. 74.

14. ESRO PAR 255/1/2/3; BM Banks 122.13; Edwards Vol I p. 113; Frederick Shoberl (ed.), *Forget Me Not* (1833) advertisement Ackermann; *Sotheby Belgravia Catalogue* 3 Dec 1980 p. 14.

15. A detailed description of the method of decorating, varnishing and finishing Tunbridge ware is contained in Ernest Spon, *Workshop Receipts for the Use of Manufacturers, Mechanics and Scientific Amateurs* (1875) p. 78 but it is unlikely that the trade manufacturers of the early nineteenth century went to such lengths.

16. *The Repository of Arts, Literature, Manufacture &c* 2nd series Dec 1816 p. 336.

17. Geoffrey Wills, *English Furniture 1500–1760* (1971) pp. 13, 138; TWM Sprange 35; *The Times* 4 Jan 1806, 5 Feb 1806; J Doran, *The History of the Town and Borough of Reading in Berkshire* (1835), advertisement of Charles Ingall.

18. *The Repository of Arts* 2nd series Jan 1822 advertisement of S & J Fuller; BM Banks 100.8, 100.11, 100.30.

19. Derrick Vol II p. 39; Burr p. 108.

20. Brian Austen, 'Tables by Tunbridge Makers', *Furniture History* XXXIII (1997) p. 265.

21. Peter Reindl, 'Early Renaissance Furniture in Basle' *Apollo* Dec 1976 p. 457; Jervis passim; Peter Thornton, *Seventeenth-Century Interior Decoration in England, France and Holland* (1978) p. 85; John Carwitham, *Various Kinds of Floor Decorations …* (nd 1739) plates 6, 11, 18,23, 25; Martyn Bramwell (ed) *The International Book of Wood* (1976) p. 106; FJB Watson, *Louis XVI Furniture* (1960) p. 105, plate 25.

22. Henry W Wolff, *Sussex Industries* (nd 1883) p. 47; Christopher Gilbert, *Pictorial Dictionary of Marked London Furniture 1700–1840* (1966) p.393; *The Times* 5 April 1806.

23. J Clifford, *A Descriptive Guide of Tunbridge Wells* (Tunbridge Wells 8th edn 1844); Edwards Vol 3 pp. 252–53; BM Heal 122, 27; *Auction Catalogue – Brackett, Tunbridge Wells* 24 Feb 1933; *Post Office Directory of the Six Home Counties* (1845).

24. Anon., *The Handbook of Turning* (1842) p. 74; Edward Vol 1 pp. 25–26; RGE Sandbach, 'Tunbridge Ware', *Practical Education* April 1972 pp. 150–51; BM Heal 122.26; TWM Sprange 35; *The Times* 9 Jan 1807; *The York Herald* 14 Feb 1795; *Sotheby Belgravia Catalogue* 3 Dec 1980 p. 39.

25. Edwards Vol 3 pp. 343, 352–53; Savidge pp. 123–24; Brackett p. 55; Clifford p. 40; Phippen (1844) pp. 88–89.

Chapter 6

1. Peter & Ann MacTaggart, 'Tunbridge End Grain Mosaic: a Misnomer', *The Chronicle of Early American Industries Association* Vol 36 No 2 pp. 33–34. The use of both end- and cross-grain tesserae provided a greater variety of effect, as cross-grain reflects more light.

2. Phippen (1840) p. 116; *Pigot & Co's London & Provincial New Commerical Directory* (1828) (1832).

3. Charles Hotszapfel, *Turning and Mechanical Manipulation* Vol 2 (1846) pp. 764, 767.

4. J Clifford, *The Tunbridge Wells Guide* (Tunbridge Wells 1837) p. 32; Pinto pp. 40–41; Phippen (1840) p. 116, advertisement G & J Burrows.

5. TWM Handbill of George Wise.

6. TWM unattributed newspaper cutting 28 May 1837; Phippen (1840) advertisement p. 17; Anon., *The Tunbridge Wells Guide and Directory* (nd *c*1845) p. 88.

7. *Sotheby Belgravia Catalogue* 3 Dec 1980 pp. 26, 30; *Brackett's Descriptive Illustrated Hand Guide to Tunbridge Wells* (nd 1863) advertisement; Robert Ellis, *Official Descriptive and Illustrated Catalogue of the Great Exhibition* Vol II (1851) p. 791; Pinto plate 25.

Chapter 7

1. Savidge pp. 124, 136, 137, 165.

2. Ibid pp. 105, 109, 114–16, 122, 131, 159, 163.

3. *The Times* 21 Jan 1965; PRO HO 107/462, HO 107/1614, HO 107/1615; RG9/491, RG9/492, RG9/493; RG10/927, RG10/928, RG10/929, RG10/930, RG10/1049; *Abstract of the Answers and Returns … Population Act 11 Geo IV c30* (1833); Pelton (1833) p. 78.

4. Ellis Vol II pp. 733, 791; *Official Descriptive and Illustrated Catalogue of the Great Exhibition – Report of the Juries* (1852) Vol I p. clxxxviip; G.R. Goodrich (ed) *Science and Mechanism: Illustrated by Examples in the New York Exhibition 1853–54* (New York 1854) p. 237; *New York Industrial Exhibition 1853 – General Report of the British Commissioners* (1854) pp. 39–409; *The International Exhibition of 1862 – Illustrated Catalogue of the Industrial Department – British Division* (1862) Vol II p. 21.

5. *The Tunbridge Wells Gazette* 23 Sept 1864, 30 Sept 1864; *The Tunbridge Wells Advertiser* 13 Oct 1899.

6. William Tiffen, *The New Hand-book and Guide to the Town and Port of Folkestone* (1850) advertisement; William Tiffen, *Excursions from Folkestone, Sandgate and Hythe* (1853) advertisement; *Craven & Co's Directory of Hampshire* (1857) KB King, *The Views Illustrated on End-grain Tunbridge Ware Designs* (Hitchin nd 1981) passim.

7. King No 81 p. 12; Swann p. 9; Alph. Giroux et Cie traded from 1837 to *c*1885, see Danielle Kisluk-Grosheide, 'Maison Giroux and its "Oriental" Marquetry Technique', *Furniture History* XXXV (1999) pp. 147–72.

8. Gilbert pp. 99, 107, 139, 155; Farrant pp. 176–78; Pimlott p. 174.

9. *Sotheby Belgravia Catalogue* 3 Dec 1980 p. 15; 5 Aug 1981 pp. 55, 60. Younghusband plate xx; King p. 7; Other items described are in Tunbridge Wells and Worthing Museums and in private collections.

10. BRL Erredge 8/53; BM Banks 122.13; *Folthorp's Court Guide and General Directory for Brighton* (Brighton 1848).

11. *Swayland & Gill's New Directory for Brighton* (1832); *Leppard & Co's Brighton Directory* (1839), (1845); *Post Office Directory of the Six Home Counties* (1866) advertisement; *Post Office Directory Sussex* (1874); *Robinson's Popular Brighton Directory* (1884). Pieces of Tunbridge ware described are from the Tunbridge Wells Museum and private collections.

12. *The Post Office Directory of the Six Home Counties* (1851), (1855), (1859); *Willis's Brighton Townsman and Visitor's Directory* (Brighton 1826); John & Jill Ford pp. 284–85, 291, 295, 305–06, 317, 321, 341; *Leppard & Co's Brighton Directory for 1839–40* (Brighton 1839) advertisement; Ibid (1843) advertisement; *Post Office Directory of Sussex* (1878).

13. *Melville & Co's Directory and Gazetter of Sussex* (1858); *Folthorp's General Directory for Brighton* (Brighton 1864).

14. For further information on James Medhurst see pp. 172–74.

15. WBC BW/P/19–20, 27–28; WM Medhurst handbill; *Pigot & Co's National London & Provincial Directory* (1832); *Lewes Parliamentary Poll Book* (Aug 1841); *Post Office Directory of the Six Home Counties* (1845); *Melville & Co's Directory and Gazetter of Sussex* (1858).

16. WM transcript of a handbill; Swann p. 8; Richard Larn, *Shipwrecks of Great Britain and Ireland* (Newton Abbot 1981) pp. 157–58. The situation is further complicated by the existence of a William Medhurst at Prospect Place (1855), turner.

17. PRO RG9/546; RG10/1007; *Post Office Directory of the Home Counties* (1855), (1865), (1874), (1878); *Melville & Co's Directory and Gazetteer of Kent* (1858); *Kelly's Directory of Kent* (1882), (1890).

18. RGE Sandbach, 'Tunbridge Ware' *Cantium* Vol 6 No 3 Autumn 1974.

19. For further information about Tunbridge ware decorated with photographs see pp. 113, 115.

20. Wadmore p. 107; Ford *passim*.

Chapter 8

1. Holtzapfel Vol II p. 764; Pelton (1883) p. 74.

2. Holtzapfel Vol II pp. 764–66; Elias Taylor, *The Lathe and its Uses* (3rd edn 1871) pp. 294–95.

3. Holtzapfel Vol II p. 766; Taylor pp. 193–95; William Tiffen, *Excursions from Folkestone, Sandgate and Hythe* (1853) advertisement.

4. Holtzapfel Vol II pp. 764–66.

5. Pelton (1833) pp. 76–77; Wadmore p. 109; Pinto plate 4; Taylor p. 292.

6. Wolff p. 48; *The Tunbridge Wells Advertiser* 28 Feb 1890.

7. Pelton (1883) p. 75.

8. Pinto p. 55, based on information supplied by Frank Hemsley, claimed that green wood was additionally produced by immersing satinwood in chalybeate water. No other contemporary reference to this practice has been noted and experimentation suggests that no such transformation takes place.

9. Pelton (1883) pp. 75–76; Taylor p. 292; Frederick AA Talbot, 'Tonbridge Ware: its History and Manufacture' *The Windsor Magazine* Vol VII Feb 1898 p. 371; *The Tunbridge Wells Gazette* 23 Sept 1864; *The Tunbridge Wells Advertiser* 12 Aug 1910.

10. *The Tunbridge Wells Advertiser* 28 Feb 1890, 12 Aug 1910; Wolff p. 52; Taylor pp. 292–94; Holtzapfel p. 767; Wadmore pp. 109–10; Mactaggart p. 33.

11. Wolff p. 52; Wadmore p. 111; Taylor p. 295.

12. *The Tunbridge Wells Gazette* 23 Sept 1864; Pelton (1883) p. 76.

13. See pp. 154–56

14. *The Tunbridge Wells Advertiser* 28 Feb 1890; Wadmore p. 111.

15. *The Tunbridge Wells Advertiser* 28 Feb 1890; Wolff p. 53; Talbot p. 373; Taylor p. 296.

16. Taylor p. 296; Richard Bitmead, *The London Cabinet-Maker's Guide* (1873) p. 89.

Chapter 9

1. Gisela MA Richter, *The Furniture of the Greeks, Etruscans and Romans* (1966) p. 126; Hollis S Baker, *Furniture in the Ancient World* (1966) pp. 97–98, 301–02; F Hamilton Jackson, *Intarsia and Marquetry* (1903) pp. 10, 14, 16, 53–81.

2. Wolff p. 46.

3. See pp. 207, 210–12.

4. Maurice Tomlin, *Catalogue of Adam Period Furniture* (1972) p. 25.

5. Holtzapfel Vol II p. 767.

6. *Sotheby Belgravia Catalogues* 3 Dec 1980 item 102; 17 Feb 1982 item 82; Ralph Edwards and LGG Ramsey (ed), *The Complete Connoisseur Period Guides* (1968) plate 72c p. 1416.

7. Edwards & Ramsey pp. 1220, 1462–63; *Colbran's Hand-Book and Directory for Tunbridge Wells* (Tunbridge Wells nd 1850) advertisement; Pelton (1883) p. 76.

8. Edwards & Ramsey p. 1460; Phippen (1840) p. 116; Clifford (1837) p. 32.

9. For a full list of the views identified and their scarcity see Appendix 3 pp. 242–45.

10. Clifford (1825) facing p. 71, (1844) p. 39; Pelton (1883) p. 77; King *passim*.

11. *Sotheby Belgravia Catalogues* 3 Dec 1980 items 14, 23, 73, 103, 206, 289, 17 Feb 1982 lots 54, 78, 165, 175; *Brackett's Catalogue* 4 Dec 1987 lot 30.

12. *The Tunbridge Wells Advertiser* 28 Feb 1890; Wolff p. 51; *Brackett's Catalogue* 24 Feb 1993 lot 377; *Sotheby Belgravia Catalogues* 3 Dec 1980 lots 324, 333, 17 Feb 1982 lot 172; Pinto p. 33.

13. Sandbach (Cantium) p. 53; *Post Office Directory of the Six Home Counties* (1855), (1865); *Melville & Co's Directory of Kent* (1858); *WE Owen & Co's Directory of Kent* (1883); PRO RG10/1007; *White's History, Gazetteer and Directory of Hampshire* (2nd edn 1878).

14. See appendix 1 pp. 237–38.

15. *Sotheby Belgravia Catalogue* 3 Dec 1980 items 41–44; Pinto plates 20, 21, 25, 26; Sandbach (*Practical Education*) p. 185.

Chapter 10

1. *Post Office Directory of the Six Home Counties* (1874); *Post Office Directory of Kent* (1878); *WE Owen & Co's Directory of Kent* (1883); *The Tunbridge Wells Gazette* 27 Mar 1891; *The Kent & Sussex Courier* 17 July 1903; *Visitor's Guide to Tunbridge Wells* (1888); Wolff pp. 44–45.

2. *The Tunbridge Wells Advertiser* 13 Oct 1899; *The Kent & Sussex Courier* 13 Oct 1899; Isabelle Anscombe & Charlotte Gere, *Arts & Crafts in Britain and America* (1978) p. 114.

3. Taylor p. 296; *The Tunbridge Wells Advertiser* 13 Oct 1899.

4. Wolff p. 53; *The Tunbridge Wells Advertiser* 28 Feb 1890, 13 Oct 1899; Pinto pp. 107–17; *Victorian Shopping – Harrod's Catalogue 1895* (Newton Abbot 1972) pp. 1126, 1128; *Yesterday's Shopping – The Army & Navy Stores Catalogue 1907* (Newton Abbot 1969) pp. 132–4, 198, 200, 203, 378, 419, 426, 1116; *Gamage's Christmas Bazaar 1913* (Newton Abbot 1974) pp. 379, 382, 404–07, 411.

5. *The Tunbridge Wells Advertiser* 28 Feb 1890, 12 Aug 1910.

6. *Chamber's Journal* 1 Dec 1894 p. 762; *The Tunbridge Wells Advertiser* 12 Aug 1910.

7. *The Tunbridge Wells Advertiser* 17 Sept 1920; Birmingham Museum (Pinto Collection) statement by AF Hemsley 14 Oct 1969; *Kelly's Directory of Tunbridge Wells* (1905), (1911), (1918), (1922), (1930); TWM Letter Porter's to C Mackintosh 1 June 1916, 22 Oct 1923.

8. *The Post Office London Commercial & Professional Directory* (1923); *The Tunbridge Wells Magazine* June 1923; *The Daily Mirror* 10 July 1923; *Catalogue of the Daily Mail Ideal Home Exhibition* (1923) p. 132, (1924) pp. 122, 177; *Christie's South Kensington Catalogue*, 31 May 1989; TWM Letter Porter's to C Mackintosh 22 Oct 1923; Birmingham Museum (Pinto Collection) statement of AF Hemsley 14 Oct 1969.

9. TWM Correspondence of the Tunbridge Wells Manufacturing Co with C Mackintosh 21 Feb 1925, 11 May 1925; *Price list of the Tunbridge Wells Manufacturing Co*; RBG (Kew) invoice 106 5 July 1924; *Catalogue of the Daily Mail Ideal Home Exhibition* (1924) p. 177, (1925) p. 205, (1926) p. 182; *Bracket* 16 May 1997 lot 68.

10. Sandbach (Cantium) pp. 53–54; RGE Sandbach, 'Tunbridge Ware', thesis Museums Association Aug 1969 p. 34. I am also indebted to Sandra Kilmington for allowing me to examine material formerly belonging to Albert Botton.

11. Much of the information in this section is based on an interview with the late LJ Green, son of Thomas Littleton Green in 1980 and an inspection of material held by him, for which I would like to express my thanks.

Chapter 11

1. I am greatly indebted to Peter and Daphne Benjamin for allowing me to see their workshop and productions, and discussing their business; *Bracket* 16 May 1997, lot 63.

2. TWM price list of Albert Fickling dated 1977.

3. Paula Davies, 'Intricate Art from Tunbridge', *Daily Telegraph* 18 Mar 1991; *Financial Times* 18 July 1991.

4. Len Garrett, 'Tunbridge Ware Revived' *The Craftsman* 11 (1986) p. 4; Mike Sherry, 'Miniature Mosaics' *Popular Crafts* (March 1989) pp. 32–34.

5. Bill Adams, 'The Many Faces of Tunbridge Ware' *Woodworker* Vol 95 No 7 (July 1991) pp. 732–36.

Chapter 12

1. PRO RG10/927; Henry R Knipe (ed), *Tunbridge Wells and its Neighbourhood* (Tunbridge Wells 1916) p. 203; *The Kent & Sussex Courier* 17 July 1903.

2. SH will of Edmund Nye d 28 June 1863.

3. PRO RG10/927; *The Tunbridge Wells Gazette* 23 Sept 1864, 20 Sept 1864; *The Kent & Sussex Courier* 17 July 1903; Pelton (1883) p. 78; *Green & Co's Mid-Kent Court Guide, Gazetteer and County Blue Book* (1874) advertisement.

4. *The Tunbridge Wells Gazette* 27 Mar 1891; *The Tunbridge Wells Advertiser* 13 Oct 1899; *The Kent & Sussex Courier* 17 July 1903; Sandbach (*Practical Education*) pp. 80–81.

5. *The Kent & Sussex Courier* 17 Jul 1903; *Kelly's Kent Directory* (1905), (1911); W Stanley Martin & Prescott Row, *Tunbridge Wells of Today* (2nd edn 1906) p. 27.

6. TWM Statement of Alfred A Brown 31 Oct 1941; Indenture of James Hollamby 25 Mar 1878; *Post Office Directory of the Six Home Counties* (1862); *The Post Office Directory of Kent* (1865), (1878), (1882); *The Tunbridge Wells Advertiser* 12 Aug 1910, 20 March 1914; *The Kent & Sussex Courier* 20 March 1914.

7. *The Tunbridge Wells Advertiser* 28 Feb 1890.

8. Birmingham Museum (Pinto Collection) statement by AF Hemsley 14 Oct 1969; TWM Letter B Ellis to C Mackintosh 1 June 1916; *The Tunbridge Wells Advertiser* 12 Aug 1910, 19 Aug 1910.

9. Savidge p. 49; Luke Pearce, *Historical Associations of the Free Churches of Tunbridge Wells &c 1642–1904* (Tunbridge Wells 1904) p. 66 states that Jordan was a Tunbridge ware manufacturer, possibly on the basis of *Colbran's New Guide for Tunbridge Wells* (1840) p. 96.

10. KCAO P344/1/5; U477/P1; U749/E15, U749/E16, U749/E17, U749/E18, U749/E19, U749/E26, U749/E27, U749/E28, U749/E35, U749/E38; TWM Sprange II 248.

11. KCAO P344/17, P344/1 Index to burials; PRO HO107/463; WRL Letter books of Hastings Nathaniel Middleton Vol 1 15 & 26 Oct 1816; *Colbran's Hand Book and Directory of Tunbridge Wells* (Tunbridge Wells 1847) p. 114, (Tunbridge Wells 1850) p. 115; *The Sussex Agricultural Express* 28 Oct 1837; Phippen (1844) advertisement p. 21; *The Tunbridge Wells Guide and Directory* (Tunbridge Wells nd 1845) p. 62; *The Post Office Directory of the Six Home Counties* (1851); Samuel Bagshaw, *History, Gazetteer and Directory of the County of Kent* (1847); *Furniture History* XXXIII 267, 269.

12. KCAO U479/E20; U785/T10; P344/11/1; Hotzapfel Vol II pp. 763–64; Phippen (1840) advertisement.

13. KCAO P344/11/1; P371 Marriage register Holy Trinity, Tunbridge Wells 14 Jan 1842. Although there is clear evidence for a partnership from 1828–31 rates thereafter were paid solely in the name of George Burrows for a number of years and separate entries appear in both the 1832 and 1834 editions of *Pigot's* directories. It is not until 1839 that George and James are once more linked. This might suggest a period of individual enterprise from 1832–38.

14. *The Post Office Directory of the Six Home Counties* (1845), (1855).

15. PRO HO107/1614; *The Tunbridge Wells Guide and Directory* (Tunbridge Wells nd 1845).

16. KCAO DRb/RT2/371E/2; *The Post Office Directory of the Six Home Counties* (1878); *WE Owen & Co's Directory of the County of Kent* (1883).

17. KCAO U749/E15; TWM Sprange 76.

18. KCAO U749/E15, U749/E19; P344/11/1; *T Barrow's Map of Tunbridge Wells* (1808); Pearce p. 30.

19. KCAO CTR 344A/344B; Phippen (1840) advertisement p. 17; Edwin Marks (pub), *A Summer Excursion to Tunbridge Wells* (Tunbridge Wells nd *c*1840) pp. 145–46; *Colbran's Hand Book & Directory* (1847) p. 114, (1850) p. 115; TWM unattributed newspaper cutting 28 May 1837; Britton (1832) p. 318; *The Post Office Directory of the Six Home Counties* (1855). I am indebted to Diana Durden for information regarding the family history of JT Ubsdell.

20. KCAO P344/11/1, P344/1 index to burials; PRO HO 107/1614; RG9/491; Phippen (1840) p. 117; Box trade card John Johnson collection; *Simpson & Co's Directory … of Canterbury, Dover & Maidstone …* (1865); *The Post Office Directory of Kent* (1865); *The Tunbridge Wells Gazette* 15 March 1867.

21. TWM Apprenticeship indenture 29 May 1831; *The Tonbridge Wells Guide and Directory* (Tunbridge Wells nd 1845); T*he Post Office Directory of the Six Home Counties* (1855); *The Official Descriptive and Illustrated Catalogue of the Great Exhibition 1851* Vol II (1851) p. 791; *New York Industrial Exhibition – 1853 – General Report of the British Commissioners* (1854) p. 39; *The Illustrated Catalogue of the 1862 International Exhibition – British Division* Vol II (1862) p. 21.

22. Pelton (1883) pp. 77–78, (1896) p. 103; TWM advertisement.

23. KCAO U749/E15; P344/11/1; U785/T10.

24. Phippen (1840) p. 117; *Brackett's Sale Catalogue* 24 Feb 1933 lot 373; *The Tonbridge Wells Guide and Directory* (Tunbridge Wells nd 1845) p. 88; Bracket p. 50; John & Jill Ford pp. 294, 297, 345; *Pigot & Co's National Commercial Directory* (1835); *Pigot's & Co's London & Provincial Commercial Directory* (1826).

25. Phippen (1840) advertisement p. 28; *The Tunbridge Wells Guide and Directory* (Tunbridge Wells nd 1845) p. 88; *The Sussex Agricultural Express* 29 Mar 1851; Robert Ellis Vol II p. 733; *Exhibition of the Works of Industry of All Nations – 1851 – Report of Juries Vol II* (1852) p. 1213; SH will of Edmund Nye d 28 June 1863.

26. PRO HO107/462; RA Y175/182, 186; *Post Office Directory of the Six Home Counties* (1851); Ellis Vol II p. 791.

27. PRO RG10/928; *Sotheby Belgravia Catalogue* 3 Dec 1980 lot 275; *Connoisseur* Aug 1920 pp. 226–27; *Post Office Directory of the Six Home Counties* (1862); *The Tunbridge Wells Journal* 2 July 1863; *A Guide to the Rides, Drives and Places of Interest in the Neighbourhood of Tunbridge Wells* (1873).

28. KCAO CTR 371A, CTR 371E; PRO HO107/463; *Pigot & Co's London & Provincial New Commercial Directory* (1823); Phippen (1840) p. 117, advertisement p. 10; Ellis Vol II index; *Melville & Co's Directory & Gazetteer of Kent* (1858).

29. PRO HO107/1614; ESRO PAR 344/1/2/1; Phippen (1844) advertisement p. 8; *Melville & Co's Directory & Gazetteer of Kent* (1858).

30. PRO HO107/462, HO107/1614; RG9/492, RG10/928; ESRO PAR 255/1/2/6, PAR 255/1/2/8, PAR 255/1/2/13; *Melville & Co's Directory & Gazetteer of Kent* (1858); *The Post Office Directory of the Six Home Counties* (1859); *Simpson & Co's Directory and Court Guide of Canterbury, Dover and Maidstone* (1865); *Bracket's Descriptive Hand Guide to Tunbridge Wells* (nd 1863?) advertisement of J Luck.

31. BL Ac5962b/5, Ac5962b/6; KCAO U55/T385.

32. KCAO P371/12/4, P371/12/5, P371/12/6; BL Ac5962b/5; *Bailey's British Directory* Vol 4 (1784).

33. TWM Sprange 9, 11, 14, 32, 39, 53, 54, 56, 104, 110, 154; John & Jill Ford pp. 345, 393; Bracket p. 50; *Maidstone Journal* 22 Jul 1800; Wadmore p. 106.

34. KCAO CTR 371C, CTR 371E.

35. E Berresford Chancellor, 'A Note on Tunbridge Ware' *Connoisseur* Jan 1935 p. 32; Wadmore p. 107; *Pigot & Co's Royal National Commercial Directory* (1840) advertisement; *Melville & Co's Directory & Gazetteer of Kent* (1858) advertisement; JF Wadmore, *Tonbridge Priory* (Tonbridge nd *c*1875) p. 16.

36. William Tiffen, *The Hand-Book and Guide to the Town and Port of Folkestone* (1850) advertisement.

37. TWM Handbill announcing the opening of Wise's Tunbridge Wells showrooms; Savidge p. 112; *Pigot & Co's National London & Provincial Directory* (1832); *The Tunbridge Wells Guide and Directory* (Tunbridge Wells nd 1845) p. 62; *The Tunbridge Wells Gazette* 26 Jan 1857.

38. Goodrich p. 237; *New York Industrial Exhibition 1853 – General Report of the British Commissioners* (1854) p. 40; Christie 10 Apr 1986 lot 86.

39. SH will of George Wise Snr d 2 Mar 1869; PRO RG9.494; *The Tonbridge Telegraph* 13 Mar 1869.

40. It may be significant that George Wise Jnr's wife was born in Warwick.

41. PRO HO107/1615; RG9/494; *The Post Office Directory of the Six Home Counties* (1862), (1878); *WE Owen & Co's Directory of Kent* (1883); Wadmore p. 106; SH Will of George Wise Jnr d 13 Feb 1899; *Tonbridge Free Press* 18 Feb 1899.

42. Only one principal may have been involved, i.e. a Serjeant John Whitten Morris, but the baptismal records of St Nicholas parish show a John and Maria Morris, parents of Abraham Morris of John Street in 1817 and a Serjeant Whitten and Elizabeth Morris of Trafalgar Place in 1814, both fathers declaring their trade as Tunbridge ware manufacturers (ESRO PAR255/1/2/1, PAR255/1/2/2).

43. ESRO PAR 255/1/2/1; BM Banks 122.13; *Baxter's Stranger in Brighton and New Brighton Directory* (Brighton 1822); John & Jill Ford, gallery 721, 722; E Wallis, *Brighton Townsman and Visitor's Directory* (Brighton 1826), p. 45.

44. BPL SB 352.1 BRI 1835 poor rate book, 1836 Church rate book; R83-872 SB 352.1 B76 poor rate book *c*1848; Erredge 8/53; PRO LC11/134; ESRO PAR 255/1/2/2, *Folthorp's Court Guide and General Directory for Brighton* (Brighton 1848).

45. PRO HO107/1645; KCAO U749/E15, U749/E35, U749/E38; ESRO PAR 255/1/2/1, PAR 255/1/2/2, 255/1/2/5, PAR 255/1/2/9; *Baxter's Stranger in Brighton and New Brighton Directory* (Brighton 1822), (Brighton 1824); *Pigot & Co's London & Provincial Directory* (1823), (1828); John & Jill Ford No 614 p. 313.

46. PRO HO107/1645; ESRO PAR 255/1/2/2; PAR 259/1/2/1; BPL SB 352.1 BRI poor rate book 1834, general rate book 1854; *Robson's Commercial Directory of the Seven Counties* (1838); *The Post Office Brighton Directory* (1846); *The Post Office Directory of the Six Home Counties* (1845), (1851), (1855), (1859); *Folthorp's General Directory for Brighton* (Brighton 1864).

47. ESRO PAC 344/1/2/1; PAR 255/1/3/11; RGP Kerredge, *A History of Lancing* (Chichester 1979) pp. 3, 5; E Wallis, *Brighton as it is* (1832) p. 70; JD Parry, *An Historical and Descriptive Account of the Coast of Sussex* (1833) pp. 363–4; Richard Dally, *The Arundel Guide* (1830) pp. 74–5; Thomas Walker Horsefield, *The History, Antiquities and Topography of the County of Sussex*, Vol. II (Lewes 1835) p. 207; WM Medhurst handbill; WBC/BW/P19–20, 64–65.

48. ESRO PAR 255/1/3/11; PAR 344/1/2/1; WM Transcript of Medhurst handbill; *The Post Office Directory of Hampshire, Dorsetshire and Wiltshire* (1846); *The Post Office Directory of Dorsetshire* (1855), (1859); *Somerset & Dorset Notes & Queries* Vol 11 (1908) pp. 64–65; John Hutchins, *The History and Antiquities of the County of Dorset* Vol I (3rd edn 1863) pp. 838–39.

49. PRO RG9/614, RG9/1349; WBC/BW/P/64–65. I am indebted to Dr WR Boon for information on the Medhurst family.

Chapter 13

1. Arthur Young, 'A Tour in Ireland … Made in the Years 1776, 1777 and 1778' in John Pinkerton (ed), *A General Collection of … Voyages and Travels* Vol III (1809) p. 847.

2. Nicholas Carlisle, *A Topographical Dictionary of Ireland* (1810); Henry D Inglis, *A Journey Throughout Ireland During … 1834* (5th edn 1838) p. 125; GN Wright, *A Guide to the Lakes of Killarney* (1822) pp 6, 9; Samuel Lewis, *A Topographical Dictionary of Ireland* (1837) Vol II pp. 126–27; James Fraser, *Handbook for the Lakes of Killarney* (1849) pp. 3, 21; Anon., *A Familar and Accurate Hand-Book from London to the Lakes of Killarney* (1846) pp. 6–10; *The Times* 2 Dec 1853.

3. Anon., *The Tourist's Picturesque Guide to Killarney and Cork* (1872) pp. 68–69; Henry Parkinson and Peter Lund Simmons, *The Illustrated Record and Descriptive Catalogue of the Dublin Industrial Exhibition of 1865* (1866) p. 303; Anon., *Picturesque Guide to the Lakes of Killarney* (Dublin 1851) tourist's advertiser p. 15; *Pigot & Co's City of Dublin and Hibernian Provincial Directory* (1824), (1826); *Killarney – The Prince of Wales's Visit* (1858).

4. Lewis p. 127; *Killarney – The Prince of Wales's Visit* (1858); *Official and Descriptive Catalogue of the Great Exhibition 1851* Vol 2 p. 675.

5. *The Dublin Evening Mail* 27 Aug 1861. The view of Muckross Abbey frequently used resembles that in Mr & Mrs SC Hall, *Ireland – Its Scenery, Character &c* Vol I (1841) p. 215.

6. John Francis Maguire, *The Industrial Movement in Ireland as Illustrated by the National Exhibition of 1852* (1854) pp. 80–81; Brian Austen, 'Tourism and Industry: Killarney and its Furniture', *Irish Arts Review* Handbook Vol 12 (Dublin 1995) p. 50.

7. Jeanne Sheehy, *The Re-discovery of Ireland's Past: The Celtic Revival 1830–1930* (1980) p. 79.

8. Arthur J Jones Son & Co, *Descriptive of a Suite of Sculptured Decorative Furniture Illustrative of Irish History …* (Dublin 1853); *The Irish Builder* Vol XXIII No 528 (1881) p. 372.

9. *Killarney – The Prince of Wales's Visit* (1858); 'How to see Killarney in one Day' *Dublin University Magazine* Vol XXIV pp. 745–48 (Dec 1844); Anon., *A Familiar and Accurate Hand-Book from London to the Lakes of Killarney* (1846) p. 27.

10. Michael Norton, 'Muckross Abbey Furniture' *Country Life* 21 Jul 1955 p. 154; Mr & Mrs SC Hall, *Handbook for Ireland – The South and Killarney* (1853) p. 64ff; *The Dublin Evening Mail* 27 Aug 1861; *Slater's Royal National Commercial Directory of Ireland 1870–71* (1870).

11. *Killarney – The Prince of Wales's Visit* (1858); *Official Catalogue of the Exhibition of Irish Arts and Manufactures, 1882, Rotunda, Dublin* (Dublin 1882), p. 42.

12. Anon., *A Familiar and Accurate Hand-Book from London to the Lakes of Killarney* (1846) p. 27; Mr & Mrs SC Hall, *Ireland: Its Scenery, Character &c* Vol I (1841) p. 255; *Killarney – The Prince of Wales's Visit* (1858); *The New York Industrial Exhibition 1853 – General Report of the British Commissioners* (1854) p. 40; *Irish Industrial Exhibition, World Fair St Louis* (Dublin 1914) p. 41.

13. *Killarney – The Prince of Wales's Visit* (1858); *Royal National Directory of Ireland* (1894) Vol I; *Kelly's Directory of Ireland* (1905) Vol II p. 278.

14. Mrs & Mrs SC Hall, *A Week in Killarney* (1850) p. 121; Mr & Mrs SC Hall, *Handbook for Ireland – The South and Killarney* (1853) p. 64; *The Dublin Evening Mail* 27 Aug 1861; *Killarney – The Prince of Wales's Visit* (1858).

15. *Killarney – The Prince of Wales's Visit* (1858) reprinted from the *The Tralee Chronicle and Killarney Echo*.

16. Ibid.; *The Tralee Chronicle and Killarney Echo* 27 Aug 1861, 20 Aug 1861; *Picturesque Guide to the Lakes of Killarney* (Dublin 1851) p. 15.

17. Maguire p. 79.

18. An Oxonian (S Reynolds Hole), *A Little Tour in Ireland* (1859) pp. 137–38.

19. *Killarney – The Prince of Wales's Visit* (1858); John Sproule (ed), *Irish National Exhibition of 1853 – A Detailed Catalogue of its Contents* (Dublin 1854) p. 412; Hole p. 163.

20. Hole p. 171; Mr & Mrs SC Hall, *A Week at Killarney* (1850) pp. 102–21; A.R.B., *Lake Lore or an Antiquarian Guide to Some of the Ruins and Recollections of Killarney* (Dublin 1853) p. 11; *Picturesque Guide to the Lakes of Killarney* (Dublin 1853) p. 15; The Knight of Glin, 'Dublin Directories and Trade Labels' *Furniture History* XXI (1985) p. 266.

21. *Slater's Royal National Commercial Directory of Ireland* (1870), (1881); *Guy's Directory of the Province of Munster* (1886), (1893); *Royal National Directory of Ireland* (1894); *Kelly's Directory of Ireland* (1905); *Cork Industrial Exhibition 1883 – Report of Executive Committee, Awards of Jurors* (Cork 1886) p. 417; Bella Sidney Woolf & Thomas Julian Goodlake, *Killarney and Round About* (Dublin 1901) p. 21.

22. The report of this method of trading in Thomas Nelson (publisher), *Souvenir of the Lakes of Killarney and Glengariff* (1892) p. 14 can be largely discounted as it is phrased in exactly the same words as used in RM Ballantyne, *The Lakes of Killarney* (1859) pp. 21–22.

23. Ward Lock & Co's *Killarney and South West of Ireland* (nd *c*1930) p. 96.

24. *Journal and Proceedings of the Arts and Crafts Society of Ireland* (1896) p. 36, (1897) pp. 175–77; Norton p. 154.

25. *Irish International Exhibition 1907 – Home Industries Section, Irish Rural Life and Industry* (Dublin 1907); *Irish Industrial Exhibition, World Fair, St Louis 1914* (Dublin 1914) p. 42; *Journal and Proceedings of the Arts and Crafts Society of Ireland* (1901) p. 202.

26. *The Irish Press* 18 July 1946; Norton pp. 152, 154.

27. One bookstand is in the collection of the Kerry Folk-Life and History Museum, Muckross House, and the other in a private collection in Dublin.

28. Wolff p. 51.

29. G. Bernard Hughes, 'Tunbridge Ware' *Country Life* 13 Aug 1948 p. 325.

30. Pinto, plate 19.

31. Edward T. Joy, *English Furniture 1800–1851* (1977) p. 287.

Chapter 14

1. Burr p. 107; Clifford (1840) p. 32.

2. Philippine Cruysmans, 'Le Charme Révolu des Bois de Spa', *Connaissance des Arts* March 1997 p. 73.

3. Ibid p. 75; Hans Huth, *Lacquers of the West* (1971) p. 107; Ivan Dethier, introduction to *Trois Siècles de Bois de Spa* (Liège 1967) p. 8.

4. Cruysmans pp. 75, 77; Huth pp. 107–08; Hugh Honour, 'European Lacquer Furniture' in LGG Ramsey, *The Concise Encyclopaedia of Antiques* Vol 4 (1959) pp. 44–45; Hugh Honour, *Cabinet Makers and Furniture Designers* (1972) pp. 62–63.

5. Dethier pp. 9, 20–22; Cruysmans pp. 75–77; Hugh Honour, *Cabinet Makers and Furniture Designers* (1972) pp. 50–59.

6. Anon., *Two Sketches of France, Belgium and Spa in Two Tours During the Summers of 1771 and 1816* (1817) pp. 47–48, 124; Cruysmans pp. 73–74; Huth pp. 108–09.

7. Cruysmans p. 75; Huth p. 109; *Trois Siècles* Nos 169, 170 pp. 51, 61.

8. Huth p. 108.

9. Ibid; *Trois Siècles* p. 16, No 28 p. 24, No 41 p. 28, No 52 p. 29, No 54 p. 30, No 79 p. 35; V & A W21-1914.

10. Huth p. 108; Cruysmans pp. 72, 75, 77; *Trois Siècles* p. 12, No 103 p. 39, No 109 p. 41, No 148 p. 46, Nos 156–57 p. 47, No 177 p. 52, No 202 p. 196, Nos 199–201 p. 56.

11. Huth p. 108; *Trois Siècles* No 98 p. 38, Nos 174–75 p. 51, No 191 p. 55, No 205 p. 59.

12. Huth p. 109.

13. Huth pp. 109, 115–16; Pinto pp. 71–72. For a fuller description of Mauchline and Scottish wares see pp. 215–19.

14. *Trois Siècles* No 203 p. 56; *Two Sketches* pp. 121–22.

15. *Trois Siècles* p. 15, No 253 p. 66; *Illustrated London News* 4 Oct 1851; *Official Descriptive and Illustrated Catalogue of the 1851 Great Exhibition* Vol III (1851) p. 1164; *Exhibition of the Works of All Nations 1851 – Reports by the Juries* (1852) p. 653, 655.

16. *Trois Siècles* pp. 16–17, 63–79; Wolff p. 50; J Radford Thomas, *Pelton's Illustrated Guide to Tunbridge Wells* (Tunbridge Wells 6th edn 1874) p. 65; *1851 Exhibition – Reports by the Juries* (1852) p. 653.

17. Cruysmans p. 77; *Trois Siècles* p. 15.

Chapter 15

1. Pinto pp. 32–33; Sandbach *(Practical Education)* p. 179.

2. Serge Grandjean, *Empire Furniture* (1966) pp. 61–62; Hugh Honor, 'Nineteenth Century Italy' in Helena Hayward (ed), *World Furniture* (1965) p. 267.

3. Alessandro Fiorentino, *L'arte della Tarsia a Sorrento* (Naples 1982) pp. 44, 46.

4. *London International Exhibition 1862 – Kingdom of Italy – Official Descriptive Catalogue* (1862) p. 341; *Report of the Juries* (1863) pp. 27, 53, 58.

5. Fiorentino p. 42.

6. *London – Exhibition of the Works of Industry of All Nations – Reports by the Juries* (1852) p. 545; George Dodd, *Where do we Get it and How is it Made?* (1862) p. 153; *New York Industrial Exhibition 1853 – General Report of the British Commissioners* (1854) p. 40; *London – International Exhibition 1862 – Kingdom of Italy – Official Descriptive Catalogue* (1862) p. 341.

7. *The Tunbridge Wells Gazette* 23 Sept 1864.

8. Fiorentino p. 34.

9. *The Tunbridge Wells Advertiser* 12 Aug 1910.

A Note on Mauchline and Scottish Souvenir Woodwares

1. John Baker, *Mauchline Ware* (Princes Risborough 1985); Larch S Garrad, *A Present From …* (Newton Abbot 1976) pp. 28–36; Edward & Eva Pinto, *Tunbridge and Scottish Souvenir Woodware* (1970) pp. 65–119, 142–149.

2. See pp. 251–52.

3. Pinto, pp. 86–87.

4. Baker, p. 5; Garrad pp. 28–30; Pinto pp. 65–73.

5. Baker, pp. 5–6; Garrad pp. 30–31; Pinto pp. 74–85.

6. Baker, pp. 3, 6, 34; Garrad pp. 31–33; Pinto pp. 90–99.

7. Baker, pp. 25–27; Garrad p. 34; Pinto pp. 99–107.

8. Baker, pp. 16–22, 30; Garrad p. 33; Pinto pp. 107–117, 142–49.

9. See pp. 136–37.

10. Baker, pp. 22–24.

11. Baker, pp. 27–29; Garrad p. 35.

12. Baker, pp. 28–29.

13. Pinto, plate 11.

14. Baker, p. 13.

Appendix 1

List of articles manufactured in print-decorated and painted (P) or inlaid and mosaic (M) Tunbridge ware

Artist's colour boxes	P	Counter boxes	M
Banjoes	M	Cribbage scorers	M
Barometer cases	M	Cribbage boards	PM
Bellows	P	Darning-eggs	M
Bezique boxes	M	Decanter boxes	M
Bilboquets (cup-and-ball)	P	Desk boxes	M
Blotter cases	M	Dice-shakers	M
Bobbin cases	PM	Draughts set (travelling)	M
Bonnet-stands	M	Easels	M
Book-bindings	M	Eggs	PM
Book-markers	M	Egg timer	M
Book slides	M	Envelope and stationery boxes	M
Bookstands	PM	Etuis	M
Brooch or stud boxes	M	Footstools	M
Brooches	M	Games boxes	PM
Button boxes	M	Games markers	M
Button hooks	M	Glove boxes	M
Buttons	M	Glove-darners	M
Cabinets of drawers	PM	Graters	PM
Caddy-spoons	M	Hair brushes	M
Cake-baskets	M	Hall letter boxes	M
Candle-arms	M	Handkerchief boxes	M
Candle-stands	M	Hand mirrors	M
Candlesticks	PM	Hand screens	PM
Card- or menu-holders	M	Hat-pin cushions	M
Chairs	M	Humming-tops	M
Cheerot cases	M	Indiarubber boxes	M
Chess boxes	M	Inkstands	M
Chess sets (travelling)	M	Jewel boxes, cabinets and	
Cigar boxes and tables	M	caskets	PM
Cigarette and cigar boxes	M	Kettle-holders	M
Clothes brushes	M	Knitting-needle protectors	M
Coin collector's cabinets	M	Knitting sheaths	M
Compass cases	M	Letter-racks	M
Cotton-reel boxes	PM	Letter-scale bases	M
Cotton-reel stands	M	Lip-salve boxes	PM

Match boxes	M	Sewing clamps	PM
Match-box holders	M	Shawl pins	M
Match stands	M	Silk-ball holders	M
Medicine chests	M	Silk-skein holders	PM
Miniature furniture	M	Silk-winders	PM
Mirror frames	M	Smelling-salts or perfume-	
Money boxes	M	bottle cases	M
Mosaic pictures	M	Solitaire boards and marbles	M
Napkin rings	M	Sovereign cases	M
Necklaces	M	Spectacle cases	M
Needle-books	M	Spice boxes	P
Needle-boxes	M	Spill vases	PM
Needle-cases	M	Spinning-tops	M
Needlework clamps	PM	Stamp boxes	M
Newspaper rests	M	String-holders	M
Notebook cases	M	Studs	M
Nutmeg graters	P	Tables	M
Panorama cases	P	Tape-measure cases	PM
Paper-knives	M	Taper cases	M
Paper-weights	M	Taper-holders	PM
Pen-and-pencil boxes	PM	Tea caddies	PM
Penholders	M	Teapot stands	M
Pen-stands	M	Teapoys	M
Pen-trays	M	Tea trays	M
Pen-wipers	PM	Thermometer stands	M
Pencils	M	Thimble cases	M
Photograph album covers	M	Thread-waxers	M
Photograph and picture frames	M	Thread-winders	M
Pin cushions	PM	Tie-pin boxes	M
Pin-tables	M	Tobacco barrels	M
Pin-trays	PM	Toilet boxes	PM
Pipe-racks	M	Tops	PM
Playing-card boxes	PM	Trays	M
Pleat-holders or weights	M	Trick-opening boxes	M
Pope Joan and Matrimony		Trinket boxes	M
wheels	P	Vinaigrettes	M
Postcard boxes	M	Visiting-card boxes	M
Puzzles and puzzle boxes	PM	Visiting-card cases	M
Razor boxes	M	Visiting-card trays	M
Reel boxes	PM	Watch stands	PM
Reticule frames	M	Whist-markers	M
Ring-spikes	M	Wool-winders	M
Ring-stands	M	Work-baskets	M
Rouge-pots	PM	Workboxes	PM
Rulers	M	Work-tables	M
Scent-bottle holders	M	Writing boxes	M
Seal boxes	M	Writing-slopes (desks)	M
Sealing-wax outfits	M	Yo-Yos	PM

1. Blocks and bandings were sometimes sold to cabinet-makers and these have been seen included in a bookcase, an overmantle, writing desks, a longcase clock case, barometer cases, and even shop display cases.

2. It is unlikely that the list given is exhaustive, but it does demonstrate the wide range of items produced in this decorative ware.

Appendix 2

Topographical prints recorded on items of Tunbridge ware

		Used by[1]	Date of print[2]	Scarcity factor[3]
Devon				
Teignmouth				D
Dorset				
	— The Arched Rock, Lulworth			D
East Sussex				
Bayham Abbey		G. Wise		D
	— Ruins			D
	— Gatehouse			D
Brighton	— Chain Pier – the Pier Head			D
	— Donaldson's Library	G. Wise, Morris	1807	C
	— The Fish Market			D
	— Mrs Fitzherbert's House	G. Wise	1807	C
	— Raggett's and Donaldson Libraries from the Steine			D
	— The Royal Crescent	Izard		D
	— The Royal Mews (Dome)	G. Wise, Morris		C
	— The Royal Pavilion (Classical building by Holland)	T. Wise G. Wise	1803 1807	C
	— The Royal Pavilion ('Hindoo' building by Nash)			A
	— Sea Front and Chain Pier	G. Wise, Upton		A
	— The Steine			C
Buckhurst				C
Hastings	— The Promenade	G. Wise	1813	D
	— Entry to Hastings from the London Road			D

	— St Clement's Church			D
Hove	— The Parish Church	T. Wise	1800	D

Essex

Southend	— Royal Terrace from the sea			D

Gloucestershire

Cheltenham	— Promenade and Pump Room	G. Wise		D
	— Well Walk	Wise		D

Kent

Broadstairs	— Ranelagh Gardens, St Peter's			D
	— Upton Cottage	G. Wise		D
Canterbury	— Canterbury Cathedral			D
Folkestone				D
Gravesend	— The Baths			D
Kingsgate	— Castle	G. Wise		D
Margate	— The Boulevard			D
	— Bettison's Library Hawley Square	T. Wise	1806	C
	— Interior of Bettison's Library	G. Wise		D
	— Dandelion Gardens	G. Wise		D
	— The Marine Library	G. Wise		D
	— The Marine Parade, storm approaching			
	— The New Church from Austin Row			D
	— North Foreland Lighthouse			D
	— Reculver Towers			D
Ramsgate Harbour	— The Brewery and Bridge			D
Reculver	— Towers			D
Sevenoaks	— Knowle			D
Tonbridge	— Mabledon House			D
	— Summerhill House	G. Wise		D
	— The Brewery and the Bridge	G. Wise		D
	— Tonbridge from the Wells Road			C
	— Tonbridge Bridge and Castle	G. Wise		D
	— Tonbridge Castle	G. Wise		C
	— Tonbridge Church	G. Wise		C
	— Tonbridge Church	G. Wise		D
	— Wise & Co's Manufactory	G. Wise		D
Tunbridge Wells	— The Bath House	T. Wise	11 Feb 1806	D
	— Chapel of King			D
	— Charles the Martyr			
	— Edgecumbe Hotel, Mount Edgecumbe			D
	— Entrance to Tunbridge Wells from London	T. Wise	11 Feb 1806	D
	— Grove House, Mount Sion			D

	— Mount Edgcumbe			D
	— The Parade	T. Wise	1805	
		E. Nye		B
	— The Rocks	W. Fenner	1824	D
	— The Tea House,			D
	High Rocks			D
	— Wellington Place			D

Lincolnshire

Louth from Thorpe Hall	D

London

The Bank of England from Bartholomew Lane	D
Greenwich Park	
Kew Palace (James Wyatt's castellated building)	D
New London Bridge	D
The Quadrant, Regent Street	D
The Queen's House	D
Regents Park	D
The Naval School and Hospital from Greenwich Park	D
Syon (Syon) House	D

Somerset

Bath	— All Saints Chapel	D
	— Bath Abbey Church	D
	— Royal Crescent	D

Warwickshire

Astley Castle	D

West Sussex

Selden Cottage (Salvington)			D
Worthing	— Stafford's Marine	G. Wise	D
	Library		

Overseas

The Wooden Theatre at Moscow (used in	D
conjunction with a view of Holland's Royal	
Pavilion, Brighton)	

Notes

A considerable number of prints exist which appear to have been intended for box decoration but have not yet been recorded as used on pieces of Tunbridge ware. Examples by Wise are in the collections of Tonbridge and Margate branches of the Kent County Libraries and the Tunbridge Wells Museum. A large number of views by Izard, Morris, Upton, Wise and others are recorded in John and Jill Ford, *Images of Brighton* (Twickenham 1981).

For the most popular print-decorated subjects, e.g. the Chain Pier, Brighton Pavilion and the Parade, Tunbridge Wells, a number of different engravings were produced and used.

1. Both Thomas and George Wise frequently marked their work by applying the description and imprint from below the print to the interior of the box. Some Wise prints lack the imprint and thus only a description will be found. Other makers, especially those in Brighton, seldom marked their wares.

2. The dates, where indicated, are those of the first publication of the print.

3. Scarcity factor:

A	Very common	above 30 examples known
B	Common	10 to 30 examples known
C	Uncommon	
D	Scarce	

APPENDIX 3

Topographical mosaic blocks

		Makers using the block	Scarcity factor
A. ENGLAND			
Berkshire			
Eton College		D	D
Windsor Castle	— The State Apartments	Wise	C
	— The Round Tower[1]	Wise	D
East Sussex			
Battle Abbey	— The Cloisters	B, D	C
	— The Gatehouse	B, D, Wise, Hollamby, Boyce, Brown & Kemp	B
	— The Gatehouse (graduated perspective block)	Barton	C
Bayham Abbey		B, D, Barton, Hollamby, Nye	B
+ Buckhurst Park		D, Barton	C
+ Eridge Castle		B, D, Barton, H. Burrows, Talbot, Nye, Hollamby, Boyce, Brown & Kemp	A
Frant Church & Depository		D, Wise(?)	D
Herstmonceux Castle[2]		B, D, Hollamby	C
Rye Windmill[3]		Green	D
Gloucestershire			
Cheltenham	— Churchill & Plough Hotel		D
Hampshire			
Netley Abbey		D	C

244

Hereford and Worcester

Eastnor Castle		Hollamby	D
Malvern Priory Church			C

Kent

Cobham Hall		Wise	D
Dover Castle		B, D	C
St Mary in Castro Church and Pharos		B	D
Hadlow Castle		Wise	D
Hever Castle		D, Barton, Hollamby, Boyce, Brown & Kemp	C
Knole			D
Leeds Castle		Garrett	
Penshurst Place	— North face	Wise(?)	D
	— West face	B, D, Hollamby, Boyce, Brown & Kemp	C
	— Solar and Buckingham Building	B, D, Hollamby, Boyce, Brown & Kemp	B
+ Tonbridge Castle		B, D, Wise, T. Burrows, Hollamby, Boyce, Brown & Kemp, Tunbridge Wells Manufacturing Co	B
Tonbridge Priory		Wise	D
+ Tunbridge Wells	— Calverley Hotel		D
	— Farnborough Lodge		D
+	— St Helena Cottage[4]	D	C
	— Holy Trinity Church		D
+	— Hurst Wood Cottage	D	D
	— The Lodge, Calverley Park		D
	— View from Mount Ephraim[5]	Russell, Talbot	C
	— The Pantiles	D, Hollamby, Boyce, Brown & Kemp	B
	— Romanoff House (or School)		D
	— The Toad Rock, Rusthall Common		D

London

St Paul's Cathedral — West front		Vorley	

Warwickshire

Shakespeare's Birthplace, Stratford-upon-Avon[6]		D, Hollamby	C
Warwick Castle		D, Wise	C

Yorkshire

Gisborough Priory		D

B. IRELAND

Muckross Abbey (Friary), Killarney	D, Hollamby	B
Ross Castle, Killarney	Hollamby	C
Glena Cottage, Killarney	Hollamby(?)	C, D

C. SCOTLAND

Abbotsford	C

D. WALES

Carew Castle	D

E. THE UNITED STATES OF AMERICA

The Capitol, Washington DC	D

General Notes

A. A number of views exist which have not yet been identified.

B. This subject is included in a collection of squared topographical designs in the Tunbridge Wells Museum which appear to have connections with blocks used in the main by Henry Hollamby (fig. 34).

C. The Hollamby attribution is on the basis of an advertisement in the Tunbridge Wells Museum collection, and the list of subjects in Henry W. Wolff, *Sussex Industries* (nd *c*1883) p. 51. Hollamby's stock was acquired by Boyce, Brown & Kemp who used many of the same blocks.

D. Blocks of this subject are in a hoard of veneers acquired by T.L. Green of Rye after the collapse of the Tunbridge Wells Manufacturing Co. There is evidence that the Tunbridge Wells Manufacturing Co. used the Tonbridge Castle block and may have used others. It is possible that Green may have used up some stock of veneers.

E. Thomas Barton appears to have used topographical blocks other than the perspective view of Battle Abbey gatehouse. These may have been bought in from Henry Hollamby.

F. The scarcity rating is on a similar basis as that used for appendix 2 for print-decorated wares, i.e. A – very common, B – common, C – uncommon and D – scarce.

G. The views marked '+' exist in more than one form. In some cases the differences in the blocks represent adjustments to account for minor changes that had taken place in the building or its surroundings. In the case of Eridge Castle, however, upwards of 20 or 30 blocks exist, differing greatly in detail and size and represent the work of a number of different makers.

H. Those interested in the views will find KB King, *The Views Illustrated on End-grain Tunbridge Ware Designs* (nd 1981) of value.

Notes

1. This design shows the Tower before it was increased in height by 33ft (10.1m) as part of the works carried out by Sir Jeffrey Wyatville between 1828 and 1832.

2. This view exists in both oval and rectangular frames.

3. There are discrepancies between this block and the smock-mill that now exists at Rye. The mill was, however, burned down in the early 1930s and reconstructed in 1932 in a rather different form.

4. An example of this view is known on an item bearing an Upton (Brighton) stamp.

5. An earlier version of this block shows a windmill to the right. This mill appears to have been demolished some time in the 1840s.

6. Ethel Younghusband, *Mansions, Men and Tunbridge Ware* (Slough, 1949) p. 162 states that this view shows some old cottages at Tenterden, Kent. Hollamby, however, advertised a view of Shakespeare's Birthplace, and this view is so described in an article by Frederick AA Talbot in *The Windsor Magazine* in February 1898.

APPENDIX 4

Tunbridge ware manufacturers and retailers

Name	Address	Period of operation	Remarks	Status
ENGLAND AND WALES				
Berkshire				
Newbury				
Waller, William	Bartholomew St	1770	Cabinet-maker	R
Dorset				
Blandford				
Bastard, Thomas, John & William	Market Place	1731	Cabinet-makers & architects	R
Weymouth				
Edney, G	Birmingham House, 10, St Mary St	c1806	Fancy repository	R
Medhurst, James[1]	Maiden St 9, Chesterfield Pl	1839–51 1851–60		M
East Sussex				
Brighton				
Arnold, Lucy	118, London Rd	1839	Toy & Tunbridge dealer	R
Bell, Elizabeth	3, Kings Rd	1822–24	Toy shop	R
Braddock, James	162, North St	1839	Toy & Tunbridge dealer	R
Brown, Audley	68, East St	1866–67	Tunbridge ware rooms	R
Brown, George	32, Carlton St Carlton Hill	1826 1828	Tunbridge ware maker	M
Buhrer, Joseph	27, North St 28, North St & 1, Ship St	1831–39 1839	Toyman Fancy repository	R R
Burrows, W	104, St James's St	1856	Tunbridge ware stores	R

Burvilme & Littlewood	39, Western Rd	1873–81	Toy & fancy repository	R
Camfield, Thomas	76, St James's St	1850	Tunbridge ware manufacturer	M
Camfield, William	76, St James's St	1851–64	Tunbridge ware & brush manufacturer	M
Chapman, W	1, North St	1822	Dealer in fancy articles	R
Chassereau, George	21, North St	1824–38	Toy dealer & juvenile bookseller	R
Chassereau, Susan	21, North St[2]	1839–52	Toy & fancy repository	R
Chassereau, Mary, Jane & Charlotte	40, Kings Rd	1844–54	Toy & fancy repository	R
Cheesman	9, Cranbourn St	c1830	Tunbridge ware manufacturer	M
Cheesman, Thomas	Riding School La	1832	Tunbridge ware manufacturer	M
Childs, William Snr & Jnr[3]	53, Kings Rd 51 & 51a, Kings Rd	1839–43 1844–73	Dealer in toys &c. Fancy, toy, cabinet warehouse	R
Choat, Thomas	136, North St & 3, Prince's Pl	1811–20	Librarian	R
Clarke, Samuel	The Market & 56, Edward St (1843)	1838–46	Toy dealer	R
Connard, Edward	21, East St	1822	Brighton ware manufactory & fancy japanner	M
Donaldson & Wilkes	7, Marine Parade	1798–c1802	Librarian	R
Donaldson, John Snr & Jnr	Steine	c1802–24	Librarian	R
Fisher, Frederick G	Steine	1800–04	Librarian	R
Fry, Richard	57 Cavendish St	1824	Tunbridge ware manufactory	M
Greenin & Co	13, North St	1839	Toy dealer	R
Greenin, Daniel Harding	20 & 21, East St & 40 Kings Rd (1856)	1839–68	Fancy & toy repository	R
Gregory, James	Steine & 2, North St (1800)	1792–c1809	Librarian, perfumery, jewellery, medicine & toy shop	R
Hewlett, George & Lamin----	72, St James's St	1805–19	Toyman	R
Holding, James	24, Little Castle Sq	1822	Toy shop	R
Hunt, John	Castle Sq	1822–35	Toy manufacturer & dealer	M[4]
Irvin	Civet cat, 111, St James's St	1839	Toy dealer	R
Izard, John	18, St James's St	1822–50	Tunbridge ware manufacturer & toyman	M

Name	Address	Dates	Trade	
Izard, Frank, William	18, St James's St	1851–55[5]	Toy dealer	R
Jaquemart, A	17, Old Steine	1839	Fancy repository	R
Littlewood, Eliza	39, Western Rd	1881–86	Toy & fancy repository	R
Medhurst, James	11, Cumberland Place (1838)	1819–38	Tunbridge ware maker	M
Melluish, Elizabeth	91, Western Rd (1832) 53, Western Rd (1838)	1832–39	Toy dealer & stationer	R
Morris, Abraham	26–28, Richmond Pl	1836–48	Tunbridge ware manufacturer	M
Morris, Edward	Richmond Gardens	1839–47	Tunbridge ware manufacturer	M
Morris, John Witten	Trafalgar Pl 26 & 27, Richmond Pl	1814–20 1820–35	Tunbridge ware manufacturer	M
Mott	West Cliff	c1815	Circulating library	R
Murray, John	86, St James's St	1822	Dealer in fancy goods	R
Paine, Susannah	9, North St	1824–35	Tunbridge ware dealer & juvenile bookseller	R
Payne, R	8, North St 9, North St (1824)	1805–24	Circulating library & bookseller	R
Perry, Robert Harding	27, Western Rd (1850) 39, Western Rd Chain Pier (1855) 31, Western Rd (1858) 51, Kings Rd	1850–58 1874[6]–84	Gutta percha dealer & fancy repository Fancy & toy warehouse	R
Pollard	Marine Parade	c1806–08	Librarian	R
Robinson, John	13, North St (1801) 30, North St (1822)	1801–22	Tunbridge ware manufacturer & perfumerer	M
Rose, John	109, Trafalgar St	1844–46	Tunbridge ware manufacturer	M
Saunders, Edward	14, Cheltenham Pl (1839) 26, New Rd (1839) 3, Western Rd, Hove (1839) 3 & 4, Western Rd, Hove (1845)	1839–78	Tunbridge ware maker, stationer and bookseller	M
Saunders, William	112, St James's St	1826–33	Juvenile bookseller & Tunbridge ware manufacturer	M
Smith, Sarah Ann	64, West St 8, Boyces St	1823–c42 c1842–50[7]	Toy dealer	R
Souch, Elizabeth & Mary Ann	50, North St (1831) 52, North St (1832) 59, North St (1852)	1827–52	Fancy repository	R
Souch, Frederick	33, Ship St (1822) 113, St James's St (1832)	1824–33	Tunbridge ware manufacturer	M

Upton, Miss	40a, Old Steine	1858–61	Tunbridge ware	R
	68b, East St	1862–64	repository	
Upton, William	Trafalgar Pl (1815)	1815–64	Tunbridge ware	M
	New Rd (1818)		manufacturer	
	26, East St & 6,			
	Boyces St (1823)			
	5 Somerset Pl (1828)			
	Pool Lane (1828)			
	1, Kensington Pl (1834)			
	94, Gloucester La (1838)			
	34, Old Steine (1845)			
	2, Marine Parade (1845)			
	19, Pool Valley (1848)			
	5, Kings Rd (1851)			
	40a, Old Steine (1859)			
	5, Kings Rd (1864)			
White, Frederick	St James's St	1822–24	Tunbridge ware	M
			manufacturer	
White, J	25, North Rd	1811	Tunbridge	R
			warehouse	
Whittaker, Benjamin	1a, Hampton Pl,	1855–59	Turner &	M
	Western Rd[8]		Tunbridge ware	
			manufacturer	
Wilkes	Marine Parade	c1802–04	Librarian	R
Ye Harlequin	16a, Kings Rd	1929–31	Antique dealer[9]	R
Antique Shoppe				

Eastbourne

Heatherley, John	Sea houses and	1823–35	Toy & Tunbridge	R
	Church St		warehouse	

Hastings

Moor, IB	Royal Pelham Arcade	c1839	Jeweller, cutler	R
			and silversmith	
Morris, Edward[10]	47, George St	1839–40	French & fancy	M
			repository and	
			Tunbridge ware	
			manufacturer	
Nye, Edmund[11]	10, Castle St, Priory	1826–35	Tunbridge ware	M
			manufacturer	
Wood, John	4, George St (1839)	1839–58	Tunbridge ware	R
	2, Wellington Pl (1855)		repository	

Lewes

Medhurst, George	High St, St Ann's	1832–41	Tunbridge ware	M
			manufacturer &	
			turner	

Rye

Green, Thomas,	Market Rd	1931–39	Tunbridge ware	M
Littleton			manufacturer	

Essex
Southend

Renneson & Tarry	The Library	1823–32	Library & fancy repository	R

Gloucestershire
Cheltenham

Bettison, Samuel	384, High St	1820–30	Librarian, bookseller & stationer	R
Selden	High Street	1813	Bookseller & librarian	R

Hampshire (and Isle of Wight)
Ryde

Hicks, W	60, Union St	1857–59	Photographic gallery	R

Ventnor

Knight & Son	147–49, High St	1852–c90	Bookseller & stationer	R

Hereford & Worcester
Worcester

Cooke, Samuel	Shambles	1841	Tunbridge … plain & fancy Turnery manufacturer	M

Kent
Dover

Barnard, David	157, Snargate St	1847–58	Fancy & foreign warehouse	R
Licence, Robert	21 (later 19), Woolcomber St (1855) & 11, Marine Parade (1865)	1855–83	Turner, Tunbridge ware manufacturer & librarian	M

Folkestone

Stock, Henry	High St & Tontine St	1848–65	Printer, bookseller & Berlin warehouse	R
Tiffen, William[12]	Kingsbridge St	1847–56	Bookseller, librarian & stationer	R

Gravesend

Tully, James	131 Windmill St	1843–47	Bazaar	R

Hever

Moon, Thomas		1829	Tunbridge ware turner	M

Margate

Name	Address	Dates	Occupation	
Bettison, Samuel[13]	Next door to Philpott's Bathing Rooms, High St (1794) NW corner of Hawley Sq (1817)	1793–c1840	Librarian, perfumer	R
Bettison, William, George	Marine Library High St	c1825–35	Librarian	R
Bousfield, Thomas & Pallister, Thomas[14]	Opposite the Assembly Rooms, Cecil Sq	1809–15	Librarians	R
Hall, Joseph	Hawley Sq	1786–95	Librarians	R
Silver, Samuel	E side of Cecil Sq	1797–1808	Librarian	R
Witherden, George	Marine Parade adjoining York Hotel	1823–32	Librarian, bookseller, printer & stationer	R

Ramsgate

Name	Address	Dates	Occupation	
Burgess, John	High St	1816	Librarian	R
Burgess, John & Hunt, William	64, Queen St	1823–40	Librarians	R

Rochester

Name	Address	Dates	Occupation	
Gillman, Webster	Phoenix Printing Office	1790	Printer & librarian	RS

Sevenoaks

Name	Address	Dates	Occupation	
Payne, James		1839–49	Stationer, printer & bookseller	R

Southborough

Name	Address	Dates	Occupation	
Burrows, William		1865–67	Tunbridge ware maker	M
Gasson, William	4, Mountview Villas Holden Park Rd	1862–67	Tunbridge ware manufacturer	M
Hollamby, John	Holden Park Rd	1874	Tunbridge ware manufacturer	M

Tonbridge

Name	Address	Dates	Occupation	
Bridger, Joseph		1839	Toy warehouse	R
Burrows, Thomas	59, High St	1877–83	Tunbridge ware manufacturer	M
Connard		c1790	Tunbridge ware manufcturer	M
Cox, Zachariah		1815–24	Cabinet-maker & Tunbridge ware manufacturer	M
Nye, John		1803–34	Tunbridge ware manufacturer	M
Wise, George[15]	High St	1746–84	Tunbridge ware manufacturer	M

Wise, George Snr	High St	1806–69	Tunbridge ware manufacturer	M
Wise, George Jnr	High St	1862–c76	Tunbridge ware manufacturer	M
Wise, Thomas	High St	1784–1806	Tunbridge ware manufacturer	M

Tunbridge Wells

Adams, John	Parade	1796–1807	Toy shop	R?
Adams, Mrs	Parade	1788–95	Toy shop	R
Allen, Mrs	12, The Parade 22, The Parade	1867 1871	Tunbridge ware repository	R
Baker, Dorcas	Parade	1772–74	Toy seller	R?
Barton, Thomas	10 (later 48), The Parade Manufactory 86, (later 93) Mount Ephraim (Premises on the Parade closed March 1891)	1863–c1910	Tunbridge ware manufacturer	M
Bennett, George	Clarence Terrace, London Rd	1838–40	Tunbridge ware manufacturer	M
Blundell, James & Elizabeth	35, Church Rd	1859–74	Tunbridge ware repository	R
Boyce, Brown & Kemp	106, Camden Rd (renumbered 130)	c1873–1916	Tunbridge ware manufacturers	M
Brown, James Snr	Violet Pl, Camden Rd (1862) Goods Station Rd (1865) Tunnel Tip (1871) 9, Mercer St (1878)	1858–84	Tunbridge ware manufacturer	M
Burrows	Lower Green near Tunbridge Wells and the Parade	1802	Tunbridge ware manufacturer	M
Burrows, George	Hanover & Lodge Parade	1845–c54	Tunbridge ware manufacturer	M
Burrows, George & James	Parade, Gibraltar Cottage & Hanover Rd	1828–45	Tunbridge ware manufacturers	M
Burrows, Humphrey Snr	Jordan House & Parade	c1800–33	Tunbridge ware manufacturer	M
Burrows, Humphrey Jnr	Jordan House & Parade	1833–45	Tunbridge ware manufacturer	M
Burrows, Mary	Parade	1772–81	Toy shop	M?
Burrows, Thomas	Parade	1782–1808	Turner	M
Burrows, William & James Snr	Parade	1820–27	Tunbridge ware manufacturers	M
Burrows, William	London Rd (1845) High St (1847)	1845–51	Tunbridge ware manufacturer	M
Cottington, Charlotte	Parade	1851–52	Tunbridge ware manufacturer	M

Cottington, George & John	Parade & Jordan House	1845–c49	Tunbridge ware manufacturers	M
Dyer, Benjamin	Market Pl (1832) Bedford Pl (1839)	1832–47[16]	Tunbridge ware manufacturer	M
Dyer, John	Market Pl	1845–51	Tunbridge ware manufacturer	M
Ellis, John Thomas	130, Camden Rd	1916–23	Tunbridge ware manufacturer	M
Fenner, John	Parade	1782–87	Turner & toy shop	M
Fenner, William	Parade & Chalet Mt Ephraim	1792–97, 1818–29, 1837–40	Tunbridge ware manufacturer	M
Fenner, William & Nye, James	Parade	1798–1809	Tunbridge ware manufacturers	M
Fenner, William & Nye, Edmund	Parade & Mt Ephraim	1810–17	Tunbridge ware manufacturers	M
Foley, William	Mt Ephraim	1792–1809	Tunbridge ware manufacturer	M
Friend, James	20 & 22 The Parade	1810–65	Tunbridge ware manufacturer	M
Friend & Allen	20 & 22 The Parade	1865–78	Berlin wool & Tunbridge ware repository	M?
Fry, John	Parade	1789–1829	Cabinet-maker	M
Fry, Mary	Parade	1772–78	Tunbridge ware maker & toy shop	M
Gardener, Edward	5, Chapel Pl	1874–87	Bazaar & fancy repository	R
Hardy		1803		R?
Hollamby, Esther	Parade	1862–67	Tunbridge ware dealer	R
Hollamby, Henry	6, Edgar Terrace High St (1845) Chapel Pl & Parade (1855) 12, The Parade & Frant Rd (1858)	1845–91	Tunbridge ware manufacturer	M
Hollamby, John	Parade & Frant Rd	1858–59	Tunbridge ware manufacturer	M
Hollman, George & William	Maryan (Marin) Cottage	1844–45	Tunbridge ware manufacturers	M
Jones, E	Parade	1847	Juvenile & fancy bazaar	R
King, David HE Ltd	130, Camden Rd	1923	Tunbridge ware manufacturer	M
Knight, Joseph		1786–94	Tunbridge ware manufacturer	M
Latter, Dorcas	Parade	1781–83	Toy shop	R?
Latter, James	Culverden Gate	c1795	Tunbridge ware manufacturer	M
Marks, Edwin	Calverley Promenade	1840–47	Librarian	R

Marks, E. Stacey	51, High St	1923–25	Artist's colourman and picture framer	R
Mercer, Jane	Parade	1772–74	Toy shop	R
Nash, John	Parade	1803–40	Librarian	R
Nye, Edmund	Parade & Market Pl (1823) Parade & Chalet, Mt Ephraim (1845)	1818–63	Tunbridge ware manufacturer	M
Nye, Henry	7 & 8, Grosvenor Rd	1839–66[17]	Tunbridge ware manufacturer, fancy repository & library	M
Nye, James	Parade	1757–98	Turner	M
Nye, Sarah	Parade	1810–24		R
Owen		1871	Stationer & toy dealer	R
Owen, Ellen	43, High St	1899–1914	Bazaar	R
Owen, Thomas, Lewin	43, High St	1889–98	Bazaar	R
Pearce, John	7, Mt Pleasant Terrace, High St	1859–67	Bookseller & stationer	R
Pollard, J	Camden Rd	1865	Tunbridge ware manufacturer	M
Porter, Rachael	22, The Pantiles (1904) 12, 14 & 16, The Pantiles (1916)	1904–23	Berlin wool, Tunbridge ware depot & fancy goods	R
Rider	Parish of Speldhurst	1737	Turner	M
Roberts, Christopher	Parade	1792–1820	Tunbridge ware manufacturer	M
Robinson, John	Parade[18]	1792–1809	Perfumer & Tunbridge ware seller	M
Russell, Robert	Vale Place (1841) Chapel Place (1862)	1841–73	Marquetry & Tunbridge ware maker	M
Sharp, Ann	Oldenburgh House, London Rd	1855–58	Tunbridge ware manufacturer	M
Sharp, John, James & Ann	Oldenburgh House, London Rd	1807–55	Tunbridge ware manufacturers	M
Stapley, John	Mount Sion	1847	Tunbridge ware manufacturer	M
Stapley, S (Miss)	Parade	1859–66	Toy & Fancy repository	R
Stidolph, Thomas		1815	Tunbridge ware manufacturer	M
Syme, A (Mrs)	Parade	1847–59	Toy, Tunbridge & perfumery warehouse	R

Syme, Alexander	Parade	1859–67	Fancy repository and Tunbridge ware dealer	R
Talbot, Alfred	Chapel Pl (1844) & 6, Bedford Terrace (1845)	1844–58	Tunbridge ware manufacturer	M
Thorpe, Josiah	98a (later 94), Camden Rd	1874–95	Stationer & fancy repository	R
Tolson, CF (Mrs)	24, The Pantiles	1891–1907	Berlin wool repository	R
Tunbridge Wells Manufacturing Co	128–30, Camden Rd[19]	1924–27	Tunbridge ware manufacturer	M
Ubsdell, John Talbot	Mt Ephraim	1829–34	Tunbridge ware manufacturer	M
Upton, Sarah	Parade	1772–87	Toy shop	R
Waterman, Thomas	Parade Mt Pleasant Terrace High St (1859)	c1851–63	Tunbridge ware manufacturer & toy dealer	M
Wheatley, Frances (Mrs)	Parade	1797	Toy shop	R
Wise, George & Co	11, Calverley Promenade Parade (by 1845)	1832–57	Retail outlet of Tonbridge manufacturer	M

London

Ackermann, Rudolph Snr	101, Strand (1796) 96, Strand (1827)	1796–1856	Print seller & repository of the arts	R
Ackermann, Rudolph Jnr	191, Regent St	1826–60	Print seller & fancy stationer	R
Alexander, John	Elephant and Coffee Mill, 29 Crooked La, Cannon St	1763–93	Ivory & hardwood turner	M
Ashley, John	Greyhound Ct, near Arundel St, Strand	c1750	Goldsmith	R
Axtell, Jonathan & Thomas	41, Bunhill Row Chiswell St (1826) 45, Bunhill Row (1828) 54, Bunhill Row (1830)	1826–38	Turner & Tunbridge ware manufacturers	M[20]
Banks, Ann	60, Bishopsgate Without	1817–25	Turnery & toy warehouse	R
Barnes, Isaac	Blue Coat Boy opposite Buckingham St, Strand	1763–77	Ivory & hardwood turner	M
Batten, HN	Clapham Common	c1820–59	Library & post office	R
Bellamy	Green Parrot near Chancery Lane	1762	Toyman	R

Bellamy, Elizabeth & J	304, Holborn	1782–90	Toy warehouse	R
Bettison, Samuel	17, Theobalds Row, Bloomsbury	1793–94	Perfumer & toyman	R
Blackman, George	362, Oxford St	1799–1823	Artist's colourman	R
Booth, Benjamin	The Rocking Horse near Serjeants Inn	1749–75	Turner	M
Brogden, James	108, Shoe Lane	1832–4		M?
Browning & Hopkins	26, High Holborn	1813		M
Burgess, Alexander	Red Ball & Case of Knives, corner of Leadenhall St, next to Cornhill	c1760	Toyman	R
Cameron, Charles	107, St John's St & 3, Dorrington St, Clerkenwell[21]	1826–35	Tunbridge ware maker	M
Cheeseman, Charles	21, French Row, Aldersgate St	1809	Cabinet-maker & Tunbridge ware maker	M
Cooper, Joseph	The Crown & Bowl, facing St Sepulchure's Church, Tower Hill	c1760	Wood & ivory turner	M
Cormack Brothers	37, Ludgate Hill	1866–89	Leather case and fancy goods maker	M
Crawley, Gerard	45, Cornhill	1743–77	Turner & umbrella warehouse	M
Dore, George	4, Carey La, Foster La	1796–1804	Manufacturer of turnery & Tunbridge ware	M
Deverell, William	The Catherine Wheel, opposite Brownlow St, Holborn	c1750	Turner & toyman	R
Dobson, William	166, Strand	1797–1848	Hardwareman & writing & dressing-case maker	M
Drew, Charles	21, Charlotte St, Gt Surrey St	1830–34		M?
Dunnett, Malcolm	154, Cheapside (1799) 3, Cheapside (1803)	1799–1846	Perfumer & toyman	R
Edlin, Edward C	34, New Bond St (1798) 31, New Bond St (1831)	1798–1832	Turner & toyman	M
Ferguson, Mary	address unrecorded	1686		M

Found, Mary	56, Bishopsgate St Within	1826–28	Toy dealer & turner	M
Fuller, Samuel & Joseph	34, Rathbone Pl	1809–55	Print sellers & stationers	R
Garton, Thomas	7, York Pl, Asylum	1817–18	Tunbridge warehouse	R
Gisbon, John	Ray St Pl, Clerkenwell	1826–41	Tunbridge ware manufacturer	M
Halford, FW	6, Baynes Row, Cold Bath Sq	1811–25	Tunbridge ware manufacturer	M
Hand in Hand Tunbridge ware shop	At the Frost Fair	1716		R
Heath, Robert	34, Brush La, Cannon St	1826–28	Tunbridge ware maker	M
Hepburn, Thomas	103, Oxford St	1817–28	Toy & Tunbridge warehouse	R
Hewlins, Peter	2, Strand (1802) 164, Strand (1807)	1802–14	Cabinet-maker & upholsterer, Tunbridge ware maker	M
Hodges, Richard	Ordinance Wharf, Pedlar's Acre	1826–28	Tunbridge ware manufacture	M
Hollyer, Matilda	31, Burlington Arcade, Piccadilly	1835	Tunbridge ware manufacturer	M
Horne, Robert	20, Barbican	c1770–1827	Turner & drum & colours maker	M
Howard, William	68, Aldersgate (1830) 63, Aldersgate (1836) 62, Barbican (1838)	1830–63	Manufacturer of pocket books, workboxes &c	M
Huguenin, Moses	33, Haymarket	1789–93	Turner & toyman	M
Ivey, John	34, Leather Lane	1781–90	Hardwood & ivory turner	M
Ivey & Jacques	34, Leather Lane	1794	Hardwood & ivory turner	M
Jacques, Thomas	65, Leather Lane	c1795–1817	Tunbridge ware warehouse	M
Jacques, Thomas & John	65, Leather Lane	1817–c1840[22]	Turner & Tunbridge ware maker	M
Jackson, John	The Unicorn, corner of Wood St, Cheapside	1710	Toyman	R
Jackson, Thomas	Golden Coffee Mill, Mutton La, near Clerkenwell Green	1763–83	Turner	M
Jarvis, Samuel & Co	41, Snow Hill	1740–84	Turner & looking-glass seller	M

Kain (late Jones)	25, Ludgate St	c1820	Toy & Tunbridge warehouse	M
Lecoust, Richard	12, Lambeth Walk	1812	Tunbridge ware manufacturer & cabinet maker	M
Lowe & Lawrence	The Coffee Mill, upper end of St John's St Clerkenwell	c1760–70	Hardwood turners	M
Lowe, John & Lawrence	20, White Cross St, Savile Row	1770–91	Hardwood turners	M
Marlborough, William	35, Plumber St, City Road	1832–48	Toy maker	M
Merrick, William	6, St John's Sq Clerkenwell	1817–45	Tunbridge ware manufacturer	M
Nesbitt, William	73, Old St Road, St Lukes	1818–39	Tunbridge ware manufacturer	M
Ordish, Louisa	49, Red Lion St, Holborn	1821–28	Tunbridge ware manufacturer	M
Ordish, Thomas &	12, Great Turnstile (1799) 49, Red Lion St, Holborn (1811)	1799–1821	Tunbridge ware manufacturer	M
Patterson, Joseph	The Crown, New Bond St	1730	Turner & chair maker	M
Pattison, James	28, New Bond St	1784–93	Turner & toyman	M
Pryer, Charles	472, Strand Manufactory: Paradise Row, Chelsea	1790–1803	Turner & cabinet-maker	M
Pryer, Samuel & Son	474, Strand	1785–90	Turners	M
Reilley, William	15, Ironmonger St, St Lukes & from 1844 also 8, Finsbury Terrace, City Rd	1835–51	Cabinet & Tunbridge ware manufacturer	M
Robinson, John	34, Duke St, St James (1795) 53, Piccadilly (1798) 51, Piccadilly (1810)	1795–1811	Tunbridge ware manufacturer & perfumer	M
Robinson, J	5, Margaret St, Cavendish Square	1812–18	Tunbridge warehouse	M
Sandoe, Anthony	4, Devonshire Sq, Queen Square	1820–22	Tunbridge ware manufacturer	M
Scott, Charles	3, Aylesbury St, Clerkenwell	1805–20	Tunbridge ware manufacturer	M
Sexton, G	23, Leadenhall St (1802) 26, Leadenhall St (1815)	1802–38	Perfumer & Tunbridge warehouse	R
Soper, Thomas	209, Borough	1784	Tunbridge & toy warehouse	R

Stephens, Timothy	6, Spread Eagle Ct, Finch Lane	1802–31	Turnery warehouse	R
Sulaman, John	3, Stockwell St, Greenwich	1860–66	Toy and fancy repository	R
Swift, Providence & Maria	7, Brighton Place New Kent Rd	1830–34	Toy dealers	R
Tomkins, Richard	Corner of Clifford St, Savile Row	1783–85	Turner	M
Vale, William	62, Fleet St	1794–1822	Perfumer & Tunbridge ware repository	R
Waite, Robert	Parrot & Star, against Bow Lane, Cheapside	c1770	Toyman	R
West, Edward	42, High Holborn	1815–18	Tunbridge warehouse	R
Wetherstone, Alexander	At the Painted Floor Cloth & Brush, Portugal St, near Lincoln's Inn back gate	1760–65	Carpenter, joiner & turner	M
Willerton & Roberts	Old Bond St	1768–75	Jeweller, & toyman	M

Merseyside
Liverpool

Hausburg, Frederick, Ludwig, Leopold	Old Post Office Buildings, 24 Church St	1845–59	Goldsmith & jewellers	R
Tooke, William	Old Post Office Buildings, 24 Church St	1860–65	Goldsmith & jewellers	R

North Yorkshire
York

Doughty, Joseph	6, Coney St	1795–1801	Toy, Tunbridge turnery & spring blind manufactory	M
Doughty, Martha	Coney St	1801–09	Toy, Tunbridge turnery & spring blind manufactory	M
Marshall & Doughty	Coney St	1795	Toy, turnery, umbrella & cabinet manufacturers	M
Stones, George	Spurriergate (1798) Pavement (1816)	1798–1823	Turner, fancy chair & Tunbridge ware manufacturer	M

Somerset
Bath

Brabant, John	Trim Bridge	1791	Tunbridge & toy warehouse	R

South Glamorgan
Cardiff

Burwell, T		c1830	Probably an itinerant trader	R

West Midlands
Birmingham

Evans, John	Upper Temple St (1821) 30, Colmore St (1828) 87, Hull St (1835)	1821–35	Tunbridge ware manufacturer	M

Coventry

Mann & Stephens	High St	1831–32	Jewellers, silversmiths & watchmakers	R
Tester, S	34a Smithford St (1866) 7 Smithford St (1874)	1866–95	Fancy repository	R

West Sussex
Bognor

Binstead, James	Library Manor House	c1790–1822 1823	Library & toyshop	R
Binstead, Charlotte & Augusta	The Promenade	1839	Library & toyshop	R
Binstead, Augusta	Waterloo Square	1850s	Library & toyshop	R

Worthing

Medhurst, George	12, (or 14) Prospect Row (or Place), and Parade 24, Prospect Place (1880)	1843–92	Turner & Tunbridge manufacturer	M
Medhurst, James[23]	11, West Buildings	1839–60	Tunbridge ware and turnery manufacturer	M
Medhurst, Robert	3, Montague St (1858) 7, Montague St (1866)	1858–78	Tunbridge ware turner	M
Phillips, John	22, South St	1832–59	Bookseller, stationer & fancy repository	R
Spooner, Mary (Mrs)	The Colonnade Library	1814–24	Bookseller, stationer, perfumer & library	R

Stafford's Marine Library	Near the Steine	1805–33	Library	R

Wiltshire
Salisbury

Fellows, C		c1795	Circulating library	R

SCOTLAND
Edinburgh

MacGill	7, Hanover St	c1910		R

IRELAND
Dublin

Kelly, B	55, Chapel St	1834–36	Tunbridge warehouse & stationery	R
Pearson, Susanna	17, Clanbrassil St	1834–36	Toy & Tunbridge warehouse	R
Philpot, Mary	9, Aungier St	1813–27	Tunbridge warehouse	R
Plunkett, Mary	37, Great Britain St	1817–36	Haberdasher & toy seller	R
Raynor, S (Miss)	2, Royal Arcade	1834–36	Tunbridge & fancy warehouse	R
Reaf, Catherine	109 Grafton St	1813	Tunbridge warehouse	R
Spence, Neal	17, Nassau St 21, Nassau St	1809 1811–36	Tunbridge & toy warehouse	R
Spence, Robert	21, Frederick St South	1834–36	Tunbridge warehouse	R

RECENT MAKERS

Adams, William	Birmingham
Benjamin, Peter	Tonbridge, Kent
Fickling, Albert	Dibden Purlieu, Hampshire
Garrett, Len	Brighton, Sussex
Vorley, Charles	Laindon (later Pitsea and Canvey Island), Essex

Notes

1. Also traded in Worthing.
2. From 1824–30 the number was 20, North St. Some directories 1831–33 show Chassereau, T but this may be an error.
3. Probably a retailer and wholesaler. Tessellated mosaic Tunbridge ware does exist with the labels of Wm Childs and Wm Childs Jnr and the latter claimed to be a manufacturer of desks and dressing-cases.
4. From 1822–24 appears to have had a toy manufactory at 44, East St.

5. *Mathieson's Brighton and Suburban Directory* (1868) lists Izard, Frank William at Lion Mansion, 6, Grand Junction Rd & Lion Lodge, Old Steine.

6. Between 1870 and 1874 traded as a house decorator and paper-hanging warehouse from 34, Duke St.

7. Traded thereafter as a marine store dealer (1851) and milliner and dressmaker.

8. Listed as 195, Western Rd in 1859, which may be the same location.

9. The label of this dealer has been seen on a number of pieces of whitewood Tunbridge ware of late Georgian date displaying Brighton views.

10. See also Edward Morris of Brighton. Probably a branch of this Brighton maker.

11. A branch of the noted Tunbridge Wells maker.

12. Also traded at Hythe. The business was continued after 1856 by his daughter Amelia Tiffen.

13. Also traded at 17, Theobolds Row, Bloomsbury, London 1793–94.

14. Successors to Silver.

15. Also had showrooms at 11, Calverley Parade, Tunbridge Wells *c*1832–35 and the Parade *c*1845–57.

16. Listed after 1847 as a cabinet-maker.

17. Only listed as a manufacturer 1839–40. Even in these years the circulating library appears to have been the major activity.

18. Also traded from 34, Duke St, St James's, London and North St, Brighton.

19. London address stated to be 36, Rusholme Road, Putney.

20. Listed until 1838 as a tooth powder box maker. The business survived until 1879.

21. In 1834–35 only 3, Dorrington St.

22. About 1839 this firm moved to 102, Hatton Garden and concentrated more on the manufacture of games equipment. The firm is still trading.

23. Also traded at Weymouth.

APPENDIX 5

Museum collections of Tunbridge ware

Major or substantial collections permanently on view

Birmingham Museum & Art Gallery (The Pinto Collection)
Brighton Museum
Guildhall Museum, Rochester
Hove Museum
Maidstone Museum
Tunbridge Wells Museum
The Victoria & Albert Museum, London
Worthing Museum

Smaller collections not necessarily on view

Dover Museum
The Geffryre Museum, London
Hastings Museum
Hever Castle, Kent
Lancaster Museum
Leith Hall, Huntly, Grampian
Muckross House, Killarney
The Museum of London
Petworth House, West Sussex
The Royal Botanical Gardens, Kew
Salisbury & South Wiltshire Museum, Salisbury
Torre Abbey, Torquay, Devon
The Castle Museum, York

APPENDIX 6

Killarney arbutus ware manufacturers and retailers[1]

Name	Address	Period of operation[2]	Remarks	Status[3]
Coakley, James	4, Main St, Killarney	1858–1905	From 1894 listed only as a bog oak manufacturer	M
Connell, Denis	Killarney (c1830) 10, Nassau St, Dublin (1846) 13 & 26, Nassau St Dublin (1851)	c1830–53	Worked at Killarney c1830–45, subsequently sold arbutus wares at Dublin	M
Connell (widow)	Killarney	1853		R?
Crimmin, Jeremiah	Main St, Killarney	c1852–62	In partnership for part of this period with Cornelius Goggin. Surname also spelt Cremmin.	M
Daly, John	Main St, Killarney	1870		R
Egan, James	New St, Killarney (1844) 8, Main St, Killarney (1846) 5, Main St, KIllarney (1870)	1844–70		M
Eager, Edward	Main St, Killarney	1856	Arbutus dealer	R
French, James	Gap House, Gap of Dunloe, Killarney	1883–c1925		M
Goggin, Cornelius	10, Nassau St, Dublin (1850) 13, Nassau St, Dublin (1851) 75, Grafton St, Dublin (1870)	c1850–83	Manufacturer of bog oak wares and partner of Crimmin in the 1850s. May have operated in the Killarney area before 1850. Sold arbutus wares in Dublin	M

Goggin, Jeremiah	74, Grafton St, Dublin Wood Quay, Dublin	1855–1901 1902–06	Bog oak manufacturer & dealer in fancy goods	M
Hudson, John	Main St, Killarney	1870	Photographer & wholesale publisher of views of Irish scenery	R
Kiernan, John	Arbutus Cottage, Gap of Dunloe, Killarney	c1925–55		M
McCarthy, Justin	Killarney	1852	Displayed furniture at the Cork Exhibition (1852)	M
Neate (widow)	Opposite the Kenmare Arms,	1841–c52	Husband may have manufactured previous to 1841. Moved to Dublin and daughter married Jeremiah Crimmin	M
O'Connell, Daniel	New St, Killarney	1886–93	Arbutus and bog oak carver	M
O'Connelly, John	Main St, Killarney	1846–47	Arbutus dealer	R
O'Connor, Jeremiah	Corner shop opposite the church, Main St, Killarney. Also (1858) additional premises opposite the Kenmare Arms, Main St, Killarney	c1835–36	Described in 1886 as a bog oak warehouse	M

Notes:

1. Only specialist retailers of arbutus wares are indicated here. Many more retail outlets sold such wares in addition to other trades.

2. Few local directories exist and general trade directories of Ireland are sparse, especially for the twentieth century. The dates given here may therefore not reflect the full span of a firm's operation.

3. M = manufacturer, R = retailer.

APPENDIX 7

Museums and houses displaying items of Killarney arbutus ware

Avondale, Rathdrum, Co. Wicklow

Muckross House, Killarney, Co. Kerry – Centre for Kerry Folk-Lore and History.

The National Museum of Ireland, Dublin.

The Ulster Museum, Belfast.

Avondale, Rathdrum, Co. Wicklow

Portsmouth City Museum.

Kensington Palace, London.

APPENDIX 8

Price Guide to Tunbridge and other decorative woodwares

Items produced in quantity, each identical – such as stamps, coins, medals and modern porcelain figures – provide a relatively easy subject for price guides. Tunbridge and other decorative woodwares do not. To try to find identical items of Tunbridge ware is very difficult, and even when larger manufacturers, such as Henry Hollamby, used a number of standard body sizes and shapes, each was veneered differently. Items were also supplied in various grades. Boxes might have only the top decorated with marquetry, the front and top so decorated, three sides and the top decorated or all four sides and the top. There were also various widths of tessellated banding, the wider ones being used for the more expensive pieces. Even the blocks used to decorate the top of boxes can considerably affect the price. Floral subjects are the most common and least expensive; birds, butterflies and animals command a premium. Amongst the views, Eridge Castle is by far the most common. Some of the views are rare, and in an auction where two or more bidders are keen to purchase, can command high prices. A glove box, of no great distinction, in a recent auction sold for £1,500 because the top was decorated with the rare block featuring the Toad Rock, Rusthall Common, Tunbridge Wells[1].

The prices given in this guide are based on actual auction realisations. They exclude buyer's premium in the range 10–15 per cent plus VAT. Retail prices would in general be higher as dealers often source from auctions. Dealers also purchase privately and may well have in stock items bought advantageously and priced accordingly. They may well be no higher in price than auction realisations, and purchase from dealers has the advantage that you can acquire items immediately, without the frustration caused in auction sales of determined rival bidders forcing prices above expectation.

Although larger items are in general more costly than small, this is not necessarily the case. Some collectors try to acquire as many different items as possible and this forces up the price of small items that were only produced in limited quantities, such as tops and yo-yos.

Damage and completeness has to be taken into account when valuing an item. Limited damage to basic veneers, often of rosewood, can be corrected, and minor damage to tessellated mosaic can also be repaired, though the cost of such restoration has to be taken into account. More substantial areas of missing mosaic present real problems however, with high restoration costs and the risk that the repair may be detectable. The purchase of such items can only be justified if they have features of great rarity or interest. Tea caddies may be found without their sugar bowls, or workboxes where the interior tray is missing or the divisions no longer there. A discount from the prices shown would be expected in these cases.

Print-decorated or painted whitewood or veneered Tunbridge wares
Although earlier in date and less plentiful, these early Tunbridge wares do not command prices higher than those for the later tessellated wares. Small boxes, including turned ones, start at around £60 and can rise to £120. Larger boxes, workboxes, etc. can cost substantially more, with £250 to £800 or more being normal. Rare items, such as the spice grater and sewing companion in the shape of the Royal Pavilion domes (fig. 6) can bring substantially more than £1,000 if in good condition.

Early veneered mosaic Tunbridge wares
Items decorated solely in cubic work, vandykes or miniature parquetry are less popular than the later tessellated wares, and command prices at a similar or slightly lower level than those shown below. Prices start at around £120 for a plainer box and can rise to £1,000 for items of particular attraction or size. Items of furniture sell at higher prices and are dealt with later.

Tessellated mosaic wares or inlaid turnery wares
Auction realisations of the most popular items are shown below. These are based on auctions that have taken place in 1999, 2000 and 2001 and exclude buyer's premium.

Blotter covers	£300–£500*	Ring spikes	£65
Book markers	£30–£42	Ring stands	£100–£150
Book slides	£80–£320*	Rouge pots	£40–£70
Book stands	£380–£480	Rulers	£40–£170
Brooches	£30–£150	Scent bottle boxes	
Cabinets of drawers	£720–£1,020	(with bottles)	£550–£850
Caddy spoons	£220–£320	Sealing wax outfits	£150–£220
Clothes brushes	£20–£45	Sewing clamps	£55–£155
Cotton reels	£70–£100	Skein holders	£190–£220
Cribbage boards	£45–£250	Sovereign pots	£50
Desk stands	£400–£1,150	Spectacle cases	£130
Dishes (small)	£22–£45	Spinning tops	£180–£400
Easels	£160–£240	Stamp boxes	£50–£80
Glove boxes	£100–£680*	Stamp boxes (double)	£95–£220
Glove darners	£75–£100	Stamp boxes	
Handkerchief boxes	£70–£300*	(single with tessellated	
Ink bottle stands	£90–£350	Queen's head)	£120–£260
Kettle holders	£30–£95	Stationery cabinets	£320–£650
Jewellery boxes	£140–£420*	Tape measures	£55–£180
Matchbox covers	£50–£65	Taper sticks	£40–£140
Napkin rings	£20–£42	Taper sticks with boxes	£70–£90
Needle boxes	£100–£270	Tea caddies (single)	£210–£350
Needle cases	£40–£160	Tea caddies (two	
Nutmeg graters	£90–£130	compartment)	£220–£880
Paper knives	£25–£85	Teapot stands	£170–£420
Pens	£85–£110	Thermometers	£190–£220
Photo frames	£45–£160	Trinket boxes (small)	£30–£200*
Pin cushions (small)	£30–£180	Trinket boxes (larger)	£70–£300*
Pin cushions (large)	£80–£280	Trays (pin)	£65–£120
Pin cushions (large		Trays (large)	£210–£520
with scent bottles)	£360–£500	Watch stands	£80–£280
Pin wheels	£50–£220	Workboxes	£480–£1,150*
Plaques, framed	£400–£550	Waxers and pin cushions	£30–£120
Playing card boxes	£150–£350	Writing slopes	£620–£1,200
Postcard boxes	£160–£300	Visiting card cases	£70–£160
Propelling pencils	£95–£160	Yo-yos	£180–£450
Puzzle boxes	£60–£90	* higher prices noted because of scarce	
		blocks or other factors.	

Items decorated with Robert Russell's distinctive Tunbridge marquetry (fig. 74) are sought after. The box in fig. 112, although less than perfect, sold for £820[2], around £100–£150 more than a comparable item decorated with tessellated mosaic.

Items bearing maker's labels or stamps command a premium. The common Nye or Barton labels will add £30 to £100, less common labels more. Even retailers' labels are of interest and enhance prices.

Tunbridge ware makers manufactured and sold items of furniture, confined to small tables, including games tables, worktables and teapoys. These are uncommon and in good condition attract substantial prices. Tables and teapoys would start at around £2,000, worktables at around £4,000 but can fetch double or more if attractive.

Killarney woodwares

Much sought after with a considerable demand from a now prosperous Ireland and the USA. Such items are found reasonably frequently in the United Kingdom. Furniture, such as tables, cabinets and Davenports range from £4,000 to £10,000 if well decorated with marquetry, especially Killarney views. Smaller items such as boxes, table cabinets, book slides and paper knives realise prices similar to those of comparable Tunbridge items. Later items of Killarney manufacture tend to be of inferior quality and as a consequence, fetch somewhat less than the nineteenth-century manufactures.

Spa woodwares

These are not often found in the United Kingdom as the main market is in continental Europe. When they are found, the prices tend to be higher than those for painted and print-decorated Tunbridge wares. Mid-nineteenth-century or later Spa items would perhaps be lower in price but are seldom to be found.

Sorrento woodwares

These are often found in the United Kingdom but do not command high prices. Fine and large items, including furniture, will always find ready purchasers at good prices. Even at this top end of the market, prices are lower than comparable Tunbridge items. A good Sorrento writing slope, decorated with marquetry including a large peasant group, will sell for about £450 compared with double that for a Tunbridge ware slope. Good early Sorrento boxes sell for around £80–£150, but much on the market is of twentieth-century date and some of indifferent quality. Auction realisations can be low, with even attractive boxes and other items c1920–50 selling for £30–£60.

Mauchline woodwares

Early penwork and painted wares are relatively scarce, in demand, and as a result are highly priced. A good early Mauchline tea caddy will sell at a price similar to a Tunbridge item of the same period. Later items are more common. Tartan decorated items are in demand, with larger boxes fetching £150 in auction and even smaller boxes £40–£100. Sycamore wares printed with views or decorated with photographs are more commonplace and in auction start at around £20–£25. Larger items decorated with a number of views, or items other than common boxes or serviette rings, command substantially higher prices though somewhat less than corresponding Tunbridge ware items. A strong international collectors group ensures the growing popularity of Mauchline wares.

Price appreciation

Like most antiques, prices of decorative woodwares have appreciated considerably in recent years. In 1970 it was possible to purchase a good Tunbridge ware tea caddy for £25–£30. Today the price would be £500. A stamp box with a tesserae head of Queen Victoria would have been sold in 1970 for £5 but now is £175. In the 1970s, early print-decorated Tunbridge wares were little understood or regarded and sold at low prices. It is not possible to predict future price movements but it seems likely that decorative woodwares will continue to appreciate. Particular antiques and collectables have in the past been subject to fashion and speculation and prices have collapsed when buyers dried up. There has been no recent sign of speculation or fashion in decorative woodwares fortunately, and prices have remained steady at times when other areas were suffering from depressed markets. Any form of collecting as an investment, especially if the purchaser lacks knowledge and interest in the field, brings with it risks and the chance of financial loss. Collectors should only buy because they find items attractive to them and are prepared to advance their study in that field. This road brings pleasure in the possession and in the hunt, and is likely also to be financially rewarding should circumstances require or suggest sale.

The photographs included in this section and the price information is derived from the following auction salerooms: Bracketts, Tunbridge Wells; Christie's, King Street, London; Gorringe, Tunbridge Wells office; Phillips, Bath saleroom; Sotheby's South, Billingshurst.

Notes:
1 Bracketts, 29 September 2000, lot 5.
2 Bracketts, 29 September 2000, lot 104.

104. Octagonal tulipwood box decorated with a print of Kingsgate Castle, Kent, attributable to George Wise. c1815. w:22cm. £190. (Phillips, 29 November 1999).

105. Painted whitewood box, the lid with a print of the Chain Pier and Marine Parade, Brighton. c1825. w:38cm. £500. (Bracketts 7 April 2000).

106. *Card box veneered with cubic work and vandykes. c1825. w:43cm. £350. (Sotheby's, 12 September 2000).* © *Southeby's South.*

107. Back row, left to right: *blotter cover with Pantiles view. c1860. w:27cm. £450; rosewood workbox c1830. w:23cm. £180.* Middle row: *box w:14cm. £110; watch stand w:9cm. £80; Mauchline tartan serviette ring £15.* Front row: *brushes w:16.5cm. £45, £35, £30, £38; postcard box w:14cm. £300. (Bracketts, 7 April 2000).*

273

108. Back row, left to right: *turned whitewood box with Queen Victoria print c1900 dia:7.5cm £30; Sorrento octagonal tray c1930 w:30.5cm £20; watchstand with Barton label h:13cm £220.* Second row: *brush w:15.5cm £30; inkstand w:14cm £160.* Middle: *paper knife £45; puzzle box £65; matchbox £75; stamp box £65; six-inch ruler £40.* Front row: *turned boxes £42–£50 each. (Bracketts, 7 April 2000).*

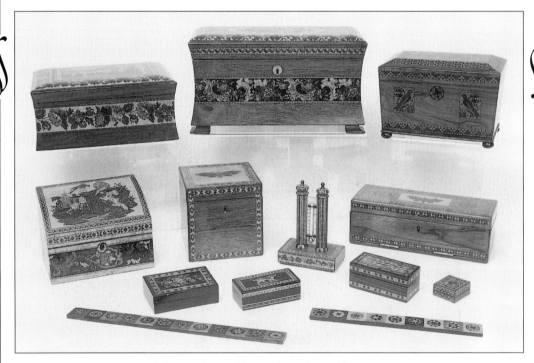

109. Back row, left to right: *workbox with Bayham Abbey view c1860 £700; tea caddy (interior missing) c1860 w:30.5cm £360; tea caddy with birds c1840 w:20.5cm £440.* Middle row: *stationery box, Prince Edward c1850 w:16.5cm £400; tea caddy, butterfly c1850 w:12cm £210; thermometer h:13cm £190; glove box, butterfly c1840 w:23cm £130.* Front row: *boxes £80, with dog £140, £140; stamp box £150; two rulers £110.* (Gorringe, 31 August 1999).

110. Back row, left to right: *stationery box, Eridge Castle view c1840 w:21.5cm £300; tea caddy c1860 w:11.5cm £350; stationery box c1860 w:21.5cm £400.* Middle row: *glove box, Eton College view w:24cm £340; glove box, Eridge Castle view c1845 w:24cm £280.* Front row: *stamp box £100; cribbage board 23 cm £45; matchbox cover £50. (Bracketts, 7 April 2000).*

111. Back row, left to right: *cabinet, Bayham Abbey view c1860 w:20.5cm £1,000; scent bottle box with four bottles c1850 w:15cm £550; tea caddy 15cm £320.* Middle row: *glove box 24.5cm £100; box, Barton label c1870 w:15cm £160.* Front row: *box 16.5cm £120; four cotton reels £350. (Bracketts, 7 April 2000).*

275

112. *Workbox with Russell marquetry. c1860. w:31 cm. £820. (Bracketts, 29 September 2000).*

113. *Rosewood games table with tilt top (some damage). c1850. w of top:46cm. £750. (Bracketts, 7 April 2000).*

114. *Large needlework box with substantial original sewing accessories, probably by Nye. c1840. w:114cm. £3,100. (Sotheby's, 26 October 1999). © Southeby's South*

115. *Work-table, ebony and amboyna veneer, attributable to Barton. c1865. w:65cm. £8,000. (Christie, 13 November 1997).*

SELECT BIBLIOGRAPHY

A. MANUSCRIPTS

East Sussex Libraries – Brighton Reference Library

SB 352.1   Brighton parish rate books 1824–64.

East Sussex Record Office

PAR 255/1/2/1–15	Baptismal registers for the parish of St Nicholas, Brighton 1813–50.
PAR 259/1/2/1	Baptismal register for the Chapel Royal, Brighton 1823–53.
PAR 344/1/2/1–3	Baptismal registers for the parish of St Alban, Frant 1813–94.

Kent County Archives Office

CTR 344A and B	Tithe award map and schedule – Speldhurst 1841.
CTR 371A and B	Tithe award map and schedule – Tonbridge 1838.
CTR 371E	Tithe award map, Tunbridge Wells, 1838.
DRb/Rt2/371A/1/1–10	Bishop's transcripts of parish of SS Peter & Paul, Tonbridge – baptisms 1813–70.
P344/1/5, 18–19	Burial register of the parish of St Mary, Speldhurst 1771–1929.
P344/11/1	Poor relief rate books, St Mary's Speldhurst 1810–45.
P344/17	Militia duty exemptions, Speldhurst 1803.
P371/12/4–6	Accounts of the overseers of the poor, parish of SS Peter & Paul, Tonbridge 1728–1805.
P371	Marriage register of the parish of Holy Trinity, Tunbridge Wells 1837–64.
TR8	Court Rolls, Rusthall Manor, 1673.
U38E1	Particulars and valuation of property on the Walks, Tunbridge Wells 1699.
U55-T385	Deed 28 Apr 1737.
U477-P1	Plan of Walks 1739.
U749/E14–20	Rent books, Walks Estate 1771–1820.

U749/E26	Lease 28 Aug 1752 – William Burrow
U749/E27	Rentals 1741–46 – Walks Estate
U749/E28	Rentals of the estate of John O'Connor 1752.
U749/E35	Sir George Kelly's memorandum book 1771–72.
U749/E38	Rental for the Walks Estate 1772–74.
U749/T2	Lease 30 Aug 1682 for property on the Walks.
U749/T16	Title deed – will of Edmund Baker of Speldhurst 1713.
U785/T10	Leases of property on the Parade 1824–74.

Public Record Office

1841 Census enumerator's returns.

HO107/462–3	Tunbridge Wells and Tonbridge.

1851 Census enumerator's returns.

HO107/1614–15	Tunbridge Wells and Tonbridge.
HO107/1644–46	Brighton.

1861 Census enumerator's returns.

RG9/491–93	Tunbridge Wells.
RG9/614	Worthing.
RG9/1349	Weymouth.

1871 Census enumerator's returns.

RG10/927–30	Tunbridge Wells.
RG10/1049	Frant.
LC 11/134	Lord Chamberlain – Bills, upholsterers &c 1846.

The Royal Archives, Windsor

Y175/182, 186	Accounts books of HRH the Duchess of Kent 1849.

Somerset House

Will of Edmund Nye d 28 June 1865.
Will of George Wise Snr d 2 Mar 1869.

Westminster Reference Library

Letter book of Hastings Nathaniel Middleton Vol I 1816.

B. COLLECTIONS OF PRINTED EPHEMERA etc.

Birmingham City Museum

Pinto Collection

Bodleian Library

John Johnson collection.

British Museum – Department of Drawings and Prints

Banks Collection.
Heal Collection.

East Sussex Libraries – Brighton Reference Library

Erredge Collection.

Guildhall Library

Trade cards.
Prints of Frost Fairs 1683–1716.

Kent County Libraries – Margate Reference Library

Parker Collection.
Printers' specimen book *c*1835–45.

Kent County Libraries – Tonbridge branch

Collection of Wise prints.

Royal Botanical Gardens, Kew

Correspondence &c relating to the acquisition of items in the Museum collection.

Tunbridge Wells Museum

Sprange collection 1793–1803.
Mackintosh collection – correspondence and accounts.
Prints, designs, trade cards, handbills and lists.

Victoria & Albert Museum – Department of Prints

Trade cards – boxes GG65A, GG66.

Westminster City Libraries – Reference Division

Gardiner Collection.

Worthing Borough Council

BW/P/20–72   Poor rate collection books – Parish of Broadwater 1839–65.

Worthing Museum

Transcript of handbill of James Medhurst.

C. PRINTED BOOKS, PERIODICAL ARTICLES AND THESES

A.R.B., *Lake Lore: or an Antiquarian Guide to some of the Ruins and Recollections of Killarney* (Dublin 1853)
Abstract of the Answers and Returns ... Population Act 11 Geo IV c30 (1833)
Ackermann's Repository of Art Dec 1816, Jan 1822
Adams W.J. (publisher), *Adam's Illustrative Descriptive Guide to the Watering Places of England* (1848)
Altic, Richard D., *The Shows of London* (1978)
Anon., *Amusements des Eaux de Spa* (1734)
Anon., *A General Description of all Trades* (1747)
Anon., *The Handbook of Turning* (1842)

Anon, *Two Sketches of France, Belgium and Spa in Two Tours During the Summers of 1771 and 1816* (1817)

Anscombe, Isabella & Gere, Charlotte, *Arts & Crafts in Britain and America* (1978)

Austen, Brian, 'Tunbridge Ware: the Collection of John Ryan Esq.' Sotheby sale *High Victorian Decorative Arts and Design* 12 and 13 November 1992

Austen, Brian, 'English Spa Souvenirs: The Tunbridge Ware Industry to about 1830', *Antiques* (New York June 1995)

Austen, Brian, 'Tourism and Industry: Killarney and Its Furniture', *Irish Arts Review Yearbook* Vol 12 (Dublin 1995)

Austen Brian, 'Brighton's Tunbridge Ware Industry', *Sussex Industrial History* 27 (Brighton 1997)

Austen, Brian, 'Tables by Tunbridge Ware Makers', *Furniture History* XXXIII (1997)

Bagshaw, Samuel, *History, Gazetteer and Directory of the County of Kent* (1847)

Bailey's British Directory (1784)

Baines, Edward, *History, Directory and Gazetteer of the County of York* (1823)

Baker, Hollis S., *Furniture in the Ancient World* (1966)

Baker, John, *Mauchline Ware and Associated Scottish Souvenir Ware* (Princes Risborough 1985)

Ballantyne, R.M., *The Lakes of Killarney* (1859)

Barrow, T., *Map of Tunbridge Wells* (1808)

Baxter's Stranger in Brighton and Guide (Brighton 1822), (1824), (1826)

Beard, Geoffrey & Gilbert, Christopher, D*ictionary of English Furniture Makers* 1660–1840 (Leeds 1986)

Beddoe, Stella, 'Thomas Barton: Tunbridge Ware Maker' thesis Postgraduate Diploma, Art Gallery and Museum Studies, University of Manchester, 1978.

Bitmead, Richard, *The London Cabinet-Maker's Guide* (1873)

Body, Albin, *Essai Historique sur les Ouvrages Peints dits Bois de Spa* (Liège 1898)

Bonner, G.W., *The Picturesque Pocket Companion to Margate* (1831)

Boore T.H., *Brighton Annual Directory and Fashionable Guide* (1822)

Bowra, John, *A Survey of Tunbridge Wells* (1738) map

Bracket, Arthur W., 'Tunbridge Wells and its Old Prints', *The Print Collector's Quarterly* Jan 1933.

Brackett, & Sons, *Auction Catalogue* 24 Feb 1933, 4 Dec 1987, 16 May 1997, 3 Oct 1997, 22 May 1998, 30 Apr 1999, 24 Sept 1999, 7 Apr 2000, 29 Sept 2000, 21 Apr 2001

Brackett, William (publisher), *Brackett's Descriptive Illustrated Handbook to Tunbridge Wells* (Tunbridge Wells nd *c*1863)

Brackett, William (publisher), *A Guide to the Rides, Drives and Places of Interest in the Neighbourhood of Tunbridge Wells* (1873)

Bracketts (Tunbridge Wells), Sale Catalogues 16 May, 3 Oct 1997, 22 May 1998, 24 Sept 1999

Bramwell, Martyn (ed), *The International Book of Wood* (1976)

Bray, William, *The Diary of John Evelyn* Vol II (1879)

Brayley, E.W., *Delineations, Historical and Topographical of the Isle of Thanet* (1817)

Brears, Peter C.D., 'York Spinning Wheel Makers', *Furniture History* Vol XIV (1978)

Brighton – *The Brighthelmstone Directory* (1790)

Brighton – *Brighton New Guide or a Description of Brighthelmstone* (Brighton 1800)

Brighton – *The New Brighthelmstone Directory* (1770)

Brighton – *The Stranger's Guide in Brighton* (Brighton 1838)

Brighton – *Parliamentary Poll Books* 1832–47

Britton, John, *The Original Picture of London* (28th edn nd *c*1832)

Burney, Fanny, *Diary and Letters of Madame d'Arblay* Vol I (1842)

Burr, Thomas Benge, *The History of Tunbridge Wells* (1766)

C.C., 'Old Tunbridge Ware', *The Connoisseur* August 1920

Calendar of Treasury Papers 8 Dec 1686

Campbell, R., *The London Tradesman* (1747)

Carlisle, Nicholas, *A Topographical Dictionary of Ireland* (1810)

Carwitham, John, *Various Kinds of Floor Decorations* (1739)

Chalklin, Christopher W., 'A Kentish Wealden Parish (Tonbridge) 1500–1750' thesis Oxford B. Lit. 1960

Chalklin, Christopher W., 'The Making of Some New Towns *c*1600–1720' in C.W. Chalklin & M.A. Hammond (ed), *Rural Change and Urban Growth 1500–1800* (1974)

Chalklin, Christopher, W., *Seventeenth Century Kent* (1965)

Chalklin, Christopher, W., 'A Seventeenth Century Market Town – Tonbridge' in *Archaeologia Cantiana* Vol LXXVI (Maidstone 1961)

Chambers Journal 1 Dec 1894

Chancellor, E. Berresford, 'A Note on Tunbridge Ware' *The Connoisseur* Jan 1935

J. Clifford (publisher), *Clifford's Visitor's Guide for Tunbridge Wells* various editions 1821–1855

Colbran's Handbook and Directory for Tunbridge Wells (Tunbridge Wells 1847) (2nd edn 1849), (3rd edn 1850)

Cooke, G.A., *Walks Through London* (nd *c*1835)

Cork Industrial Exhibition 1883 – Report of Executive Committee, Award of Jurors (Cork 1886)

Craven & Co's Commercial Directory of Hampshire (Nottingham 1857)

Cruysmans, Phillippe, 'Le Charme Révolu des Bois de Spa' *Connaissance des Arts* March 1977

Daily Mail Ideal Home Exhibition Catalogues 1923–7

The Daily Mirror 10 July 1923

The Daily Telegraph 18 March 1981

Dally, Richard, *The Arundel Guide* (1830)

Derrick, Samuel, *Letters Written from Leverpoole, Chester, Corke, The Lake of Killarney, Dublin, Tunbridge-Wells, Bath* (1767)

Dodd, George, *Where do we get it and how is it made?* (1862)

Doran, J., *The History and Antiquities of the Town and Borough of Reading in Berkshire* (1835)

The Dublin Almanack and General Register of Ireland (Dublin 1834–47)

The Dublin Evening Mail 27 Aug 1861

Dublin – *Exhibition of Irish Arts and Manufactures 1882 – Official Catalogue* (Dublin 1882)

Dublin International Exhibition of Arts & Manufactures 1865 – Official Catalogue (Dublin 1865)

Dublin – *Irish Industrial Exhibition of 1853 – A Detailed Catalogue of its Contents* (Dublin 1854)

Dublin – *Irish International Exhibition 1907 – Home Industries Section – Irish Rural Life and Industry* (Dublin 1907)

Dublin – *The Post Office Annual Directory* (various editions 1835–50)

Dublin – *The Treble Almanack* (Dublin various editions 1801–35)

Dublin University Magazine Vol XXIV Dec 1844

Edwards, Ralph (ed), *The Dictionary of English Furniture* (2nd edn 1954)

Edwards, Ralph & Ramsey, L.G.G. (ed), *The Connoisseur Complete Period Guides* (1968)

Ellis, Robert, *Official Descriptive and Illustrative Catalogue of the Great Exhibition* (1851)

Erredge, John Ackerson, *History of Brighthelmstone* (Brighton 1862)

Evans, John, *An Excursion to Brighton, A Visit to Tunbridge Wells and a Trip to Southend* (1823)

Evelyn, John, *Sylva, or a Discourse of Forest Trees* (1664)

Farrant, Sue & John, 'Brighton 1580–1820: From Tudor Town to Regency Resort' *Sussex Archaeological Collections* Vol 118 (Lewes 1981)

Finch, W., *An Historical Sketch of the County of Kent* (1803)

The Financial Times 18 July 1981

Florentino Allesandro, *L'ante della Tarsia a Sorrento* (Naples 1982)

Folthorp's General Directory for Brighton (Brighton various editions 1848–69)

Ford, John, *Ackermann 1783* (nd *c*1980)

Ford, John & Jill, *Images of Brighton* (Twickenham 1981)

Fraser, James, *Handbook for the Lakes of Killarney* (Dublin 1849)

Freeman, H.A. 'Experiments in Tunbridge Ware' *Woodworker* Nov 1969

Fry, T. (publisher), *The Fashionable Guide & Directory to the Public Places of Resort in Great Britain* (1840)

Gamage's Christmas Bazaar 1913 (reprint, Newton Abbot 1974)

Gilbert, Christopher, *Pictorial Dictionary of Marked London Furniture 1700–1840* (1996)

Gilbert, Edmund M., *Brighton Old Ocean's Bauble* (1954)

Gill, Margaret A.V., *Tunbridge Ware* (Princes Risborough, 1985)

Goodrich, C.R. (ed), *Science and Mechanism: Illustrated by Examples in the New York Exhibition 1853–54* (New York 1854)

Gore's Directory for Liverpool and its Environs (Liverpool various edns 1845–67)

Gorringe's Sale Catalogue (Tunbridge Wells) 31 Aug 1999

Goulden, R.J., 'Edmund Baker and Jasper Sprange', *Factolum* No. 38 Feb 1994.

Green & Co's Mid-Kent Court Guide, Gazeteer and County Blue Book (1874)

Guy's Directory of the Province of Munster (Cork 1886) (1893)

Hall, S.C. Mr & Mrs, *Handbook for Ireland – The South and Killarney* (1853)

Hall, S.C. Mr & Mrs, *Ireland – Its Scenery, Character &c Vol I* (1841)

Hall, S.C. Mr & Mrs, *A Week at Killarney* (1850)

J.G. Harrod & Co's Postal and Commerical Directory of Hampshire (1865)

Hinckley, F. Lewis, *Directory of the Historic Cabinet Woods* (New York 1960)

Hinton, I.T. (publisher), *The Watering Places of Great Britain and Fashionable Directory* (1831), (1833)

Holden's Annual London and County Directory (1811)

Holden's London Directory (various editions 1799–1817)

Holden's Triennial Directory (1809)

Holtzapfel, Charles, *Turning and Mechanical Manipulation* Vol II (1846)

Honor, Hugh, *Cabinet Makers and Furniture Designers* (1972)

Honor, Hugh, 'Nineteenth Century Italy' in Helena Hayward (ed) *World Furniture* (1965)

Horsfield, Thomas Walker, *The History, Antiquities and Topography of the County of Sussex* (Lewes 1835)

Hughes, G. Bernard, 'Tunbridge Ware' *Country Life* 13 Aug 1948

Hughes, Therle, *More Small Decorative Antiques* (1962)

Hutchins, John, *The History and Antiquities of the County of Dorset* Vol I (1863)

Huth, Hans, *Lacquer of the West* (1971)

Illustrated London News – issues for 1851

Inglis, Henry D., *A Journey throughout Ireland … in 1834* (5th edn 1838)

The Irish Press 18 July 1946

Jackson, F. Hamilton, *Intarsia and Marquetry* (1903)

Jervis, Simon, *Printed Furniture Designs before 1650* (1974)

John Bull 7 April 1822

Johnstone's London Directory (1817), (1818)

Jones, Arthur J, Son & Co, *Description of a Suite of Sculptural Decorative Furniture Illustrating Irish History and Antiquities* (Dublin 1853)

Journal and Proceedings of the Arts and Crafts Society of Ireland (1896–1901)

Joy, Edward T., *English Furniture 1800–1851* (1977)

Kelly's Directory of Ireland (1905)

Kelly's Directory of Kent (various editions 1870–1927)

Kelly's Directory of Kent, Surrey and Sussex (various editions 1887–1905)

Kelly's Directory of Sussex (various editions 1867–1938)

Kelly's Directory of Tunbridge Wells (various editions 1889–1930)

Kent – Parliamentary Poll Books 1734–1847

The Kent & Sussex Courier 13 Oct 1899, 17 July 1903

Kent's London Directory (various editions 1794–1825)

Kerridge, R.G.P., *A History of Lancing* (Chichester 1979)

Killarney – *A Familiar and Accurate Hand-Book from London to the Lakes of Killarney* (1846)

Killarney – *Picturesque Guide to the Lakes of Killarney* (Dublin 1851)

Killarney – *The Tourist's Picturesque Guide to Killarney and Cork* (1872)

King, K.B., *The Views Illustrated on End-grain Tunbridge Ware Designs* (nd 1981)

Kisluk-Grosheide, Danielle, 'Maison Giroux and its "Oriental" Marquetry Technique', *Furniture History* XXXV (1999)

Knight of Glin, 'Dublin Directories and Trade Labels', *Furniture History* 1985

Knipe, Henry R. (ed), *Tunbridge Wells and Neighbourhood* (Tunbridge Wells 1916)

Legg, Polly, 'The Bastards of Blandford: An Inventory of their Losses in the Fire of 1731', *Furniture History* XXX (1994)

Leppard & Co's Brighton and Hove Directory (Brighton 1839), (1843), (1845)

Lewes – *Parliamentary Poll Book* (Aug 1841)

Lewis, Samuel, *A Topographical Dictionary of Ireland* (1837)

Llanover, Lady, *The Autobiography and Correspondence of Mary Granville, Mrs Delany* Vol I (1861)

London – *Exhibition of the Works of Industry of All Nations – Reports by the Juries* (1852)

London – *The International Exhibition of 1862 – Illustrated Catalogue of the Industrial Department – British Division* (1862)

London – *The International Exhibition of 1862 – Kingdom of Italy – Official Descriptive Catalogue* (1862)

London – *The International Exhibition of 1862 – Reports by the Juries* (1863)

Lowndes, H., *A London Directory* (1774), (1778), (1791), (1794), (1795)

M. M'Corquodale's Annual Liverpool Directory (1848)

Mackcoull, J., *A Sketch of Worthing* (Worthing 1813)

Mackinnon, Donald D., *History of Speldhurst* (Tunbridge Wells 1902), (Speldhurst end edn 1930)

Mactaggart, Peter & Ann, 'Tunbridge End Grain Mosaic: A Misnomer' *Chronicle of the Early American Industries Association* Vol 36 No 2 June 1983

Maguire, John Francis, *The Industrial Movement in Ireland as Illustrated by the National Exhibition of 1852* (Cork 1854)

The Maidstone Journal 22 July 1800

Margate – *The Margate Guide – A Descriptive Poem* (1797)

Margate – *The New Margate, Ramsgate and Broadstairs Guide* (8th end nd *c*1825)

Marks, Edwin (pub), *A Summer Excursion to Tunbridge Wells* (Tunbridge Wells nd *c*1840)

Martin, W. Stanley & Row, B. Prescott, *Tunbridge Wells of Today* (2nd end 1906)

Mathieson's Brighton and Suburban Directory (1868), (1869), (1871)

Mathieson's Tunbridge Wells and Tonbridge Directory (Tunbridge Wells 1867)

Melville & Co's Directory & Gazetteer of Kent (1858)

Melville & Co's Directory & Gazetteer of Sussex (1858)

Mercer & Crocker's Directory of Hampshire (1871)

Messengers/Cavendish (Derby) Sale Catalogue 21 July 1995

Morris, Mary S., *A Catalogue of English Painted Enamels 18th and 19th Century in the Wolverhampton and Bilston Collections* (Wolverhampton 1973)

Mortimer's Universal Director (1763)

Morris, C., *The Journeys of Celia Fiennes* (1947)

Musée de Spa, *Les Bois de Spa* (Spa 1978)

Musée de la Vie Wallonne, *Trois Siècles de Bois de Spa* (Liège 1967)

Musgrave, Clifford, *Life In Brighton* (1970)

Musgrave, Clifford, *Regency Furniture* (1961)

Nessel, Edmond, *Traité des Eaux de Spa* (Spa 1699)

New York – *New York International Exhibition 1853 – General Report of the British Commissioner* (1854)

Norton, Michael, 'Muckross Abbey Furniture' *Country Life* 21 July 1955

Owen W.E. & Co, *Directory of the County of Kent* (1883)

An Oxonian (S. Reynolds Hole), *A Little Tour in Ireland* (1859)

Page's Court Guide and General Directory for Brighton (Brighton 1870)

Parkinson, Henry & Simmons & Peter Lund, *The Illustrated Record and Descriptive Catalogue of the Dublin International Exhibition of 1865* (1866)

Parry, J.D., *An Historical and Descriptive Account of the Coast of Sussex* (1833)

Pearce, Luke, *Historical Associations of the Free Churches of Tunbridge Wells* (Tunbridge Wells 1904)

Pelton's Illustrated Guide to Tunbridge Wells (6th edn 1874), (10th edn 1883), (12th edn 1888), (15th edn 1896)

Petigrew and Oulton's Dublin Directory (Dublin 1834), (1836)

Phillips & Patching, *Brighton Pocket Directory and Tradesman's General Advertiser* (Brighton 1827)

Phippen, James (ed), *Colbran's New Guide for Tunbridge Wells* (Tunbridge Wells 1840), (2nd edn 1844)

Pigot & Co's City of Dublin and Hiberian Provincial Directory (1824), (1826)

Pigot & Co's London and Provincial Commercial Directory (various editions 1816–30)

Pigot & Co's Metropolitan New Alphabetical Directory (1827), (1828_, (1838)

Pigot & Co's Royal National and Commerical Directory (various editoins 1832–40)

Pike's Directory of Brighton (Brighton 1929–31)

Pike's Tunbridge Wells, Tonbridge and Southborough Directory (Brighton 1894), (1895)

Pimlott, J.A.R., *The Englishman's Holiday* (1947)

Pinkerton, John, *A General Collection of the … Voyages and Travels* Vol III (1809)

Pinto, Edward H. & E.R., *Tunbridge And Scottish Souvenir Woodware* (1970)

Post Office Brighton Directory (1846)

Post Office Directory of Dorsetshire (1855), (1859)

Post Office Directory of Hampshire (1852), (1855)

Post Office Directory of Hampshire, Dorset & Wiltshire (1848)

Post Office Directory of Liverpool (1864)

Post Office London Directory (various editions 1800–1928)

Post Office Directory of Kent (various editions 1859–82)

Post Office Directory of the Six Home Counties (various editions 1845–78)

Post Office Directory of Sussex (various editions 1855–87)

Ramsey, L.G.G. (ed), *The Concise Encyclopaedia of Antiques* Vol 4 (1959)

Reindl, Peter, 'Early Renaissance Furniture in Basle' *Apollo* Dec 1976

Richter, Gisela M.A., *The Furniture of the Greeks, Etruscans and Romans* (1966)

Roake, Margaret & Whyman, John, *Essays in Kentish History* (1973)

Robinson's Popular Brighton Directory (1884), (1886)

Robson's Commercial Directory of the Seven Counties (1838–39)

Robson's London Commercial Directory (various editions 1820–39)

Rowe, Ronald E., *English Dial Clocks* (Woodbridge 1978)

Royal National Directory of Ireland (1894)

St Louis, *Irish Industrial Exhibition, World Fair St Louis 1914* (Dublin 1914)

Saint-Sernin, *Healthful Sports for Young Ladies* (1822)

Sandbach, R.G.E., 'Tunbridge Ware' thesis Museum Association Aug 1969

Sandbach, R.G.E., 'Tunbridge Ware', *Practical Education* Apr, May, July/August 1974

Sandbach, R.G.E., 'Tunbridge Ware' *Cantium* Autumn 1974

Savidge, Alan, *Royal Tunbridge Wells* (Tunbridge Wells 1976)

Shearsmith John, *A Topographical Description of Worthing* (Worthing 1824), (new edn 1832)

Sheehy, Jeanne, *The Rediscovery of Ireland's Past: the Celtic Revival (1830–1930)*, (1980)

Shoberl, Frederick (ed), *Forget Me Not* (1833)

Sicklemore, R., *An Epitome of Brighton* (Brighton 1815)

Simpson's Brighton and Cliftonville Directory and Court Guide (1864), (1867)

Simpson & Co's Directory and Court Guide of Canterbury, Dover, Maidstone … (1865)

Slater's Classified Directories of … Important English Towns (1847)

Slater's National Commercial Directory of Ireland (1846), (1847)

Slater's Royal National Committee Directory of Ireland (various editions 1856–94)

Slater's Royal National Commercial Directory of Manchester and Liverpool (1858)

Somerset & Dorset Notes & Queries Vol 11 (1908)

Sotheby Belgravia Sale Catalogue 5 Aug 1981, 17 Feb 1982

Sotheby London Sale Catalogue 12–13 Nov 1992

Sotheby South Sale Catalogue 26 Oct 1999, 12 Sept 2000

Spa – *Amusements des Eaux de Spa* (1734)

Spon, Ernest (publisher), *Workshop Receipts for the Use of Manufacturers and Scientific Amateurs* (1875) (new edn 1921)

Sprange, Jasper, *The Tunbridge Wells Guide* (1780), (1817)

Stapley, William, *Stapley's Tunbridge Wells Visitor's Guide* (1847)

Steven's *Directory of Tunbridge Wells, Tonbridge & Neighbourhood* (1886)

The Sussex Agricultural Express 28 Oct 1837, 29 Mar 1851

Swann, Flavia, Introduction to *Sotheby Belgravia Catalogue for Tunbridge Ware Exhibition and Sale* Nov-Dec 1980

Swaysland, T.A. & Gill, J., *A New Directory of Brighton* (1832)

Talbot, Frederick A.A., 'Tonbridge Ware: its History and Manufacture' *The Windsor Magazine* Feb 1898

Taylor, Elias, *The Lathe and its Uses* (3rd end 1871)

Thom's Irish Almanac and Official Directory (Dublin 1851), (1867)

Thornton, Peter, *Seventeenth Century Interiors in England, France and Holland* (1978)

Tiffen, William, *Excursions from Folkestone, Sandgate and Hythe* (1853)

Tiffen, William, *The New Hand-book and Guide to the Town and Port of Folkestone* (1850)

The Times (various editions 1803–21), 2 Dec 1853, 21 Jan 1965

Tomlin, Maurice, *Catalogue of Adam Period Furniture* (1972)

The Tralee Chronicle and *Killarney Echo* 27 Aug 1861, 30 Aug 1861

The Tralee Chronicle and *Killarney Echo – The Prince of Wales's Visit* (1858)

Tunbridge Wells – *The Tunbridge Wells Guide and Directory* (nd 1845)

Tunbridge Wells – *Visitor's Guide to Tunbridge Wells* (1888)

The Tunbridge Wells Advertiser 28 Feb 1890, 13 Oct 1899, 12 Aug 1910, 19 Aug 1910, 17 Sept 1920

The Tunbridge Wells Gazette 26 June 1857, 23 Sept 1864, 30 Sept 1864, 15 Mar 1867, 27 Mar 1891

The Tunbridge Wells Journal 2 July 1863

The Tunbridge Wells Magazine 1 June 1923

The Universal British Directory (1791–98)

Varley, A, *A History of Libraries in Cheltenham from 1780–1900* (1968)

Victorian Shopping – Harrod's Catalogue 1895 (reprint Newton Abbot 1972)

Vigus, A.W.E., 'Tunbridge Ware' *The Marquetarian* Spring 1961

Wadmore, Beauchamp, *Some Details in the History of the Parish of Tonbridge* (1906)

Wall, Col. F., 'Tonbridge Burials 1547–1832; typescript British Library Ac 5962b/5

Wall, Col. F., 'Tonbridge Baptisms – Parish of SS Peter and Paul 1553–1812' typescript British Library Ac 5962b/6

Wallis, E., *Brighton as it is* (new edn 1830), (1832)

Wallis, E., *Brighton Townsman and Visitors Directory* (1826)

Ward Lock & Co, (publishers), *Killarney and the South West of Ireland* (nd c1930)

Watson, F.J.B., *Louis XVI Furniture* (1960)

White, William (publisher), *History, Gazetteer and Directory of the County of Hampshire* (2nd edn 1878)

Whyman, John 'A Hanoverian Watering Place: Margate' in Alan Everitt (ed) *Perspectives in English Urban History* (1973)

Willis, Geoffrey, *English Furniture 1500–1760* (1971)

Wilson's Dublin Directory (Dublin various editions 1808–28)

Wolff, Henry, W., *Sussex Industries* (nd 1883)

Woolf, Bella Sidney and Goodlake, Thomas Julian, *Killarney and Round About* (Dublin 1901)

Wright, C., *The Brighton Ambulator* (1818)

Wright, G.N., *A Guide to the Lakes of Killarney* (1822)

Wrightson's Directory for Birmingham (1821)

Yesterday's Shopping – The Army & Navy Stores Catalogue 1907 (reprint Newton Abbot 1969)

The York Courant 2 Mar 1807, 28 Mar 1814, 18 Mar 1816

The York Herald 27 Mar 1790, 14 Feb 1795

The Yorkshire Gazette 24 May 1823, 7 June 1823

Younghusband, Ethel, *Mansions, Men and Tunbridge Ware* (Slough 1949)

INDEX

Abergavenny, Marquis of 106, 139
abstract designs used in Tunbridge
　ware 109, 130, 132
Acid Springs of the Ardennes Forest – The
　(1560) 196
Ackermann, Rudolph Jnr 25
Ackermann, Rudolph Snr 24–6, 47,
　49–50, 53, 80–81, 167
Adams, Alfred E. 123
Adams, William 133–34, 263
Adelaide Crescent, Hove 73
Aesthetic Movement 118
Aghadoe 180, 184
Aix-la-Chapelle (Aachen) 201, 206
Albert, Prince Consort 139, 184, 195
Allen, —— (Mr) 148
Alyth 217
amateur decoration of woodwares
　52–3
Amusements des Eaux de Spa (1734)
　198–9
animals depicted in Tunbridge ware
　66, 104–6, 269
Anne, Queen 16
antiquities, exhibition of 173–4
Arbutus Cottage 190, 193
arbutus wood 41, 178, 180–7, 190–1,
　194
Army & Navy Stores 120
Arts & Crafts Exhibition
　Society 118
Ashenhurst, Thomas 21
Ashford 14
Astley Castle 26, 243
Aston Hall, Birmingham 56
Athol, Earl of 23
Atkins, James 58
Auchinleck 218
Augusta, Princess 173
Austen, Jane 20, 47
Australia 220
Axtell, Thomas 28, 267
Ayr, county of 218

backgammon 58–9, 192
Baker, Dorcas 16, 254
Baker, Edmund 30
Baker, Thomas 20
Balmoral Estate 219

Banks Collection 21–2, 76
Banbury 114
Barker, W. 58
Barrow, T.T. 143, 146, 156
Bartolozzi (artist) 47
Barton, —— (Miss) 141
Barton, Thomas 15, 52, 59, 68, 71–2, 82,
　91–2, 95, 97–8, 104, 109–10, 115–17,
　121, 135–41, 153–54, 214, 244, 254,
　271, 275
Basle 55
Bastard, Thomas, John & William 27,
　248
Bath 13–14, 20, 35, 199, 243, 261
Battle Abbey 72, 89, 95, 110, 138, 142,
　244, 246
Bayham Abbey 71, 108, 110, 241, 244,
　274–5, 277
bazaars 40, 180, 242
Bedford, Stephen 49
Belgium 196, 218
Bellamy (toyman) 45, 257
Benjamin, Daphne 130
Benjamin, Peter 130, 263
bergamote 200
Bergavenny, Lord (*see also*
　Abergavenny, Marquis of) 14
Berlin 197
Berlin embroidery 102–4, 118, 148
Bettison, Samuel 28, 36, 252, 257
Bettison, William George 36–7, 253
Beyreuth 204
Bilston enamels 35
Birch, —— (Miss) 20
birds, depiction in Sorrento ware 213
birds, depiction in Tunbridge ware
　65–6, 71, 75, 95, 100, 102, 104, 106,
　123, 129, 149, 274
Birmingham 40, 49, 133, 219, 262
Birmingham Museum 67, 81, 89, 104,
　159, 266
Blackman, George 26–7, 257
Blandford 27
Blickling 46
blocks, manufacture of 82–3, 86, 88,
　92–5, 101, 132
Body, Albin 206
bog oak 41, 179–80, 182–4, 187–8
bog yew 179, 181–2

Bognor 35, 37, 262
Borders, Scottish 72
Botton, Albert 104, 123, 128
Bouchier, Francois 201
Boulle, André-Charles 198
Bourbon Condé, Duc de 205
bourdoniers 197
Bousfield & Pallister 37, 253
Bowra, John 142
Boyce, Brown & Kemp 89, 92, 94–5, 97,
    109–10, 114–6, 120–1, 123, 128, 141–2,
    151, 214, 246, 254
Boyce, Thomas Amos 141
Brabant, John 35
Brandenburg 197
Brighton 8, 29–34, 40–1, 44, 48, 58, 73,
    148, 161, 164, 168–73, 220, 241, 270,
    272
Brighton makers and sellers of
    Tunbridge wares 18–19, 29–34, 37,
    45, 49, 51, 57, 69, 73–7, 132–3, 168–73,
    248–51
Bristol 13, 174, 179
British Museum 21–2
Brixhe, Vincent 205
Broadstairs 36, 164, 242
Bronfert, H. 207
Brooker, Richard 18
Brooks, John 164
Broomhill 117
Brown, Alexander 219–20
Brown, Alfred 141
Brown, James Jnr 89, 120–1, 141–2, 214
Brown, James Snr 116, 141, 254
Bruno, Henri 206
Buck, I. 49
Burney, —— (artist) 47
Burney, Fanny 20
Burns, Robert 218, 220
Burr, T. Benge 14, 30, 43, 53, 196
Burrows, family 16, 56, 142–5
Burrows, Frances 16, 143
Burrows, George 66, 101–2, 109, 144,
    148, 254
Burrows, Humphrey Jnr 15, 20, 143–4,
    254
Burrows, Humphrey Snr 20, 59, 67, 86,
    107, 143–4, 244, 254
Burrows, James 64–6, 82, 96, 101–2,
    104–5, 107, 109, 144, 148, 167, 254
Burrows, (Lower Green) 143, 254
Burrows, Mary 16, 143, 254
Burrows, Thomas (Tonbridge) 116, 145,
    168, 245, 253
Burrows, Thomas (Tunbridge Wells)
    143, 254
Burrows, William 16, 99, 143–4, 254
Burton, Decimus 146
Burville & Littlewood 77, 249
Buscot Park 115
Butler, Jane 146
butterflies depicted in Tunbridge ware
    66, 71, 73, 95, 100, 102, 104, 132, 134,
    137, 151, 274–5, 277
Buxted 173

Buxton 13
Byzantine mosaic work 99

Cabinet Directory, The (1803) 214
Caledonian Box Co. 219–20
Calverley Estate, Tunbridge Wells
    66–7, 69, 146, 167, 245, 264
Cambridge, Duke of 186
Camfield, William 77, 249
Camilla (1796) 20
Canada 220
Canterbury 242
Canvey Island 132, 134, 263
Capitol, Washington DC 73, 107, 246
Carnegie Trust 7
Carlisle, Earl of 186
Carter, Charles 51
Casson Gallery 134
Castle Inn, Brighton 30
Castle Museum, York 41, 265
Castleross, Viscount & Viscountess of
    184, 186
Castletown, Co. Kildare 46
Catherine of Braganza, Queen 14, 58
Catrine 218
Chain Pier, Brighton 31–2, 241, 243
Chalet, The 138, 145–7
Chantilly 205
Chatham 132
Charles I, King 56
Charles II, King 14, 53, 197–8
Charles, Prince of Wales 130, 132
Cheesman, —— 34, 74, 249
Cheesman, Thomas 74, 249
Cheltenham 35, 164, 242, 252
chess 117, 165, 192
Childs, William Jnr 76–7, 152, 249, 263
Childs, William Snr 76–7, 249, 263
China 120
Chinese taste of the Regency 50–1
Chinoiserie subjects used in Spa
    woodwares 197, 201, 207
Chlorosplenium aeruginosum 90–1
Civil War, English 14
Clarendon, Earl of 186
classical subjects in the decoration of
    Spa woodware 204
Clemens August, Emperor of Cologne
    204
Cleopatra's Needle 92, 114–5, 221
Clerkenwell 23, 135, 258–60
Clifford's Tunbridge Wells Guide 106
Coakley, James 183, 187, 266
Cobham Hall 168, 245
Colbran's New Guide for Tunbridge Wells
    (1840) 64
Colbran's New Guide for Tunbridge Wells
    (1844) 142, 159
Cologne 204
Colonnade Library, Worthing 40, 262
Columbine 174
Commonwealth period 14
competition of foreign imports with
    Tunbridge ware 119–20
composite veneer 95–7

Connard, J. 42, 45, 253
Connell, Denis 180, 266
Connemara 186
Coo, la Cascade de 156
Cormack Brothers 111, 114
Cornwallis, Lady 156
Cosmorama 27
Cottington, George & John 143–4, 254
Country Life 195
County Committee for Kent 14
Coventry 40, 262
Crab, W. 218
Crane, Walter 118
Crehay, G.A. 206–7
Crehay, G.J. 206–7
cribbage 192
Crimmin, Jeremiah 180, 182, 184, 266
Crossley's 104
Crumnock 205, 218
Culverden Down 156
Cumberland, Duke of 30
Curran & Son 186

Dagly, Gerard 197, 204
Damora, Antonio 209, 213
Dawson, Lady Ann Marie 156
De La Rue & Co. 110
Deal 29
Decalcomanie 97
Delahauf, —— 208
Delany, —— (Mrs) 20
Delices du Pays de Leige, Les 202
Deprez, Henri 207
Derrick, Samuel 20, 53
Devonshire, Duke of 186
Diana, Princess of Wales 130, 132
Dibden Purlieu 130, 132–3, 263
Disraeli, Benjamin 139
Disertation on the Use of Sea Water (1850)
    29
Dodd, C. Tattershall 118
dogs, depicted in Sorrento ware 213
dogs, depicted in Tunbridge ware 66,
    75, 104, 213
Dome, the, Brighton (*see* Royal Mews)
Donaldson & Wilkes 31–2, 169, 249
Donoghue, John 192–3
Doughty, Joseph 40, 261
Doughty, Marie 40–1, 261
Dover 39, 72, 89, 112, 115, 245, 252, 265
Dublin 179–84, 187
Dublin – bog oak woodware makers
    179–80, 184, 187
Dublin – Tunbridge ware sellers 41,
    263
Dudley, 3rd Baron North 14
Dumfries 218
Dunloe Castle 180, 184
Dunloe, Gap of 181, 188, 190, 266–7
Dunnett, Malcolm 24, 52, 57, 59, 258
Durrant, E. 110
Dutch marquetry 198

Earl of Abergavenny 174
East India Companies 197

Eastbourne 29, 37, 220, 251
Edinburgh 262
Edward VIII, King 129
Edward Prince of Wales (later Edward
    VII) 101–3, 109, 139, 183–4, 274
Egan, James 182–4, 186–7, 266
Egan, Thomas 183–4
Eglington, Earl of 186
Egypt 128
Egyptian inlay techniques 99
Ellis, John Thomas 120–1, 255
Elizabeth I, Queen 13, 15
Emma (1816) 20
enamel plaques 35
Epsom 14
Eridge 14, 91
Eridge Castle 66–7, 77, 87, 89, 106–7,
    110, 121, 142, 149, 159, 161, 244, 246,
    269, 275
Eton College 72, 244, 275
Eugenie, Empress of France 184
Eurydice, H.M.S. 79
Evans, John 16
Evelyn, John 15
Exhibition – Cork 1852 181–2, 185–6
Exhibition – Cork 1883 183, 188
Exhibition – Dublin 1853 181–2, 186
Exhibition – Dublin 1865 182
Exhibition – Dublin 1882 182–3
Exhibition – Dublin 1895 188
Exhibition – Dublin 1907 188, 190
Exhibition – London 1851 68, 71, 89,
    135, 167, 180–2, 212
Exhibition – London 1862 72, 182–3,
    206, 211–12
Exhibition – London 1923 (Fair &
    Market) 121
Exhibition – London 1923 (Ideal Home)
    121
Exhibition – London 1924, 1925, 1926
    (Ideal Home) 123
Exhibition – London 1932 (Ideal Home)
    128
Exhibition – New York 1853 71–3, 167,
    180, 212
Exhibition – Paris 1855 182
Exhibition – St. Louis 1914 (World Fair)
    183, 190
Exmouth 29

fabrics for lining boxes 97
Fassotte, D. 207
Fenner & Co. 145–7, 195
Fenner & Nye 20, 32, 44, 47, 59, 67, 146,
    149, 151, 168, 255
Fenner, John 145, 255
Fenner, William 15, 27, 47, 59, 67,
    145–7, 151, 242, 255
Ferguson, John 21
Ferguson, Mary 21, 258
fern-decorated wares 150, 221
Fickling, Albert J. 130, 132–3, 263
Fiennes, Celia 16, 21, 39, 42
Fisher's Library, Brighton 31, 249
Fleming, Michael 184

floors, stone and marble inlay 56
floors, parquetry 56
floral subjects depicted in Tunbridge
    ware 104, 132, 139, 151, 161–2, 269
Floyer, Sir John 29
Foley, William 118, 146, 255
Folkestone 37, 72, 167, 220, 242, 252
Forget Me Not (1831) 25
France 56–7, 73, 128, 220
Francis I, Emperor 204
Franklin, Lady 156
Frant, parish of 15, 148, 159, 173
Fredrich Wilhelm, Elector of
    Brandenburg 197
French, James 188, 190, 266
Friend & Allen 148, 255
Friend, Ann 148
Friend, James 52, 60, 118, 148, 255
Friend, John 148
frost fairs on the River Thames 21–2
Fry, John 53, 255
Fry, Mary 16, 255
Fuller, Samuel & Joseph 25–6, 258
Funeral, The (1720) 20
furniture, Tunbridge ware 57, 59, 100,
    112, 115, 117, 121, 124, 130–1, 137,
    139–40, 143–4, 146, 165, 167, 271,
    276–7

Gamages 120–1
gaming at spas 39–40, 200
Gardenstone, Lord 205, 217
Gardiner, C. 18
Garguilo, Guiseppe 212
Garguilo, Luigi 209–11
Garrett, Len 132–3, 263
Gay, John 20
Geary, Stanley 123
George III, King 164
George IV, King 76, 167, 179
George V, King 81
George VI, King 129
George Frederick, Prince of Wales 18,
    30, 50
Géronstère, la 203
Ghent 56
Gibraltar Cottage 144
Gilpin, William 177
Giroux, Alph. & Co. 73
Glena Cottage 177, 180, 190–1, 193,
    195, 246
Glengariff 187
Gloucester, Duke of 30
Godmanchester 80
Goggin & Crimmin 182, 184, 186
Goggin, Cornelius 180, 182, 184, 187,
    266
Goggin, Jeremiah 187, 267
Goudhurst 47–8
Grammont, Comte de 58
Grandville, Michel 209–12
Granville, Mary 20, 45
Gravesend 35–6, 242, 252
Great Malvern 72, 108, 110, 174, 245
Green, Thomas Littleton 122, 128–9, 251

Greenwich 35, 243, 260
Groombridge, John 18
Guiseppe, Claudio 212
Gustavus III, King of Sweden 198

Halifax 104
Hall, W.T. 47
Hampson Silks 134
Hampstead Heath (1706) 20
Hand in Hand Tunbridge workshops
    22, 259
Hanover Lodge 144
Hanse, H. 207
Harborne 133
Harding, Lady 56
Harris, William Jnr 163
Harrods 120
Hastings 37–8, 110, 151, 164, 171,
    241–2, 251, 265
Hausburg, Frederick 73, 261
Headly, Lady 186
Heal Collection 23
Healthful Sports for Young Ladies (1822)
    47, 49
Henrad, Hubert 205–7
Henrietta Maria, Queen 14
Herculaneum 209
Herstmonceux Castle 89, 244
Heveningham 46
Hever Castle 142
High Rocks, Tunbridge Wells 220, 242
Hill, Viscount 186
Historisches Museum, Basle 55
History of Cold Bathing (1702) 29
History of Tunbridge Wells (1766) 14
Hole, S. Reynolds 186
Hollamby, Henry (Brighton) 33
Hollamby, Henry Jnr (Tunbridge Wells)
    33, 67, 71–3, 87, 89, 92, 94–5, 97, 104,
    106, 108–10, 115–6, 123, 129, 141–2,
    148–51, 160, 167–8, 194–5, 221, 244–7,
    255, 269
Hollamby, James (apprenticed 1878)
    141
Hollamby, James (baptised 1813) 33
Hollamby, Stephen 33
Hollamby, Thomas 33
Holland 21, 220
Holland, Henry 241
Holtzapfel, Charles 65, 82–3, 86, 88
Holywell 13
hones, razor 218
Hooper, —— (Mrs) 214
Hope Mill, Goudhurst 47–8
Horne, Robert 43, 259
Hotel d'Hare-Skenluyse, Ghent 56
Hotham, Sir Richard 37
Hothamton – see Bognor
Hove 31, 73, 242, 265
Hunt, John 34, 249
Hythe 264

India 120, 128
Ingall, Charles 52–3
Innisfallen 180, 184

inscriptions in tessellated mosaic 110, 129, 195
invisible hinge 217–8
Islington 121
Italy 55, 213, 215
Izard, Frank William 249, 263
Izard, J. 34, 241, 243, 249

Jackson, John 21–2, 259
Jacques, Thomas & John 28, 259, 264
James I, King 14
Jannicelli, Matteo 212
Janson, Sir Thomas 21
Japan 120
japanning 50–3
Jarvis, Samuel 59, 259
Jensen, Gerreit 198
Jerin, Henri-Joseph 206
Jones, Arthur Son & Co. 181
Jones, William 181
Jordan, —— (Mr) 142
Jordan House, Tunbridge Wells 15, 20, 59, 67, 107, 142–4

Kalabergo, G. 114
Kemp, Amos 121
Kemp, John 141
Kemp, Richard 128
Kemp Town, Brighton 73
Kenmare, Earl & Countess of 179, 186, 188
Kensington Palace 21, 268
Kent, Duchess of 59, 69, 148, 151, 155, 167
Kew 46, 119, 243, 265
Kiernan, Eleanor 192–3
Kiernan, John 190, 192
Kiernan, John Peter 192–3
Killarney, development as a resort 177, 179
Killarney House 180, 184
Killarney School of Arts & Crafts 188, 190
Killarney – Tunbridge ware depicting views of 72, 195
Killarney – Tunbridge ware inscribed 110, 195
Killarney woodwares 8, 177–95, 266–7, 271
Killarney woodwares – influence of Tunbridge wares on 193–5
Killarney woodwares – museums containing 268
Killarney woodwares – size of industry 182–3
King, David H.E. Ltd. 121–2
Kingsgate Castle, Kent 272
Kingswinford 134
Kirk, Mary 58
Knight, Joseph 42–3, 256
Knight, Stephen & Son 115, 252

lacquer 21, 50, 197–8, 200, 205, 221
Laindon 132, 263
Lanark 219

Lancaster 265
Lancing 173
Landseer, Sir Edwin 104
Lanesborough, Earl of 186
Lang, Anton 188
Lathe and its Uses, The (1871) 93
Latter, Darino 18
Latter, Dorcas 18
Latter, James 18
Latin America 215
Laurencekirk 205, 217–8
Lauzum, Duke of 200
Ledin, Alfred 207
Leeds (Yorkshire) 58
Leeds Castle (Kent) 133, 245
Leloup, Antoine 202–3, 205
Leloup, Remacle 202
Lewes 29, 78–9, 144, 251
libraries, subscription 20, 28, 30–2, 34, 36–40, 78, 80, 143, 146, 167, 241–3, 249–53, 255–7, 262
Licence, James 80
Licence, Robert 79–80, 115, 252
Liège, Bishop of 200
lignum vitae 16, 21, 23, 43–4, 58
Limbourge, J-P de 202
Lisburn 186
Liverpool 73, 89, 150, 261
lodgings, provision by Tunbridge ware makers 20, 143, 147, 157
London 8, 21–8, 52–3, 89, 121, 123, 146, 180, 219, 265
London – makers and dealers in Tunbridge ware 18–19, 21–8, 41, 43, 45, 53, 57–9, 69, 81, 111, 114, 135, 146, 167, 204, 243, 257–61
Loo (card game) 39–40
Lorne, Marchionness of 139
Lorne, Marquis of 70
Louis XIV, King of France 198
Louis XV, King of France 215
Louis Phillipe, King of France 70
Louth 243
Lowe, John 58, 260
Lymborth, —— (Dr) 196
Lymington 146
Lynch, James 184

Macdonald, Robert 218
McEwen, John 45
M'Guirk, —— (Mr) 179
Mackenzie & Meakle 218
Maguire, John Francis 185
Maidstone 128, 164
Maidstone Museum 89, 137, 265
Mallow 179
Malvern (see Great Malvern)
Man, Isle of 110
Manchester Unity of Oddfellows 141
Mansions, Men and Tunbridge Ware (1949) 7
marble table tops 55–6, 58
Maresfield 173
Margate 28–9, 36–7, 39–40, 164, 167, 220, 242–3, 252–3

Margate Guide, The (1797) 36
Marie-Améilie, Queen of France 70
Marin, Jonas-Etienne 206–7
Marine Parade, Brighton 31–2, 241
marquetry, Russell 67–8
Marshall & Doughty 40, 59
Marshall, William 112
Marks, Edwin 146
Massardo, Jean 206
Matrimony (card game) 44
Mauchline wares 50, 120, 123, 205,
    217–21, 271, 273
Mayo, Earl of 190
Medhurst, Edmund 173–4
Medhurst, George 78–9, 260
Medhurst, James Jnr 173–4
Medhurst, James Snr 78–9, 172–4, 248,
    262
Medhurst, Mary 173
Medhurst, Phoebe 174
Medhurst, Robert 79, 173–4, 260
Medhurst, Sarah 173–4
Medhurst, Thomas 173
Medway, River 164, 168
Meekison, G. 218
Mercer, Jane 16, 255
metal inlay 198
Metamorphoses 204
Milner, W. & G. 218
Mission, Aristide 207
Mission, Emile & Louis 206
Molyneux, F.G. 70
Montpelier Estate, Brighton 73
Montagu, Elizabeth 20
Morris (Tunbridge ware manufacturers)
    33–4, 50–1, 74–6, 168–72, 234, 241, 243
Morris, Abraham 76, 170, 234, 250
Morris, Edward 171, 251, 264
Morris, S.J. 169–70, 234
Morris, S.W. 32, 169, 234
Morris, William 105
mosaic, tessellated – Sorrento 212–15
mosaic, tessellated – Tunbridge ware
    28, 63, 65–8, 71, 74–7, 79, 83, 86–115,
    118, 120–1, 123, 129–34, 139, 142, 144,
    160, 170, 172, 239–40, 269–77
mosaic, tessellated – Tunbridge ware,
    design of 88–9
mosaic, tessellated – Tunbridge ware,
    methods of production 89–97
mosaic, tessellated – Tunbridge ware,
    origins of 99, 101–2, 209
mother-of-pearl 197–8, 200, 203
Mount Ephraim, Tunbridge Wells 15,
    18, 44–5, 135, 139, 141, 144–6, 151,
    156, 160, 245
Mount Pleasant, Tunbridge Wells 17,
    146, 167
Mount Sion, Tunbridge Wells 45, 142,
    146
Muckross Abbey, Killarney 110, 149,
    177, 180, 184, 190–5, 246
Muckross Hotel 187
Muckross House 191–2, 194, 265
Musee de Spa 198, 201

Museum of London 26, 81, 265
museums containing Killarney
    woodwares 268
museums containing Tunbridge wares
    265
museums of antiquities maintained by
    James Medhurst 78, 174

Naples 209, 211–12
Napoleon I, Emperor 205
Nash, John 241
National Museum of Ireland 184,
    268
Neate, ——— (Mr) 182
Nessel, Edmund 197–8
Netley Abbey 72, 161, 244
New York 71–3, 167, 187, 212
New Zealand 188
Newbury 28, 248
Newport (I.O.W.) 146
Nice 212, 215
Nonsuch Green 164
Noveaux Amusements de Spa (1763, 1782)
    202
Nye & Fenner 146
Nye, Edmund 7, 15, 17, 20, 37, 58,
    67–8, 71–2, 88, 90–2, 95, 102, 104, 107,
    109–10, 135, 137, 146, 149–54, 161,
    212, 256, 271, 277
Nye, James 146, 151, 256
Nye, Sarah 151, 256

O'Connell, Daniel 188, 267
O'Connor, Jeremiah 178, 180–2, 188,
    267
Oberammergau 188
Ochiltree 218
Oeben, J-F. 56
Oldenburgh House, Tunbridge Wells
    156
orangette 200
Ovid 204
oyster veneer 58
Oxford 40, 46

painted decoration on Spa woodwares
    197–204, 206–8
painted decoration – Tunbridge wares
    28, 41, 50–3, 139, 169, 204, 239–40, 270
Pam (game) 39–40
Pantheon Bazaar, London 180
Pantiles, the (also known as the Walks
    or the Parade) 16–19, 21, 33, 39,
    91–2, 94, 110, 116, 120, 135, 139,
    143–6, 148–53, 161–2, 167, 172, 223,
    242, 254–7, 273
panoramas 25, 44, 52
papers, lining 97
papier mâché 115
Parade, the, Tunbridge Wells (*see*
    Pantiles, the)
Parc des Sept Heures 203
Paris 200, 219
parquetry 41, 50, 53–60, 63, 73–4, 82,
    86, 99, 114, 145

parquetry – miniature 54, 63, 65–7, 74, 80–4, 86, 88, 96, 100, 102, 144, 147, 167, 270, 273
Payne, R. 34, 250
'Pendarves' (Mrs) 20
Penshurst Place 87, 89, 142, 245
penwork 38, 41, 50, 167, 169, 202–4, 217
Peres, —— (Mr) 212
Perry, Robert Harding 77, 250
perspective cube work 54–9, 63, 67–8, 74–5, 82–3, 86, 109, 129, 132, 134, 139, 147, 154–5, 159, 172, 215
Peter the Great, Tsar of Russia 200
Pett, Richard 17–18
Philpott's Bathing Rooms, Margate 28
photographs used to decorate Mauchline wares 129, 220
photographs used to decorate Tunbridge wares 81, 113, 115, 123, 220
picturesque scenery, taste for 177
Pinto, Edward & Eva 7–8, 66, 195, 229
playing cards 47, 157–9
Pollnitz, Baron 197, 200–1, 204
Pompeii 209–10, 212
Pope Joan (card game) 44
Porter, Rachel 120–1
Porter's Warehouse, Tunbridge Wells 120-1, 142, 256
Portsmouth 29, 146
Portsmouth Museum 268
postage stamps used for box decoration 110, 114, 123, 128
Practical Education 7
print-decorated Tunbridge wares 19, 26, 31–2, 34, 40–1, 46–50, 53, 73–4, 77, 270
prints published by Tunbridge ware makers 17, 20, 32, 37, 78, 151, 164, 167, 169–70, 173
Putney 123
pyrography 130, 178, 189, 191–4

Queen's Wells, The (1632) 14

Ramsgate 37, 220, 242, 253
Rankin, —— 206
Rawle, S. 49
Reading 52–3, 132
Redgrave 80
Reeves & Inwood 26
Regency style 59–60, 148
Regent's Park 25, 44
Reigler, P. 207
Rener, —— (Mr) 206
Renaissance, The 55, 118
Renaissance intarsia work 99
Renson, Victor 207
Rets, Jean 208
Rich, Colin 7
Rider, John 18
Roberts, Christopher Jnr 144, 256
Roberts, Derek 130
Robinson, John 18–19, 28, 32, 41, 46–7, 52, 59, 250, 256, 260

Rochester 35
Rochester, Guildhall Museum 81, 111, 163, 265
Rococo style 201, 204, 215
Roidkin, Renier 204
Rokeby 46
Roman mosaic stone work 99, 101, 209
Roman pavement, Lancing 173
Rosapini, P. 112, 114
Rose, Lady Mary 156
Rose Hill School, Tunbridge Wells 123
Ross Castle, Killarney 149, 177, 180, 190–1, 194–5, 246
Rousseau, Vincent 199, 202
Rowzee, Lodwick (Dr) 14
Royal Botanic Gardens, Kew 119, 123, 265
Royal College of Art 118
Royal Crescent, Bath 35
Royal George 174
Royal Mews, Brighton (The Dome) 32, 169, 241
Royal patronage 59
Royal Pavilion, Brighton 30–2, 41, 241, 243, 270
Royal Society of Arts 27
Ruskin, John 165
Russell, Robert (Dr) 29
Russell, Robert (Tunbridge ware maker) 67–8, 71, 95, 109, 155–6, 160, 256, 271, 276
Russia 120
Rusthall Common, Tunbridge Wells 99, 245, 269
Rye 122, 128–9, 244, 246, 251
Rye Windmill 244, 246

St. Helena Cottage, Tunbridge Wells 75, 245
St. Martins-in-the Fields, parish of 21
St. Paul's Cathedral 132, 245
St. Peter's Church, Brighton 76, 169
Salerno 212
Salisbury 262, 265
Salomons, David 117
Saltdean 132
Sandbach, R.G.E. 7–8
Sandy, John 217
Sardinia, Kingdom of 212
Saunders, Edward 77, 250
Saunders, William 34, 77, 250
Sauveniere, la 203
Scarborough 29, 41
Scarborough Spaw (1667) 29
Scott, Sir Walter 220
Scottish souvenir woodwares 205, 217–221
sea bathing 29–30, 35, 199
Sefton, Earl of 70
Shakespeare's birthplace, Stratford-upon-Avon 110, 147, 245, 247
Sharp, John, James & Ann 20, 47, 156–9, 256
Shawle, —— (artist) 49
Sheraton, Thomas 214

ships depicted in Tunbridge ware 71,
  89, 109, 121
Sidmouth 174
Silver's Library, Margate 36–7, 253, 264
simulated wood finishes 49, 52–3
Smith, Andrew 218–9
Smith, T.R. 49
Smith, William 218–9
Smith, William & Andrew 50
Sompting 173
Sorrento 209, 211
Sorrento woodwares 8, 101, 209–16,
  271, 274
Sorrento woodwares – size of industry
  215
South Africa 220
South Eastern Railway 67
Southborough 117, 253
Southend 35, 242, 251
Southport 40
Southwark 37
Spa 14, 91, 196–7, 199–200, 205–6
Spa varnish 197, 202
Spa waters 13–14, 91, 200–8
Spa woodwares 8, 91, 196–208, 271
Spa woodwares – size of industry 206,
  208
Spain 220
spas, seaside, rise of 16–17, 69
Speldhurst, parish of 15, 18, 33, 70
spinning wheels 41
Spith, Baroness de 156
Spithead 174
Sponberry, ——— (artist) 49
Sprange, Jasper 18, 27, 35, 37, 40, 48,
  164
Stafford's Marine Library, Worthing 37,
  49, 243
stained woods used in Sorrento
  woodwares 211, 215–16
Steine, The (Brighton) 30, 32, 169, 241,
  249–51
Steyne, The (Worthing) 37
Stiven, Charles 205
Stolberg 24
Stones, Dorothy 41
Stones, George 41, 261
Stratford Saye 46
Stratford-upon-Avon 72, 132, 147, 149,
  245
Sussex Advertiser, The 116
Sussex Industries (1883) 56, 246
Switzerland 187, 215
Sylva (1664) 15

Talbot, Alfred Davies 109, 158–60, 256
Talbot, Frederick A.A. 247
Talbot, Harriet 159
Talbot, Sarah 159
tartan decorated Scottish woodwares
  205, 219–20
Taylor, Elias 93, 118
Temple Newsam, Leeds 48
Tenterden 247
Thirty Years War 196

Thrale, ——— (Mrs) 20
Tiffin, Amelia 264
Tiffin, William 72, 167, 252, 264
Tillier, ——— (Mrs) 20
Toad Rock, Rusthall Common 269
Tomkins, Richard 23
Tomkins, P.W. 49
Tonbridge 15, 20, 31, 37, 49, 51–2, 116,
  128, 130–1, 141, 162–8, 242–3, 253
Tonbridge Castle 51, 89, 112, 123, 133,
  142, 162, 168, 242, 245
Tonbridge Priory 67, 245
Tonbridge School 128, 130, 168
Tooke, William 73, 150, 261
tools used in the Tunbridge ware
  industry 7, 90, 120, 129
tortoiseshell inlay 198–9
tortoiseshell, simulation of 52
Traité des Eaux de Spa (1699) 197
Tralee 179
Tralee to Killarney Railway 186
Tulley's Bazaar, Gravesend 35, 252
Tunbridge and Scottish Souvenir
  Woodware (1970) 7
Tunbridge, parish of 18, 33, 70
Tunbridge – occupation of tradesmen
  15
Tunbridge ware industry – size of
  70–1, 139, 168
Tunbridge ware industry – influence on
  Killarney arbutus wares 193–5
Tunbridge ware industry – new mosaic
  (see mosaic, tessellated)
Tunbridge ware industry – relationship
  to Spa woodwares 196, 204
Tunbridge ware industry – supply of
  veneers to cabinet-makers 112–13,
  240
Tunbridge Wells 14–15, 30–1, 39, 48, 59,
  72, 78, 106, 133, 141, 146, 167, 172
Tunbridge Wells – development of the
  town 14, 16–18, 21, 69–70
Tunbridge Wells – sale of woodwares at
  14–16, 18–20, 33, 35, 44, 51, 66–7, 72,
  75, 112–3, 116, 121, 123, 135–62, 217,
  254–7
Tunbridge Wells – spa season 14, 16,
  20, 69
Tunbridge Wells – spa water 13–14, 69
Tunbridge Wells Manufacturing Co.
  15, 119, 122–7, 220, 246, 257
Tunbridge Wells Museum 7, 19, 75, 86,
  89, 104, 107, 112, 128, 132–3, 138,
  210–11, 216, 243, 265
Tunbridge Wells Technical Institute
  116–18
Tuogh 192
turnery, inlaid 63–4, 84–5, 97, 144, 170
turnery wares 18–19, 21–3, 31, 33, 40,
  43–6, 65, 74, 77–9, 81, 115, 118, 123,
  139, 143–4, 156, 164, 173, 181, 197,
  201, 221
turnpike roads 30

Ubsdell, John Talbot 15, 144, 146, 257

Ulster Museum 184–5
United States of America – export of Mauchline wares to 220
United States of America – export of Tunbridge wares to 73, 167
Uppark 46
Upper Medway Navigation 163
Upton Cottage, Broadstairs 36, 242
Upton, ——— (Miss) 77, 172, 250
Upton, John 75, 172
Upton, Sarah 16, 33, 172, 257
Upton, William Jnr 172
Upton, William Snr 32–3, 49–50, 75, 77, 92, 170–2, 241, 247, 251

Vale, William 23–4, 41, 47, 50, 52, 152, 261
Valentine, Charles 50
Van Sompel, ——— 208
vandyke parquetry 54–9, 63, 67, 82, 86, 96, 134, 168, 270, 273
varnish 52, 97, 197, 202, 217
Vaux Hall, le 203
veneer woods used in Tunbridge wares 95, 97
Venice 197
Ventnor 115, 252
veré eglomisé 42, 45
Victoria & Albert Museum 117–8, 199, 202–3, 207–8
Victoria, Princess 59, 69, 80–1, 143, 146, 148, 156, 167
Victoria, Queen 73, 76, 92, 110, 118, 139, 147, 151, 180, 184, 274
views topographical depicted in Spa woodwares 202–3
views topographical depicted in Tunbridge wares 19, 26, 31–2, 36–8, 46, 48, 67, 76, 80, 87, 91, 94, 105–9, 113, 125–6, 133, 138, 145, 147, 149, 156, 159, 161–3, 166, 170, 241–7, 269
Vintman, Richard 18
voiders 20
Vorley, Robert 132, 134, 245, 263
Vyne, The 46

Wadmore, Beauchamp 15, 81, 95, 97
Wales, South 72, 261
Walks, The (*see* Pantiles)
Waller, William 28, 248
Walsh, ——— (Father) 192
Warwick 234
Warwick Castle 72, 134, 168, 245
Washington DC 73, 107, 246
water, chalybeate used to effect colour change 91, 207, 229
Waterman, Thomas (Brighton) 161
Waterman, Thomas (Tunbridge Wells) 140, 160–2, 257

Waterman, Thomas & Son 162
Wedgwood, Josiah 47
Westall, Richard 47
Weymouth 78, 172–4, 248, 264
whitewood Spa woodwares 197, 199, 201–2, 207–8
whitewood Tunbridge wares 19, 26–7, 31–2, 34–5, 38, 40–1, 43, 45–53, 55, 63, 73–4, 77, 79, 139, 143, 148, 151, 169, 173
Whittaker, Benjamin 77, 251
Wight, Isle of 73, 115, 220, 252
Wilkes, ——— (Mr) 102
Willerton & Roberts 23, 261
William IV, King 76, 218
Williams, E. 123
Willington, John 18
Wilson & Amphlet 219
Winchelsea 128
Windsor Castle 67, 72, 80–1, 163, 167, 244, 247
Windsor Magazine, The 247
Wise, George (d. 1779) 15, 18, 163–4, 253
Wise, George Jnr 116, 145, 166, 168, 253
Wise, George Snr 20, 24–6, 32, 36–8, 47, 49, 52–3, 59, 67, 72, 78, 80–1, 89, 95, 97, 106–7, 109, 112, 135, 148, 164–5, 167–8, 174, 253, 257
Wise, Simon 18, 163
Wise, Thomas 20, 27, 31–2, 37, 49, 53, 164, 168, 253
Wishaw, ——— 112
Witherden, George 37, 253
Wittie, Robert (Dr) 29
Wolff, Henry W. 56, 116, 119, 246
Wolseley, Lady Capel 123
woods – treatment of 91, 207, 229
woods – used in Tunbridge ware 41, 43, 53, 58–9, 88, 90–1
Woodworker, The 132
Woodhall Park 46
Woodham, William 164
World War I 121, 142
World War II 57, 129
Worthing 37, 39–40, 78–9, 110, 164, 172–4, 220, 243, 262, 265
wrecks, use of timbers from 78–9, 174
Wyatt, James 243
Wyattville, Sir Jeffrey 67, 247

Xhrouet family 199, 204
Xhrouet, Lambert 198, 204

Young, Arthur 177
Younghusband, Ethel 7, 247
York 40–1, 261, 265